Black & Blue Cheryl Dorsey

Also Author of

**The Creation of a Manifesto
Black & Blue**
*By Cheryl Dorsey*

Coming Soon

**The Creation of A Whistle Blower
Black & Blue**
*By Cheryl Dorsey*

# BLACK AND BLUE

## VOLUME II

### THE CREATION OF A SOCIAL ADVOCATE
## CHERYL DORSEY
#### A LAW ENFORCEMENT MEMOIR

Copyright © 2018 Sgt. Cheryl Dorsey All rights reserved.
ISBN: 978-1725511811

In Loving Memory of my neighbor, childhood best friend and the sister I never had

Janet Maria Harrison Headge

Sunrise August 19, 1956 – Sunset September 4, 1993

Dedicated to Los Angeles Police Department Commander James David Tatreau (EOW April 29, 2007) for being my mentor, my friend, my counsel and the only one willing to stand for me and with me. I am eternally grateful to you and appreciate your walk with me.

In Memoriam to the countless, nameless police officers who committed suicide when the department let you down, beat you down and because of the way you died, your names will never appear on their memorial wall, I recognize that your lives mattered – to your family, partners and friends. Gone but not forgotten.

# ACKNOWLEDGMENTS

As always, I want to first thank my Lord and Savior for continuing to open doors that no man can close. I acknowledge that none of this would be possible without His mercy and grace.

I thank my parents and am so glad that God chose you to show me the way. My goal is to always make you proud. I am certain that you are.

To my cubs; Gregory, Darrnel, Malik and Bilal; you are my heartbeat. Each of you are amazing in your own unique way. Change nothing. I love you to the moon and back, the Lioness,

To my extended family, small though we have become, know that I love you bunches. The big cousins Pat, Wendell, Kim and Onnie - times spent together have been few due to distance but know that you are always and forever in my heart. I must also acknowledge cousin Kaye, gone too soon; but not forgotten. 94th place shenanigans with all of you made being an only child more than just tolerable.

And to my team- Robert and Susan. There are no words that sufficiently express the appreciation and gratitude that I have for each of you individually and as a whole; IncuBiz Marketing Group is a beast. The ways in which you have guided, watched over and helped me has been a blessing. God definitely places people in your path for a reason. I thank Him for you. A special shout out to Travis Wilson, my creative director and recipient of "the daily call." I appreciate your patience and understanding.

Say their names-

To the families that I have come to know and fellowshipped with along the way – thank you for allowing me to share your space and speak truth to power in the name of your loved ones; gone too soon. It is because of you and for you that I challenge and expose injustice, disparity and institutionalized racism within the ranks of some police departments. And so, we must never forget these families and others who have (and regrettably will) suffered the loss or injury of a loved one at the hands of an over-zealous, drunk-with-power cop. For us, time marches on but for these families- time stands still.

Uncle Bobby & Aunt Bee (Oscar Grant); Tritobia Ford (Ezell Ford) Sharon Cooper (Sandra Bland); Lezley McSpadden and Mike Brown Parents of (Mike Brown); Angie Hammond (Zachary Hammond). I pray for peace and comfort that surpasses all understanding.

# FOREWORD

I thought I knew my friend Cheryl Dorsey and I understood her deep experience in law enforcement. I always knew her to be a fountain of information and someone I could rely on to provide honest, insightful commentary. We have shared many hours together on radio and television and I rely on Cheryl for her honest, forthright appraisals. I knew her opinions were informed by experience. What I did not know was the profundity of her experiences and how important they are for us all to come to grips with the historical sweep of the last 30 years and the scars these difficult years have left upon America. Cheryl reminds us of James Comey's words: "All of us in law enforcement must be honest enough to acknowledge that much of our history is not pretty.... At many points in American history, law enforcement enforced the status quo, a status quo that was often brutally unfair to disfavored groups." Cheryl herself gives us these chilling words, "Police abuse and excessive, unnecessary force, deadly force is not an aberration. Police abuse is a too frequent occurrence in communities of color and where poor whites reside. Be clear, everyone is in danger." This is an opinion not lightly offered. This is her profession, these are her peers, and we are the people served. She bemoans this state of affairs but offers us insights and solutions: "I realized I had a story that needed to be told. And in telling my story I quickly realized that my experiences as a patrol officer and a patrol supervisor would become a critical and vital part of the discussions that were to come." We have in these pages that story as well as many other insights and prescriptions for going forward.

I thought I knew Cheryl Dorsey. I did not. My respect and admiration for her have truly expanded. She rewards the reader with an inside first-hand account of law enforcement. Her career and the extraordinary narratives shared in these pages will change you. If you have difficulty understanding why an NFL player would risk his career in his effort to raise awareness of a chronic problem, you will find your answers in these pages. Cheryl's story will change your perspective. She gives you no alternative as she ferries the reader in to her world and across a career that not only bore witness to difficult history; but also offers insights and perspectives that could only be provided by her unique perspective as a woman; an African American woman; and a professional deeply committed to her career willing to honestly examine the shortcomings of that profession. In summing up this perspective Cheryl simply reminds us, "There is not another female, black or white on the Los Angeles Police Department with twenty, solid years of patrol experience- then or now. Those twenty years I spent in patrol were under the command of Police Chiefs Daryl Gates, Willie Williams and Bernard Parks; and my experiences will never to be duplicated." And that is simply a fact. That being so, we turn away from the wisdom offered here at our peril.

She faces head on a history that is summed up by remarks Cheryl points out were delivered in a speech in 2016 by Terrence Cunningham, president of one of the largest police organizations in the United States, the International Association of Police Chiefs "this dark side of our shared history has created a multigenerational—almost inherited—mistrust between many communities of color and their law enforcement agencies." Cheryl is not willing to leave this heritage to embitter the future. In addition to providing primary documentation of a monumentally important piece of our history, this book is packed with evidence and commentary from within the world of law enforcement. It also provides a wealth of practical information about dealing with law enforcement. Cheryl does not hold back on her observations. Cheryl laments, "Twenty-five years after Rodney King was beaten senseless by four LAPD officers at the end of a car chase- not much has changed" But I say things have changed. We have Cheryl's account and her contributions to law enforcement. That is change. And part of the solution she reminds the reader, is us; our education about law enforcement and how to deal with our encounters with them. This book provides that practical wisdom in detail.

That is change. I had the great good fortune to know Rodney King, a man of profound heart and humanity. It was his wish, he expressed to me many times that we all participate in this change. His words will remain with us always. We must get along. There is reason to be optimistic. After all, we have Cheryl Dorsey.

- Dr. Drew

# PROLOGUE

I had a supervisor tell me once that the LAPD is a machine- it will chew you up and spit you out. As an officer on the Los Angeles Police Department, one needs to recognize very early on, that you are nothing more than a cog in their wheel. On August 25, 1980, I became serial number 22607. Failure to wrap your heard around this concept can cause, vomiting, sleepless nights, alcoholism, diarrhea, loss of appetite and in some cases death; by your own hands.

Anyone who tries to describe the allegations of racism, unfair disciplinary practices and discrimination made by fired LAPD officer- turned murderer, Christopher Dorner in February 2013, as "old news" is being intellectually dishonest. I am a first-hand witness and subsequent recipient of the backlash that awaits any officer who dares to take on the LAPD.

The Los Angeles Police Department will manufacture charges of police misconduct, force you to appear before a capricious administrative Board of Rights (BOR) and then terminate you at will. Then, when that officer complains publicly, the department creates an image of that officer in such a way that makes that officer appear distasteful and therefore anything that they say or do is rejected.

The department uses the press to create an image that the department can now justify. The press unwittingly becomes an accessory, after the fact; by repeating what the LAPD purports to be factual.

The department, by its mere existence, is designed to tear an officer down in the police academy and then re-create that officer in an image the department likes. A subtle form of brainwashing occurs for some.

I resisted that treatment. I was my own woman. I needed a job true enough and I was damn good at what I did. I remained professional, courteous and compassionate when dealing with the citizens of Los Angeles. But, I never bled blue. I stayed the course. I fought the good fight. And as a result, after twenty years, I earned my service pension. Although I was beaten down and betrayed by the LAPD in the process, I managed to get out "alive". I didn't go on a murderous rampage when the department came after me in the twilight of my career. I understood that I was still in control. I just needed to hold on.

I was raised by a strong and independent mother who taught me, all my life, to stand my ground. My father was a proud man from the south who didn't scratch if he didn't itch. I listened and held on to those life lessons taught to me by my working-class parents. I grew up middle-class and enjoyed a comfortable lifestyle. My father was a metal-fitter at McDonald Douglas Aircraft in Torrance, California where he worked the swing shift until he retired in the late 70s. My mother worked as an accountant and was the only black employee in all-white McKesson-Robbins, a pharmaceutical company, in Anaheim, California during the 60s and 70s before she retired in the 80s. She managed to thrive and prosper in that environment. Zango and Frankye Mae taught me well. It was my upbringing that provided the foundation I needed to overcome obstacles and pursue my goals with passion and determination. This drive and can do-will do mind set would, later in my life, enable me to stay the LAPD course, retire and walk away with my sanity and most importantly, my dignity.

As an advocate for those who continue to suffer racial injustices, disproportionate and selective enforcement, intolerance at the hands of a police force that swore an oath to protect and serve yet seems to lack empathy and compassion in certain areas of the community; I am here for you.

For anyone who has been the victim of police abuse under the color of authority and is tired of police command staff double speak and code talk after a deadly use of force incident; I am here. I will empower and educate communities with a common sense, step-by-step approach to first surviving the police encounter, understanding police culture, combating institutionalized racism that seemingly permeates many police departments around the nation by providing a clear and direct path to filing administrative complaints, demanding officer accountability and changing police policy.

My opinions have been formed because of my lived experiences as a woman, mother and veteran sergeant of the Los Angeles Police Department. I will provide a candid, honest and unique perspective on social and institutional abuses with a level of credibility that is effective, relevant and irrefutable.

# WHY...

# ONE:
# YOU HAVE BEEN WARNED

In this new era of Jim Crow which consists of trumped up traffic stops, unnecessary deadly police shootings, and mass incarceration, I will be your social justice advocate. I will shine a light on mistruths, misconceptions and mistakes that could get you killed by a cop. I will demonstrate how "protect and serve" has become more about protecting errant officers and serving minorities grief, financial harm, and unspeakable heartache. Indeed, racial profiling, dishonest cops, abuse under the color of authority and disparate selective enforcement of the law is how injustice is served.

I had no idea where I was headed when I decided to share the story of my life as a young black woman on the white, male dominated, Los Angeles Police Department (LAPD). However, I realized I had a story that needed to be told. And in telling my story I quickly realized that my experiences as a patrol officer and a patrol supervisor would become a critical and vital part of the discussions that were to come. As I reviewed and responded to a spate of deadly police encounters around the nation, I knew that in some cases an officer's expressed fear of an individual, usually a man of color; and subsequent need for deadly force to gain control or compliance from said individual had been over-stated at most times and downright dishonest at others.

My mission became one of educating communities on how to best survive police encounters, advocating for victim families who demanded justice for their loved ones murdered by police and creating opportunities for dialogue, understanding and bridge building in an effort to bring about improved police reform and officer accountability.

As an honorably retired, twenty-year veteran sergeant of the LAPD I knew that I could speak for these families regarding the cops' actions before, during and after a fatal police encounter in a way that they could not. After all, I had once been a cop but I was also part of the community that was being so disproportionately affected by what appeared to be excessive and unjustified police force. I knew, based on my professional knowledge which questions needed to be answered by these police chiefs to help family members understand how and why a police encounter could led to a death. As I watched police chiefs give lip service, regarding a thorough investigation and transparency, I felt especially compelled as a parent to step forward; it was my duty to stand in the gap for these grieving mothers and fathers.

Perhaps what I am saying is common knowledge to some and I may be preaching to the choir; but let's go ahead and address the big, blue elephant in the room; the thin blue line; police culture. This big blue behemoth is not selective in who it crushes. Be clear, it tramples on everything that comes across its path that is contrary to its predetermined way forward. No one is immune. Community gets crushed on the outside of the system and [some] officers get crushed on the inside.

Historically, rampant, unabated police abuse in minority and poor white communities has been an all too frequent reality for some, and this abuse continues today. To illustrate that point, a New York city police officer choked an unarmed black man to death because he refused to submit to officers' orders; a Ferguson, Missouri, police officer shot and killed an unarmed black teenager because he jaywalked; a Texas State Trooper snatched an unarmed black woman out of her car because she refused to put out a cigarette. There was plenty of outrage and disgust surrounding those tragedies, but no one in the minority community was surprised based on their lived experiences. Even though many of these images repeatedly splashed across television screens around the world, police department chiefs invoked the idea that there was something that had occurred moments before police cameras began recording, or some culpability existed on the part of the deceased that would surely justify what had been shown.

It was commonplace in the days that followed deadly police shootings for some police chiefs to further exacerbate the situation by metaphorically poking their finger in the family's eye with smear campaigns and character assassination of the deceased. These tactics were designed to impugn the integrity of the person that died at the hands of one of their officers as if to infer that person had it coming. You've heard the police explanations, "he refused to comply", "he ran" or "he scared me.".

The continued abuses under the color of authority, ranging from assault to homicide, against men and women of color, young and old was happening too frequently with apparently no end in sight. So, you understand that if not you right now – you could be next. Your husband could be next. Your child could be next. I am here to help you survive police encounters.

So be clear, in this era of mass incarceration, police agencies seem committed to their perceived role of provider. That-is-to-say, the provider of a steady stream of black, brown and poor white folks into the system; they are the pipeline to the prison system. According to research by the University of California Irvine reported in March 2017 blacks are only 13% of the American population but a majority of innocent defendants wrongfully convicted of crimes and later exonerated. They constituted 47% of the 1900 exonerations listed in the National Registry of Exonerations as of October 2016 and the great majority of more than 1,800 additional innocent defendants who were framed and convicted of crimes in 15 large-scale police scandals and later cleared…"

Here's an example, in Phase One of the mass incarceration process.

Seemingly under the guise of the Broken Windows theory, crime reduction, safer communities and traffic enforcement, police chiefs have directed their patrol officers to engage minority community members in a variety of ways. A time-honored method of engagement is an officer initiated activity such as a traffic stop or their favorite; an investigative stop. For the uninformed, an investigative stop is the method that some police officers use when they think someone (usually a black man) looks suspicious. Or, when an officer sees someone (usually a black man) in an area that the officer does not think that person should belong; or the individual is driving a car that in the officer's opinion that person should not be able to afford. The detention then becomes contentious, physicality ensues on the part of the officer and next thing that person discovers is that they have been arrested for interfering with the officer's official investigation, battery on a police officer or some made up criminal charge. What I like to refer to as contempt of cop ™ . That is, if you live. Because the alternative that has been witnessed time and time again is that the officer(s) escalates the use of force to a deadly force incident and now there is a death.

Contempt of Cop™ is a phrase I coined to describe what happens when a police officer gets angry during a police contact. Contempt of Cop ™ is what happens when an officer decides to step outside of the boundaries of training and policy and punish someone who failed to follow an order. Should that person survive the officer's physical assault, that person will next find themselves on the back end of an arrest. They will certainly go to jail. You see, there is an unwritten but well-known rule in street policing; if an officer puts hands on you, he can't just leave you; you must go to jail for something. It may not be you right now – but it might be you next.

And in those instances where a detention ends with a police shooting, chances of surviving that police encounter are highly improbable; this we have been shown. Why? Because officers are not trained to "shoot to stop" – police are trained to kill. I have often been asked, "why didn't the officer just shoot him in the arm or leg?" My honest response has always been, "because we are trained to kill." Now, you won't find any police chief saying that. But it is a fact. And if the reader understands that police officers perform like they practice then what I am about to say next will make perfect sense.

As a young, police recruit I spent hours at the LAPD academy gun range practicing to kill. Yeah, the firearms instructor told us that we were being trained to "stop the threat" but I was being evaluated and graded on my shooting proficiency, among other things. The overall goal was to accurately affect two rounds to center body mass (heart) followed by a head shot. Now, as the reader I ask you, "Am I being trained to stop, or am I being trained to kill? "You be the judge.

Although I was being told that I am being taught to stop the threat, in my mind I thought these two things could not be true; being told that I was shooting "to stop" while simultaneously aiming at vital body parts. This is what I like to refer to as police code talk; double speak. You've heard it many times being spoken by police chiefs as they try to convince the public during a press conference for instance that six shots needed to be fired by an officer to stop a jay walker or that an individual selling CDs wouldn't stop moving as officers straddled him and sat on his chest therefore, the only way for the officers to gain compliance was to shoot the man. Although I had been trained to fire my weapon as a last resort not a first; and I had been trained in the use of non-lethal devices and grappling techniques the notion of shooting someone because they won't be still was non-sensical. So, here's where the duality of language comes in. My humanity tells me that if I want to stop a threat, why am I not trained to shoot in the arm or leg. I was trained to shoot center body mass with a double-tap (two rounds fired in rapid succession) and if the threat continued then a head shot followed, which was known as a "failure drill".

I am sure that my training at the LAPD academy was not unique and so like many of my co-workers and cops around the nation, I participated in weekly shooting exercises at the gun range.

The purpose was to obtain a shooting medal to be worn on my uniform which indicated my level of shooting proficiency; a badge of honor if you will. In addition to bragging rights, there was a financial incentive offered by the LAPD; a monthly cash bonus for officers with high shooting scores. I wanted to be good. I needed the extra pay. So, I became a trained and decorated killer.

Now that the reader has become familiar with Phase One, the stop; here's Phase Two - let's "get this person into the system." - the penal system.

Stanford University Professor Jennifer Eberhardt conducted and co-authored a series of research studies which dealt with linguistics used by Oakland (OPD), California police officers. There was a disparate difference noted in the way OPD officers communicated with the public. Two of the studies; Perceptions of Officer Treatment from Language and Racial Disparities in Respect revealed that officers had spoken in a less respectful tone when dealing with black community members than they had when dealing with white community members. If the way an officer spoke to a detainee and vice versa was a predictor of impending conflict or animus it is my belief that an individual might recognize the need to temper their tone thus de-escalate a potentially contentious situation before things get out of hand. With that in mind, understand the significance and the importance of being able to recognize the moment when a police encounter is about to go side-ways in the hopes of avoiding Contempt of Cop ™.

Now, you have survived the stop, you didn't get shot; so let me explain a quick overview of what, "get you in the system" tactic/trickery, in my estimation, looks like. In police jargon on the LAPD, we called this "humming you to jail". For example, a foot pursuit generally occurs at the end of a police car chase. Suspects are known to jump out of the car and scatter in different directions. Officers are amped up, at the end of a car chase. Adrenaline is coursing through their bodies. And, by this time the officers are also most likely furious that the driver refused to yield to their red lights and siren. Contempt of Cop ™ is about to go down. The pursuing officers managed to grab one of the fleeing suspects; problem is, this was the passenger. The driver, got away; eastbound through the houses- as we used to say. Well, guess what, tag you're it. The slow guy just became the driver. This "driver" gets booked for an alleged offense and you're in the system. Your public defender will need to work out those details of your capture later. My guess, you will be encouraged by the public defender to plead guilty to something- anything to lighten their caseload and off you go. It may not be you right now, but you might be next.

Or, what about when a police officer has detained you for whatever reason and then conveniently finds drugs or a gun on you? That's humming you to jail.

Or an officer arrested you on a Friday night on a trumped-up charge that will surely end up being a district attorney reject on Monday morning, due to insufficient cause to prosecute; but that individual just spent an entire weekend in custody. Why? Because they did not have the financial wherewithal to make bail? That's humming a person to jail.

Come on now, don't act naive. Yes, this happens. Police officers have tremendous authority. And [some] police officers have been known to falsify an arrest report. It may not be you right now, but you might be next.

One such example occurred in early November 2017. Here's how it went. A fifty-two-year old black man was detained and arrested by two Los Angeles Police Department officers according to local news reports. It involved an LAPD officer whose bod-cam allegedly recorded him planting cocaine in the wallet of a black man who had been detained after being involved in a suspected hit and run traffic accident. The officer's body camera recording caused an internal investigation to be launched. This individual may have just been saved. But how many others may have been wrongly jailed and convicted due to the lack of body cam evidence? Often, it has been the officer's version of the encounter that is deemed most credible. It is my often-proven belief, that great deference is given to an officer's testimony. So, if not you right now – you could be next.

Shortly after that arrest, on November 16, 2017, it was reported that the Cook's County State Attorney General dropped all criminal charges which had been filed against fifteen different men who had been framed by former sergeant Ronald Watts and his officers. According to WGN 9 news reports; "The men alleged that Watts and his team of officers planted drugs on them, framed them and falsified police reports."

Joshua Tepfer of the Exoneration Project at the University of Chicago represented the accused men. According to Tepfer, "the officers targeted men living in South Side housing projects from the early 2000s for over a 10-year period by framing them by creating evidence and planting drugs on them . . . it was systemic in nature and those at the highest levels of the Chicago Police Department knew about it and did nothing to stop it . . . It was swept under the rug."

This type of abuse under the color of authority is not unique to Chicago. A research paper, conducted by the University of California Irvine (UCI) National Registry of Exonerations, Newkirk Center for Science and Society, titled, Race and Wrongful Convictions in the United States stated in part, while it is impossible to "know the motives of the dishonest officers who framed all these defendants, but there are a few obvious possibilities . . . many black defendants – especially poor, inner-city dwellers in Philadelphia, Camden, Oakland and elsewhere- have limited resources and little political clout. They are unlikely to be able to defend themselves successfully, even if innocent." This, is why I advocate for you. To help you survive that initial police encounter. Because it may not be you right now, but you might be next.

Now that we have discussed Phase One – the stop, and Phase Two – the detention this brings us to Phase Three, which is [mass] incarceration.

According to author, Michelle Alexander, in her book The New Jim Crow, Mass Incarceration in the Age of Colorblindness there's "overwhelming evidence that these institutions create crime rather than prevent it." Michelle Alexander, continues that "mass incarceration operates as a tightly networked system of laws, polices, customs and institutions that operate collectively to ensure the subordinate status of the group defined largely by race . . . Large numbers of African-Americans continue to be arrested and labeled drug criminals, they will continue to be relegated to a permanent second-class status upon their release, no matter how much (or how little) time they spend behind bars. The system of mass incarceration is based on the prison label, not prison time."

Once labeled a "convict" the issue now becomes one of being disenfranchised, and the stigma attached to that label has created great hardship for the individual as well as their family. The previously referenced UCI Race and Wrongful Convictions research study put forth this question and answer, "Why do police officers who conduct these outrageous programs of framing innocent drug defendants concentrate on African Americans?... Because that's what they do in all aspects of drug-law enforcement. Guilty or innocent, they always focus disproportionately on African Americans. It may not be you right now, but it might be you next.

What better way to add to prison population numbers than through a carefully, manufactured police encounter coupled with a creatively written arrest report. You know the kind of encounters I am speaking of; like when an officer stops someone because the third tail light on their car is burnt out. Maybe you are just standing around on the sidewalk and the beat cops don't particularly like you; because there's history. Or how about, you JDLR (just don't look right) in the area. Could it be that you didn't have any gloves in your glovebox? No, Bumps on your bumper? Police officers are adept at creating probable cause or reasonable suspicion on the fly.

And know this, the vehicle code is massive. It is unreasonable to expect that a driver would have such knowledge of all vehicle code violations in their particular state. So, as a result it is unlikely that a driver would fully understand that there are many ticky-tack reasons an officer can legitimately develop to stop someone at any given time. An officer well-versed in the vehicle code can create all manner of foolishness. It is for this reason that I advise, when stopped by an officer; comply with the officer's orders. On any given day, an unknowing driver may have committed an infraction that would have given the officer probable cause to stop and detain. Failure to comply could end badly. Trying to hold court curbside with an officer is never a good idea. There is a great likelihood that you will be found guilty of Contempt of Cop ™. I am here to help you survive that police encounter.

The myriad reasons a police officer can put forth as a justification for detaining an individual can sometimes be difficult for most citizens to understand and most probably impossible to argue against. And since great deference is given to an officer's version of events, most juries are unwilling to find fault with an officers' actions when things end badly.

As in the case of Akai Gurley, who was shot and killed in a Brooklyn, New York housing development. Former NYPD officer Peter Liang avoided prison on his conviction and received probation. Liang was ordered to personally pay the family $25,000 in addition to the $4.1 million city settlement and $400,000 agreed upon by the housing authority. Indeed, jury convictions of police officers in the fatal shooting deaths of black men seem rare. It may not have happened to your family yet, but they might be next.

In the case of Walter Scott who had been stopped for a traffic violation and had eight bullets pumped into his back as he ran away from former South Carolina officer Michael Slager; the jury deadlocked during the first trial. One of the jurors who heard the evidence presented during Scott's murder trial reportedly said, "Slager had done nothing malicious in the shooting." Well, I imagine if lying and accusing Scott of taking his taser after shooting him in the back eight times, unnecessarily, was not considered malicious, then that statement might be true. Michael Slager was ultimately tried a second time and this time, the jury convicted Slager on second degree murder for which he received a twenty-year federal prison sentence. It may not be your family right now, but they could be next.

Justice for Walter Scott and his family. Not so much in the fatal shooting of twelve-year-old Tamir Rice. A grand jury declined to indict former Cleveland police officer Timothy Loehmann in that police shooting. It may not be your family now, but they could be next.

If police chiefs and police commissioners refuse to admit that there is problem, then there is nothing to fix. If police chiefs refuse to purge over-zealous, drunk with power cops from their roles nothing will change. If these officials continue to circle- the wagons, minimize and mitigate officers' bad behavior, those officers will continue to engage in police misconduct. If police chiefs and sheriffs refuse to admit that there are ill-suited, ill-tempered officers within their ranks and mandate psychological re-evaluations on a regular basis- nothing will change.

And if citizens don't get involved and engaged with their legislators to draft law and/or policy that will hold errant police officers personally and financially liable when they use deadly force as a first resort rather than as a last resort as trained this will continue. You. Have. Been. Warned.

And now that there is a plethora of conscious black folks, around the nation, speaking out against these tragedies there is an effort afoot to silence the voices of those who would advocate for communities of color. This new enemy has emerged in the form of social justice activists being labeled as Black Identity Extremists (BIE) by the U.S. Department of Justice.

You have been warned. However, I have solutions. SOP (Standard Operating Procedure) in communities of color must change; so, I am delivering an SOS. In other words, I am here to advocate for you.

# TWO:
# BLAH… BLAH… BLAH…

(reprint from the LA Wave Newspaper April 2018 – by Sgt. Cheryl Dorsey)

"I feared for my life …thought I saw a gun … don't know why I shot"

Isn't that the way the story begins?

Shortly after unarmed, Stephon Clark had been shot and killed by Sacramento, California police officers, Mayor Darrell Steinberg acknowledged what has been the lived experience of minority communities; that is- implied racism and bias is a major factor.

Sacramento police officers pumped twenty bullets into the body of Stephon Clark because they "thought" Clark had a gun. Factually, he was holding a cellphone in his hand.

As a twenty-year veteran sergeant of the Los Angeles Police Department, I know firsthand that officers are expected to "know" when they fire their weapon.

Name another group of professionals, whom routinely deal with the public, allowed to act so carelessly and capriciously without repercussion. Imagine, a top chef in a five-star restaurant who mistakenly served a chicken breast to a customer who had requested a filet mignon and was then allowed to just simply respond, "I thought it was beef."

That chef would be fired. Why then does society and law makers allow police officers to get away with, "I was in fear. I thought he had a gun. I don't know why I shot."

Polices officers are trained professionals and expected "to get it right" – every time.

Having spent my entire career in uniform as a patrol officer and supervisor I know first-hand that suspects attempting to avoid arrest are sometimes uncooperative, combative and will run. I have chased, fought and arrested many suspected criminals; and Guess what? I shot no one.

The officers in the Clark shooting were shown on video to be in a position of cover and concealment at the corner of his grandmother's residence with an air unit overhead; what was the urgency to confront Clark? The officers had the benefit of an air unit overhead.

Why not request additional units, set up a perimeter to contain the suspect in the backyard? And why did those officers mute the audio on their bodycam after the shooting?

According to Sacramento Police Chief Daniel Hahn, there are "various reasons why somebody would." I can't think of one.

Shortly after the murder of Stephon Clark, 34-year old, Danny Ray Thomas was shot and killed by Texas Deputy Cameron Brewer. Thomas, who was unarmed, had been walking in the middle of the street with his pants down around his ankles moments prior to the fatal police encounter.

While a "thorough, transparent and expeditious" investigation has been promised by Harris County sheriff Ed Gonzalez, it is my hope that expediency does not replace common sense and reasonableness.

Although it was reported that Brewer had a taser in his possession and had been previously trained on the use of non-lethal force when dealing with a mentally ill person he claimed, "fearing for his safety", as the justification for firing a single shot striking Thomas in the chest.

We've seen this before. In July 2016, a North Miami SWAT team member with four years on that department, officer Jonathan Aledda shot an unarmed, black man, Charles Kinsey as he lay prone on the ground with his arms extended. Kinsey attempted to explain to officer Aledda that he [Kinsey] was assisting an autistic client who was also seated on the ground next to Kinsey at the time the officer fired his rifle. Thankfully, Kinsey did not die. When asked why he shot, Aledda responded, "I don't know."

Evidently the Miami-Dade State Attorney figured it out. Former officer Aledda was subsequently charged with attempted manslaughter and culpable negligence with injury in the shooting of Kinsey; And with attempted manslaughter culpable negligence without injury for Arnaldo Soto, the autistic patient who was with Kinsey at the time of the shooting…"

Unless and until there are substantive consequences for officers who use deadly force as a first resort rather than a last resort as trained – there will continue to be copy-cat, "fearful" killers offering nothing more than, "I was scared" as a reason.

Mere criminal charges against errant officers are insufficient. We need Convictions. Convictions. Convictions.

As 2018 mid-term elections near, it is important for citizen voters to get involved and engaged. Demand action from our legislators and accountability from our police officers.

While those communities most directly affected by police abuse and injustice have been demanding and expecting change and reform from their respective police chiefs- what can't be forced upon them is the "want". Change will come only when police chiefs' "want" it.

So, black, brown and poor white communities must demand action from legislators with regard to accountability from our police officers.

To that end, Sacramento, California Assembly member Kevin McCarty reported that state legislators recently introduced a measure, AB 931, allowing officers to use deadly force "only when necessary" rather than "when reasonable."

Let's demand that the law makers also take a page out of the book of the Baltimore city solicitor who has adopted a policy that would hold its police officers financially responsible in civil litigation for punitive damages. The time to act is now.

# A LAW ENFORCEMENT
# MEMIOR

# THREE:
# THE EARLY YEARS

Cheryl Ann was raised in an area now known as "South Central Los Angeles." I don't recall this part of the city of Los Angeles being referred to in that manner when I was growing up—that designation came later. I was raised on the 1900 block of West 94th Place in LAPD's 77th Division. Our house was near Western Avenue and Century Boulevard, in the flight path of airplanes bound for LAX.

Our family had the distinction of being the first black family to move onto 94th. My parents were both hard-working people who had migrated to California from the South looking for a better life, and they found it. I was their only child. As such, my mom, especially, doted on me. I wanted for nothing. I was Frankye's little girl. My mom loved to shop and therefore loved to dress. Her love of fashion extended to me as well. Birthdays and holidays were a big deal—especially Easter. My mom always made sure that I had the perfect Easter outfit, replete with gloves and bonnet. Personally, I would have been okay without the netted hat. This was a yearly tradition. By the time I turned twelve, stockings (or pantyhose, as they were referred to back then) were a must. Growing up was not always so rosy—my mom had rules, and I had to follow them. At times, I thought she was downright mean. I had to be in the house by the time the streetlights came on and there were way too many places that I just could not go. I didn't appreciate it then—but now I understand completely.

Our home on 94th was not their first. Before that we lived in an apartment that my parents owned on Gage Avenue, near Denker Avenue. As an adult, I came to understand what a great source of pride our three-bedroom, two-bathroom house with the big den (family room) was for my parents. They purchased our home back when paying off a mortgage was possible, and they did just that. When the deed came in the mail stamped "paid," my mom did a jig. She was so happy to finally own her home.

As I got older, my mom told me stories about how our neighborhood had changed after we moved in. She described the neighborhood on the weekends as "circus-like." She talked about all the waving realtor flags staked in the front yards of our white neighbors. Seemed like our white neighbors had decided that they didn't want to live near a black family, so as a result, open house events and parades of prospective buyers occurred every weekend. I often wondered how this made my parents feel, but they never discussed racial tensions they may have experienced in their lives. My parents never showed any animus toward whites. As a matter of fact, my mom was the only black person working at her job. I used to tease her when I found out that she was the only black on the office bowling team. I would joke that she was the blackest thing in the bowling alley beside the bowling balls. She would playfully hit at me and tell me to "stop it." She seemed comfortable in her environment.

As more and more white neighbors moved, my mom shared the vacancy news with her relatives from Little Rock. Her first cousin, Essie and her husband Roosevelt moved directly across the street from us. They had on daughter, Karen. She was just Kaye to the family. Kay was five years older than me and acted more like a big sister than an older cousin. Eventually Essie told her sister Shirley who moved around the corner on 94th Street. Shirley was married and had two children; Wendell (Wendy) and Kim. They were closer in age to me. Not long after that, Ma'maw and Pa'paw, Essie's parents moved into a corner duplex at the end of the block where 94th Place and Manhattan Place intersected. It was great having cousins nearby. Kaye not so much. She really played the role of the oldest. She always told us what we could and could not do when the family would get together at her house. Essie's house was the meet up spot. When our cousins from North Carolina came to visit with their mom, Essie's sister, Hester it was party time. Faye, Pat and Jr. Brown were a little older than I was. They were closer in age to Kaye. The kids would all go in the backyard where Essie had a rumpus room which was attached to the garage. We would play and rough house back there until the adults called us inside to entertain them. Essie had a large hi-fi stereo cabinet in the living room. They would put on 45s, which is the term used to describe the old records and the kids would do the latest dance to the delight of all the adults.

My older cousins loved to torment me. I'm not sure why. Maybe it was just because I was the bratty little cousin. My cousin Faye loved reptiles. One time she threw a lizard at me and the darn thing stuck on my back. I started running around yelling like a crazy person and the lizard held on tighter. The faster I ran trying to shake this thing, the more it held on. The lizard was riding my back like I was a horse. I was forever scarred. To this date, I run every time I encounter a lizard. I refer to them all as Komodo dragons. I carry on so that my children, well at least two of them are just as scared of all things four-legged.

Growing up the little cousin wasn't all bad. By the time Kaye made it to high school she allowed me to hang out with her more. She and her friends from Washington High taught me how to drive a stick shift, our term for a manual car. Kaye had a 1974 Chevrolet Vega. Not only did Kaye let me driver her car, she let me smoke. Now that was cool; so, I thought. At least until my daddy found out. When Zango discovered my partially consumed pack of Benson & Hedges cigarettes he made me sit down with him and finish the whole pack. He leisurely smoked his non-filtered camels while I went through about six or seven cigarettes. I was sick as a dog. That didn't cure me though. I continued to smoke cigarettes between the ages of fourteen and about eighteen. I liked hanging around Kaye, but she was the big cousin; I needed somebody my own age to play with.

# FOUR: MOMMA LYNDEE

I was like every other little girl growing up during the sixties and seventies. Life was simple. I had a best friend who lived a few houses away on the same street. We were inseparable. Jan was a couple of years older than me and one of six children. Being an only child could get lonely, so I loved going to the Harrisons' house. I was a daily presence. Mrs. Harrison became my second mother. Like most black families during those times, if I misbehaved, Mrs. Harrison would just handle it. Then my mom would find out, and I'd get it all over again.

Jan had an older sister, which meant I did too. We loved to hang out with her when she allowed it. She seemed to go out quite a bit, so we were always begging to tag along. It worked out well for her, because if we were with her, she could go—win-win. However, she would make us call her "Momma Lyndee." We were teenagers by now, and this whole "momma" thing didn't sit well, but we wanted so desperately to go we agreed.

Momma Lyndee was now a student at Cal State Los Angeles and very involved in the black student union (BSU). She also loved plays. Momma Lyndee would take us along whenever she had a role, and we got the chance to hang out on the college campus. One time, Momma Lyndee even let us act as hosts at one of the plays, passing out pamphlets to attendees. There was one play that I really enjoyed; it was called Tambourines to Glory. In addition to the plays, Momma Lyndee took us to the yearly Festival in the Park, which was held on Avalon and 51st Streets. Jan and I always looked forward to the concerts in the park because Momma Lyndee would let us walk around without her, and that was our opportunity to meet boys. South Park was located on the east side of town, and the boys who lived near there seemed a little rough—just the way we liked them.

Back in our own neighborhood, our parents trusted us to walk to the nearby park, Sportsman Park on Century and Western Avenues. In our small eyes, this park was huge. There was an indoor swimming pool, tennis court, swing sets, and a large gymnasium where dances where held. Jan and I would spend endless days at Sportsman Park now renamed Jesse Owens. That was before a street gang, infamously known in the '90s as a faction of the Crips, took over the neighborhood and made it dangerous to be out alone as a little girl.

Another of our favorite activities involved a car ride down to Rosecrans and Western Avenues. There was a go-cart track, a giant slide, and a skating rink: more great places to meet the boys.

# FIVE: PRIVATE SCHOOLS

Even though my parents were practicing Baptists, I attended Catholic schools. My mom believed that parochial schools offered a better education, and she would have nothing less than that for me. I attended St. Eugene's Elementary School on Van Ness Avenue. My mom worked during the day and my daddy worked the swing shift at Mc Donald Douglas. I would get home from elementary school around 2:30pm and my daddy would leave for work shortly after I arrived home. My mom didn't get home until 5:00p.m.; that meant I had two full hours to get into as much mischief as I could unsupervised. I spent most of the time rummaging through my parents' papers and cabinets when I wasn't watching the soap operas.

One day I stumbled upon some papers that had Los Angeles County Adoption Agency across the top. I wasn't sure what this meant at first, so I consulted my big cousin Kaye. She told me that I had been adopted. Well this was a news flash. Not had Kaye told me that I had been adopted by my parents but that someone had found me in a trash can before I was given to my parents. Well how could she know this? I mean, I knew she was the big cousin and all, but this could not be true. I waited a few days and then I asked my daddy just before he left for work. My daddy told me that it was true that I had been adopted but when I pressed for more information I noticed a tear well up in his eyes. I was still pretty young and not sure what to make of all of this but what I did know was that I did not like seeing my daddy cry. I immediately dropped the conversation and not another word was spoken about my adoption.

I eventually graduated from St. Eugene's and moved on to the all-girls high school, St. Michael's. I think she was trying to keep me away from the boys. St. Michael's was located near the corner of Manchester and Vermont Avenues.

I tried not to disappoint my mom in terms of my grades in the subjects that mattered most: reading, writing, and arithmetic. But "personal conduct"—well, that was a different matter. I was a bit of a class clown. According to my mom, schoolwork came easy to me, and once I finished my work, I went about disrupting my classmates. My mom spent many days in the principal's office. Our principal at St. Michael's was a short, heavyset nun, who still wore the long white habit like the kind worn by Sally Field in the Flying Nun television series. She was named Sister John Dominic. The girls called her "JD." We all thought JD was mean and way too strict. In my teenaged mind, she was a brute. JD used to patrol the sidewalks in front of the school at the end of the day, trying unsuccessfully to run the boys away who came from the nearby all-boys high school, Mount Carmel.

I was always a tall child, taller than the tallest boy in my class. This was a source of embarrassment for me, especially in elementary school. I hated being the tallest girl; I was always at the end of the line for everything when we would line up by height. This didn't seem fair. Why didn't they ever line us up in the reverse? Not only was I the tallest girl in my class, I was the skinniest too. It was not uncommon for some of my classmates to try and pick on me. I quickly gained the reputation of being "the wrong one." I was a tomboy and not afraid to fight. I was not going to allow anyone to bully me; fighting was something I came to enjoy. As a result, my mom was often called into the principal's office. I had been taught that if somebody hit me, I had a right to defend myself. Unfortunately, I didn't always "wait" for the hit.

The physical confrontations continued in high school. I guess I was an official member of St. Michael's version of "the bad girls club." I didn't fight because I was defending myself—it was usually because of some perceived slight by another female. Fights on the RTD, on the way home from St. Michael's, were commonplace. The RTD was what the public bus system was called back then—Rapid Transit District. Whenever the girls from St. Michael's were cutting up on the bus, word would get back to JD. It was not hard to identify the bad actors—we all wore the same funny-looking brown pleated skirts and white shirts with the Peter Pan collars and oxford shoes. JD knew which students took the Manchester bus, so she would drag us into her office the following day for interrogation. That meant another phone call to Frankye. I sure did give her grief.

There was one girl in my ninth-grade class who was often involved in the bad-girl cat fights. She had gone to a different Catholic elementary school than I did. Cliques were formed based on your prior elementary school. We would alternate between being friends one day and not speaking the next...the usual high-school stuff. By the time we moved up to the tenth grade, we were on pretty good terms. But I noticed something different about her after our summer break: she was wearing wigs. Being young and stupid, this was a reason to make fun of her and start a fight. I soon realized that she was sick— really sick—she had cancer. I had never known anyone with this disease before and didn't fully comprehend the severity of her illness. But when she had a leg amputated, I knew this was awful. I never tried to pick a fight with her after she lost a leg. St. Michael's was a very small school, and we had friends in common who helped me to better understand what she was going through. Then, one day, she just didn't come to school anymore. She died a short time later.

This was my first experience with the death of a peer. Her funeral was a Catholic one, but one like I had never seen. There were these large, oversized photos of her propped up on easels in the front of the church. She was such a pretty girl. I wondered how her parents were able to get these jumbo-size pictures of her printed, showing her at various stages of her short life. I would later discover that her father was a very prominent figure on the LAPD and that the pictorial tribute was similar to the type used by the department at the funerals of fallen police officers. I did not know it then, but I later learned that I would have a kind of love/hate relationship with this prominent LAPD figure.

I just turned sixteen and had been worrying my mom for a car. I had a couple of classmates who were driving, and I wanted to drive also. Most of my friends had cars that their parents passed down to them. My mom had only one car—the one she drove to work every day. So when I said I wanted a car, she took me to the Mercury dealer on Crenshaw Boulevard near the Coliseum, and we left with a brand-new, sun-yellow 1974 Mercury Capri. I was ecstatic. Of course, there were rules associated with being a young driver: no late-night driving and no friends in the car. Man, what was up with all the restrictions? I didn't like it, but I listened and followed my parents' directives (most of the time).

After my mom bought me the car, I decided that I wanted to get a job to help pay for gas. My mom was against it. Again, I had some classmates who were working at a nearby fast-food restaurant, so I begged and begged until my mom relented. My very first job was at the Burger King on Manchester and Normandie Avenues. I worked at Burger King for about three months before I had a falling-out with the manager, a senior at Mount Carmel. He made me sick. He was just too damn bossy for me. When I told my mom how he treated me, she told me to quit. I did. I had enjoyed having my own money; I just didn't like him. Oh well, Frankye would continue to spoil me, and a job was not really something I needed to have.

# SIX:
# OUT ON MY OWN

Despite all of my foolishness, I managed to graduate in June 1976. I landed a full-time job working at a button manufacturing and dye company located in downtown Los Angeles that same month. It was cool. I was the youngest person working there at the time. This company received orders from stores like J.J. Newberry, Sears, White Front, and other sewing shops. I worked inventory control. I pulled and filled the orders.

My mom wasn't too thrilled about this job either. My cousin across the street worked at the employment development office and told me about a job with the State of California. She thought a career change was in order. I applied for a clerk position and was hired by the State of California Worker's Compensation Insurance Fund. This was great, because right after graduation, I had plans to get married, something else a few of my classmates were doing. I was ready to get out from under Frankye's control. I had been dating this guy for the last two years of high school, and we both thought that we were ready for the next step. I remember having a conversation with my then-boyfriend, who was twenty years old, about how we were both "ready" to get married. He told me that he "had done everything he wanted to do already," and I agreed with a resounding "Me too"—at eighteen years of age. What a laugh now when I think back. What did we know?

I would have been happy with a simple wedding—but Frankye would have none of that. I was her only daughter, and she was going all-out. I contacted a bunch of girls I had graduated with and ended up assembling a wedding party of twelve bridesmaids and groomsmen, two junior bridesmaids, a ring bearer, and a flower girl. I chose the most amazing wedding cake from Hansen's Cakes in Beverly Hills. Our wedding reception, which included about one hundred and fifty guests, was held at the Cockatoo Inn off Imperial Avenue in the city of Hawthorne. My parents spared no expense for their little girl's wedding.

Well, my young husband and I certainly should have been able to make the marriage work—we both had good-paying jobs (for our age) and supportive parents. He worked for the County of Los Angeles Department of Parks and Recreation, and I was working for the state. His parents gave us five hundred dollars as a wedding gift, which we used for a down payment on our first home. It was a small eight-hundred-square-foot house in the Hyde Park area off West Boulevard in the city of Inglewood. It was tiny—a "walk-thru" bedroom led to another bedroom, and it had just one bath—but perfect for a young couple embarking on a new life together with a child on the way. This was a lot of responsibility. I didn't really appreciate that at the time.

We tried to hold everything together as best as we could with an eighteen-year-old and a twenty-year-old brain. The fact of the matter was we were just too damn young to get married. It took the birth of our son to cement the obvious: we didn't need to be together.

I went back to night school and took a course in stenography. I was ambitious and wanted more for myself. Besides, I needed more money. I was a single mother with a mortgage, car note, and credit-card debt galore. Of course, my ex-husband helped with child support, but I spent a lot of time shopping for my little boy—I wanted nothing but the best for him. I was, after all, Frankye's child, and shopping was my middle name. I spoiled Lazelle just like Frankye had spoiled me. Frankye was just as bad. All he had to do was say, "Granny, I want," and she would fill in the blank. We both spoiled him. I filled his little closet with expensive clothes and way too many tennis shoes named after basketball players. Then there were the birthday parties with uniquely designed specialty cakes from Hansen's Cakes in the shape of a hot dog, hamburger, or basketball. Who spends a hundred dollars on a cake for a two-year-old? I am certain that I/we ruined him (sorry, Kiona).

I applied for and was later promoted to "stenographer" as part of a secretarial pool with the Department of Justice (DOJ). DOJ was located in a big multi-story building on the southwest corner of 1st and Broadway in downtown LA (now a vacant dirt lot).

As a stenographer, it was my job to type police reports submitted by the special agents working in the Bureau of Narcotic Enforcement (BNE) and Bureau of Investigation (BI). Shortly after I started there, another young lady came to work as a dispatcher. We became fast friends. We had so much fun at work that we began socializing together after work. Joni too became the sister I never had, and she remains my dearest, closest friend some three decades later.

# SEVEN:
# THE DEPARTMENT OF JUSTICE (DOJ)

We had a great time working for and with the special agents. There were a lot of twenty-something guys assigned as special agents to the Los Angeles office, and we were in our early twenties, so naturally the young ladies in the secretarial pool felt as if we had died and gone to heaven. The young special agents often took us to lunch and out for drinks after work. We were impressed with their spending power.

During the late '70s and certainly in the early '80s, there was an emergence of a drug called phencyclidine (PCP). Sales and use were on the rise. The agents in our office assigned to the Bureau of Narcotics Enforcement (BNE) had been working a case that involved a young black male drug dealer. The agents devised a scheme to use a woman as a lure to get him to a specific location for a meet and then arrest him on the spot. Since I was the only black female in the clerical pool at the time and there were no female agents, they asked me if I would help. Well, while this was exciting at first blush, I was also a little bit scared. I agreed to go along once the agents assured me that I would be in no danger. I knew these guys pretty well by now, and I trusted them emphatically. Plus, the idea of going out in the field with them was thrilling.

The setup worked. I called this guy and pretended to be a friend of a friend. I told him I was in town and needed a place to stay for a few days. He agreed to meet me with the intended purpose of letting me "hang out" with him until I could obtain other living arrangements. Men—he let the little head think for the big head, and it cost him big-time.

We met at Pann's Restaurant over on La Tijera near Slauson Avenue, and everything went off just like the agents had promised. There were one or two patrons inside the restaurant when the suspect came in, and all of the other occupants were special agents. Some were seated in a booth in front of me, and others were nearby. When ole boy entered the restaurant, he came in and sat down next to me, and the agents immediately converged on him and took him into custody without incident. That was so cool. I decided I needed to be a special agent with the DOJ. This had just been too easy. I couldn't believe that this was "all" the agents did all day. DOJ actually pays you guys to do this? I'm in. My son and my shopping habit were both growing.

Every day for lunch, Joni and I—instead of eating—would shop. When we weren't shopping at the underground Los Angeles Mall on Temple Street, we were at the 7th Street Plaza on Figueroa frequenting the boutiques that we just could not live without. Long story short—I was in a lot of debt.

In early 1980, Joni and I decided that we were both going to pursue careers in law enforcement, because the clerical stuff was not helping us get the quantity of merchandise that we desired from the local dress stores. I began to apply to a multitude of different police departments. The timing was perfect. In 1979, the Los Angeles Police Department had a consent decree in place as a result of Blake v. City of Los Angeles. The lawsuit, which was filed by a former female sergeant, Fachon Blake, alleged that the LAPD's past hiring practices discriminated against women and minorities. The department was now required to proactively hire more women and minorities. I quickly moved along the application process with the LAPD and, at the age of twenty-two, was given a hire date of August 25, 1980. I took it. My intent was to complete my probationary period on the LAPD and then laterally transfer back to DOJ after I received my POST (Police Officers Standard Training) certificate.

I chose to join the LAPD because it was a large department and offered a variety of assignments. At that time, the LAPD had divided the city into four geographic bureaus: South, Central, West, and Valley, with a total of eighteen patrol divisions. The

South Bureau was always a much sought-after assignment, because it was believed that a new officer would learn the most if assigned to a busy division. Contained within South Bureau's operations were the Southwest, 77th, Newton, and Harbor Divisions. My friend Joni decided to stay with the state system and joined the California Highway Patrol. She already had several years invested in the PERS (Public Employee Retirement System) and did not want to start all over.

To help potential police recruits physically prepare for the rigors of the academy, the LAPD offered physical training (PT) classes, which were given twice a week at the Elysian Park Police Academy. The PT classes were supervised by sworn training officers who held the rank of Police Officer III (P-3). There were about four or five components to the testing process, and a candidate was required to pass each one before moving forward to the next. Completion of the entire hiring process could take several months. Police candidates were encouraged to take part in the PT classes. There was much discussion about the "wash-out" rate among police recruits, and it was highly suggested that candidates participate in the weekly training, so I did. At that time, I was five-nine and weighed only 118 pounds. I was not in any particular physical shape. I was just tall and skinny.

# EIGHT:
# RECRUIT CLASS 8-80

August 25, 1980. Most every day started pretty much in the same way and at the same hour: what we call on the PD (police department) call "zero dark thirty." That just means it's really too damn early for any sane person to be up doing anything, least of all standing at attention. The recruits gathered every morning on a ramp that was located just outside of the main academy building. This was the designated spot where we would form into a squad and then march as a unit to our classroom at the top of the academy grounds. The police academy was situated in Elysian Park, right across from Dodger Stadium. This location is no longer used to train recruit police officers—a more modern academy was built on Manchester Boulevard near the 405 Freeway in the Westchester area. We started every morning with a march, singing some sort of military cadence led by our Drill Instructor (DI), who was another recruit officer.

Most mornings I would arrive on the Academy grounds, pulling up to the parking lot in my little convertible MG Midget, only to find that my class was almost ready to march away. That meant I now had to sprint to the women's locker room to hurry and change into my recruit uniform before the official start of our day. I ran late so often that I had perfected the clothing change; I could make the switch in about forty-five seconds. It was uncanny. My DI hated me. I could tell by the look of contempt he gave me when I went running by that he was hoping and praying that I could not make it back in time. But I was good. I made it each and every time. He had to wait until the exact official starting time before he could call the class to attention and march them away. If the recruit class marched off without me, it would be cause for discipline. I would need to write on a form known as a 15.7 the reason for my tardiness. This 15.7 would be given to the P-3 in charge of supervising our recruit class.

It was official—I was Police Recruit Officer Hamilton, Class 8-80. The recruit class designation was based on the month and year that the group started the police academy. The Academy Class 8-80 was the last recruit class to be issued the beige khaki uniform. Tradition is a big deal around the LAPD, and this particular tradition was one that I was proud of. We were also one of the last recruit classes to join the department under the "old" pension plan. This simply meant that I was eligible to retire on a service pension after twenty years of employment. The pension tier system would change in 1981, requiring a new hire to remain until the age of fifty-five or thirty years of service before he or she would become eligible for a lifetime check. Whew! Made it just in time. I already knew that I did not want to do this for more than twenty years. I was looking forward to retiring at the tender age of forty-two.

As recruits, we had to run everywhere we went on the academy grounds. We could never stroll around casually. Even though we were all "adults," we were treated like children. I didn't understand that the Academy was designed to "tear us down" and "build us back up" mentally, much like the military. LAPD was, at that time, quasi-military. The police officers who were charged with "teaching" would often yell and try to intimidate the young recruits. I was not accustomed to this kind of treatment, but I figured if that's what they wanted to do—fine with me. I was making, at the time, a ridiculous amount of money to get in the best physical shape I could obtain to start this new career. I was determined to make it. I was not going to "buy into" the whole LAPD thing—I would not "bleed blue"— but I would certainly fake it long enough to graduate.

Our academy class was unique and the subject of much observation from the veteran police officers who visited the Academy. These officers came to the Academy for a variety of reasons: lunch, firearms qualification, or to shop at the Los Angeles Police Revolver and Athletic Club (LAPRAAC).

The Class of 8-80 was small—it consisted of only forty recruits.

There were exactly twenty men and twenty women in our class. This was the first time in the history of the department that an academy class was evenly divided between the sexes.

One day a group of male white officers had been standing around, watching our recruit class and as I ran past the group, one of the officers yelled, "Hey buddy," in my direction. I was in my recruit uniform and wearing the department's dress hat. I wore my hair in a very small Afro. I thought, at first, the officer was trying to get my attention. We had been told that officers and maybe even the public might come around, out of curiosity, to observe our recruit class because of the large number of women and we were told to be polite and professional when responding to any questions that they may have. Being a new recruit, I was ready to respond and answer his question. But it took a few seconds for my brain to translate the phrase he directed at me. He had said, "Hey buddy." This was immediately followed by a chorus of laughter and finger-pointing from the other male white officers standing with him. I realized that the officer was trying to be funny and had referred to me as a "guy" because of my short hairstyle. There was nothing "male" about me. There was no way he could have mistaken me for a male officer. I went out of my way to look (and act) like a lady. I wore makeup to the extent that we could in the Academy: a little lipstick and mascara. I walked like a girl. I wore perfume so that I would smell nice. What the hell was he talking about—"hey buddy." Making sure that I maintained my femininity in this male-denominated profession was always important to me and something that I would just flat-out not give up. I was a girl—proud to be one and damned determined to look like one. I didn't respond to his taunt. I kept running and just thought to myself, "This is some bullcrap."

I was one of only two black women in my recruit class; there were also two black males in my class. The females in my class had come from a variety of former occupations. Some had worked as cashiers or waitresses in restaurants. A couple had prior military experience, but most were women like myself who just needed a good-paying job and had no prior thought or preparation for becoming a police officer.

Our PT instructors at the Academy were intense. We were led through a two-hour session by a veteran white male P-3 and a relatively "young on the department" black male P-2. They would take us on runs through the streets of Elysian Park at speeds that I never knew a human could attain. Our P-2 would sometimes run right next to me and get right in my ear and start yelling something about dying if I didn't pick up the pace. He asked what I would say to his wife after his death (all because I couldn't run any faster, really? I thought to myself, "This man can't have a wife—he's subhuman." He was like a bullet with feet. There was no way I would ever be able to keep his pace during a run. It was not uncommon for me to receive extra punishment at the end of our daily five-mile run because I couldn't keep up with the pack. There were two other women in my class who were also slow runners, we formed the Turtle Squad.

Both PT trainers were, of course, in phenomenal physical shape. They worked out for a living—what do you expect. They would lead us through a series of calisthenics and then take us on a five-mile run. Now, they didn't do the exercises with us, but they would run like they were possessed and expect us to keep up after an hour and a half of exercise. Maybe they really didn't expect us to keep up, but we would attempt to do so, as to avoid being subjected to an additional twenty-five or fifty "burpees" at the end of the run. Burpees were just a way of life for me and the Turtle Squad. I actually started to look forward to them. I knew without a doubt that I would be doing burpees on the field while the rest of my class went off to shower before lunch.

I managed to get through the extra burpees to the amazement of my PT instructors, which only led to more controversy. They accused me of "sandbagging" on the run, because I seemed to have so much energy at the end for the burpees. It wasn't that

I had been slacking as accused. I ran as fast as I could for the five miles—which wasn't very fast—and then did what I had to do to survive the PT session and be on my way. I accepted the fact that I was not a runner, but I was not a quitter either. I never stopped or walked on the run. I may have slowed way down, but I never stopped. That meant something to me, and I think ultimately to the P-3 who led our class. Toward the end of our academy training, he kind of gave me a wink and a knowing nod during one of our PT sessions to show he appreciated that I couldn't match the physicality of the guys in my class and a few of the female runners, but I persisted and that was what wanted to see. He would often yell at us during PT when we were wrestling or involved in other hand-to-hand combat techniques, "Are you going to just give up? Or are you going to fight?" I'm a fighter—had to be.

There were several days when one recruit—sometimes me—would be the cause of the entire class being punished. Punishment usually came in the form of many trips up and down a steep hill on the backside of the Academy. This hill was known as "Discipline Hill." Sometimes we were forced to run this hill in sweats and tennis, other times in our full recruit uniform and boots.

The days, weeks, and months were moving on, and I was still in the police academy. I had watched several of my classmates "wash out." That was not an option for me. I had quit my job with the DOJ to start the police academy, and I was determined that nothing and no one was going to take this opportunity away from me. I looked at it like I was being paid a tremendous amount of money to get in the best physical shape of my life. PT was only two hours out of my day. I would suffer through it and make the best of it. Sometimes, being obstinate is a good thing.

# NINE:
## "SUSPECT GET AWAY"

In addition to the physical training that we received at the Academy, there were also several hours of classroom curriculum. We were taught and later tested on police procedures and policies and the penal code. We also had an array of visitors during our first couple of months in the Academy, who spoke to us regarding the various benefits that would be made available to us once we graduated. One of the most important and significant revelations to me was the department's pension plan. I knew that I would be offered great medical and dental benefits, but it was the LAPD's offering of a lifetime wage at the end of a twenty-year career that was of particular interest. Of course, an officer, if he or she chose, could remain active-duty beyond twenty years and increase his or her pension base for retirement, but I had no thoughts of that foolishness. The longer you worked, the larger the percentage. At age fifty-five, the city would totally subsidize your medical and dental benefits. The idea of being able to "retire" at the tender age of forty-two was most alluring. I knew that I would have to pay for my medical and dental until I reached fifty-five, but I didn't care. That would be a small price to pay for an early retirement. I decided right then and there that I would not try to laterally transfer back to the DOJ but remain within the ranks of the LAPD. I had been told that the LAPD had a myriad of opportunities available for its officers, something the smaller police agencies did not enjoy. Oh, it was true. As I mentioned before, the LAPD had four Bureaus—South, West, Central, and Valley—which consisted of a total of eighteen geographical divisions. Each patrol division was divided into a patrol unit, where the uniformed officers were assigned and detective unit, where the plain-clothes officers worked. Then there were the specialized units like Metropolitan Division, which included SWAT, K-9, and the Mounted Unit. There were also a host of administrative positions, many of which were located in the police administration building (PAB) known as Parker Center

The assignments in PAB were most sought-after and coveted. It was known that if an officer wanted to promote within the department, a "tour" through PAB and Internal Affairs was a résumé requirement. I thought this was pretty neat. I could retire and still go out and get another job doing something completely different if I desired earning two paychecks a month. Oh, the shopping I would be able to do.

There was one little caveat that I had to be mindful of. The big bad boogie men from Internal Affairs came to speak to every new recruit class about the dangers of being charged with police misconduct. Our class was warned that if in the discharge of our duties in the field as police officers we crossed the line and got into trouble, we could be terminated and as a result would forfeit all monies we had paid into our retirement accounts.

We were told that we would be on probation for the first eighteen months after graduation from the Academy, and during this period we could be terminated "at the drop of a hat." It wouldn't take much, since we would not have the full protections afforded to other officers covered under the Police Officer's Bill of Rights. We were told that poor field performance, poor report writing, or failure to deploy the proper tactics when making an arrest could be grounds for dismissal. Clearly, making probation was critical. Police recruits joining the department after December 1980 were hired under a different pension tier, and the rules were very different upon termination/resignation. It was kind of an all-or-nothing situation as I saw it. Well, I had no problem with that, because doing the right thing was how I was raised. That threat was quickly dismissed as having little import to me.

What I later found out, some eighteen years after that classroom revelation, is that the department had been negligent. No one within the department had talked to us as new, wide-eyed recruits about the internal struggles that officers would be subjected to by their fellow officers and supervisors within the confines of the divisional walls, nor did they describe the numerous obstacles officers were expected to overcome. Like my favorite, the "phone-jack," and the names and racial slurs that you may hear directed toward you and the citizens we were supposed to protect and serve from other police officers, and the tight-rope balancing act between right and wrong that an officer must perform. More importantly, the LAPD never told us that the department would cut an officer down with the efficiency of a surgeon's scalpel if it believed him or her to be errant. No, the department kept that little nugget a secret for us to learn on our own time and in our own individual way.

Nonetheless, I continued in my training with my only thoughts being of the day I would graduate from the Academy and begin this new journey. As a little girl, I thought I wanted to be a teacher, or even a probation officer. I never envisioned myself being a police officer. It never crossed my mind. I grew up in the 77th Division. I remember as a small child seeing something on television about riots in Los Angeles and then seeing uniformed white men with big guns riding in tanks as they patrolled through my neighborhood. I remembered my parents putting me in the family car after the violence had subsided and driving around our neighborhood and saw that the police were positioned along with the National Guard, and they had signs placed on the street in front of their vehicles that read, "Turn around or get shot." I remembered thinking, "Really, you're going to shoot my parents if we don't turn around?" I recall as a teenager in the late '70s the proliferation of a street gang called the Crips and the way in which the police officers in 77th Division interacted with many of my male and female friends, both those in the gang and those not. Gang activity during that time seemed to claim the lives of many young men either by involvement or incarceration, plus the occasional female associate who had a love for a bad boy or in street terms, "a roughneck." I managed to stay far away from that gang lifestyle due to the influence of my parents and their involvement in all things Cheryl. However, I still really didn't like the police. Actually becoming a police officer was kind of odd and I lost some friends as a result of this choice.

Attrition was starting to grip our recruit class. We numbered fewer than thirty recruits as we neared the six-month academy completion date. I don't remember the exact reason, but a decision was made by department brass to shorten our academy training by one month, and each of us was asked to give three choices for a division of assignment upon successful completion of our recruit training. We were also given the choice of choosing a division where we would like to go and participate in a "ride-along." As a police recruit on a ride-along, we were assigned two uniformed training officers for a weekend. We would sit as the third officer in a basic A-car (two-officer unit) and act as an observer for the shift to give us a taste of what it was like to be an officer in patrol. I choose Wilshire Division.

In the early '80s, in my young-on-the-job eyes, Wilshire Division had a high number of black officers assigned, both in patrol and detectives. I was assigned to a pair of tenured black patrol officers for my first weekend ride-along, a P-3 and a P-2. I was placed on the PM watch, which is commonly referred to in other occupations as the swing shift. I remember the ride-along with my training officers was overwhelming. There was so much to know and remember as an officer in patrol. The most alarming thing was trying to know my exact location at all times. I had never been in this part of town, and the street names were unfamiliar to me. I had heard stories from other recruits who had started the Academy a few months before I did that it was imperative that I know my location, because the training officers might ask you at any point during the shift to report your location. My head was spinning and hurting at the same time. I did not believe it was humanly possible to maintain the street names in my head with each and every turn that the driver was making. You have to be kidding me. Who could be expected to really know their exact location?

Well, as promised, at some point during the shift, my training officer (TO) stopped the car and asked, "Where are we?" I began to gasp for air briefly and then shouted out what I believed was the last street our black-and-white had turned onto. Luckily, I was right. No more tests or tricks for the night. I say "trick" because it seemed as though the driving TO made a series of quick, sharp turns onto little side streets before he stopped and asked the question about our location. Once I correctly answered, the remainder of the shift became more relaxed.

The ride-along continued for another two or three weekends. I was again assigned to the same pair of officers on subsequent ride-along. What I noticed about these two was that they seemed to get along. I had the impression that they may have spent time together when off duty. They joked and laughed a lot as we went from call to call. During code-7 (lunch), you could tell they used that time to step away from the drama of police work and just relax. They actually talked to me and included me in their conversation.

After the ride-along, each recruit returned to the Academy and continued to participate in and be evaluated during sit-sims (simulated radio calls), PT, classroom studies, and firearms training. We were gearing up for the end, and that meant two terrifying things: the final PT test and the Pride Run. I had heard horror stories about both. I heard that if a recruit officer did not get a passing score on the final PT test, it would be grounds for termination. One of the surest ways to flunk the PT test was to allow the "suspect" officer to get your gun during the simulated combat situation that would occur at some point during the test. Well, that wasn't going to happen to me. Of this I was sure. Recruits were expected to demonstrate proficiency in applying department-approved pain compliance holds, baton strikes, and the ultimate challenge: what you would do in a physical-combat situation if confronted by a suspect.

We were also expected to participate in and "finish" the Pride Run. Failing to complete the Pride Run could be problematic, but I wasn't sure if one could be fired. I did know that the

Pride Run was longer than our daily five-mile run up and down Discipline Hill.

Discipline Hill was often used to punish recruits when someone did anything that the Academy staff didn't like. The entire recruit class would pay a price. Most times when we were forced to run Discipline Hill, we wore sweatpants and sweatshirts. But if any of the recruits had done something deemed particularly egregious, then we had to "run" in our long-sleeve recruit uniform, Sam Brown dress shoes, and bulletproof vest. That was a miserable time. If we were in our sweats, after two or three trips up and down Discipline Hill, then we were led off the Academy grounds and onto the streets through Elysian Park. The police academy was located in Rampart Division. The routes that our PT instructors chose served a purpose that was twofold, in my opinion: to torture us and break us down in the beginning and then later increase our endurance. These routes encompassed many of the steepest and more difficult areas like Marathon Street, the "Stairway to Heaven," and a nearby water tower. Some of the streets near and around Dodger Stadium were infamously named like "Cardiac" due to its steep incline. The hills were so steep that you might think you were going to go into cardiac arrest if you were made to run up that hill. I was terrified. I quickly learned that the department had a way of dealing with whiners and complainers. In the Academy, you didn't want to be labeled as either. I had to "go along to get along." I was taught to take what was being given or said, without question, or there would be hell to pay. Hell could be in the form of a long and grueling run, or it could be standing and polishing a statue just outside the Academy lounge for hours. I never had to polish this statue, but I had seen a recruit in another class doing just that. As a recruit, it was drilled into our heads that the single most important thing for any officer to understand is that you are expected at all times to back your fellow officer. For some that meant not reporting misconduct committed by your partner.

Our class was no longer composed of a fifty-fifty split between the sexes. There were far fewer women in our class now. I prayed for a female recruit officer to play the role of the suspect in my combat scenario. Boy was I mistaken.

Not only did I not get a female partner, I was given the oldest male in our class. I was the only female recruit who had to wrestle a male recruit for the final PT test. Was this a coincidence? I can't say. I certainly could not prove the selection was anything untoward. Like everything that is the LAPD, if it smells like a duck and walks like a duck and quacks like a duck—it could just be a chicken.

My recruit "suspect" was thirty-five years old. This guy was so awkward and stiff, I had no idea how I was going to successfully place his hands behind his back and cuff him without having to actually break one of his old, brittle bones. Well, I assumed that his bones were brittle, because I was only twenty-two at the time, and anyone over the age of thirty to me seemed "old." (When talking to my girlfriends, I always referred to people over thirty as "you know that older guy.") I had seen my classmate during PT when he had to wrestle and grapple with other classmates, and I was not encouraged by what I had witnessed.

Thankfully, I was not selected to go first when the time came to test. When our PT instructors finally called me and my "suspect" partner to the mat, I sighed heavily. This was it. Months and months of training, and it was all coming down to this one last exercise, demonstration, fight—whatever you wanted to call it. I just knew that I could not lose my gun. I could not fail this PT test. I had invested too much. I had come too far to be sent home. I had a four-year-old son at home, depending on me to get past this hurdle. I had no doubt in my ability to properly execute and demonstrate the pain-compliance holds we had been taught, like wrist locks, twist locks, baton strikes, and the shoulder smash with the subsequent bar-arm choke hold (one of my favorites ). I was prepared. I just didn't want my "suspect" officer" to take my gun during my demonstration.

Everything was seemingly going pretty good. I was correctly placing the various compliance holds as directed by our instructors. My "suspect" partner was not giving me a hard time. His arm was going limp at just the right moments. He wasn't tensing up and struggling against my efforts to control his movements. I was able to get him right to the point of actual pain and simulate my knowledge of the proper application of the hold without actually hurting this guy. I was in my happy place. Then, all of a sudden, one of the PT instructors yells, "Suspect get away!" This would usually signal the beginning of an altercation between the recruit officers. To my dismay and out of no damn where, this guy decided to be cute, and he reached around my waist for my gun. Okay, no problem—I jumped away, got in the stance known as the "position of advantage," and simulated a baton strike to his hand. I didn't want to hurt him—he was, after all, my classmate. But this idiot wouldn't stop. He kept advancing and reaching for my gun. Now he had a firm hold on the butt of my gun. Oh, this can't be. I was going to have to really hurt this nut. He continued. He wouldn't relent. So I opened my mouth as wide as I could, and I bit his arm as hard as I could. What do you know—he let go of my gun. Then he screamed in what I guess was intense pain. Whatever, I passed my test. He (the suspect) didn't get my gun. I immediately looked in the direction of the P-3 who was in charge of our class. He was laughing and smiling; I think I saw him wink.

Now, all of my classmates and the other PT instructor were tending to this wailing recruit. I kind of sashayed away with a satisfied smirk. I passed. I was going to graduate. I did it. He should have let go of my gun when I simulated the strike, like all of the other "suspects" did with their "officer" partner. Why didn't he? Was he trying to make me fail this test? I had no answer. All I knew was that he had been unsuccessful and earned a trip to the local area hospital for a tetanus shot. Some of the other females in my recruit class thought the whole thing was pretty funny. A few of the white male recruits—not so much. I didn't care. I would see my classmate over the years when our paths crossed at an in-service training day or some other city-wide tactical event, and we were able to laugh about the incident. He even showed me the lifelong scar he sported as a result of my bite. (Sorry 'bout that, ole chap.)

There was one last hurdle that we had to overcome. Before we could graduate, the Academy staff would "gas" us. That is, they took us to an abandoned building, filled it with tear gas, and made us walk through the building from end to end. We were told to grab the waist of the recruit in front of us and form a human chain. We were told it would be impossible to run through the building, so we shouldn't even try. We were told to not let go of the person in front of us and don't stop walking. I was not really sure why we needed to know about the effects of tear gas to graduate—but the staffers seemed to really, really enjoy this lesson.

So gas canisters were thrown into the building, and we watched the smoke come out of the back door as we stood in a long line, waiting to enter the building. The first recruit started what seemed like a death march into the smoke-filled chamber. Before I even entered, I could hear gulps, cries, and coughing coming from inside. As I entered the building, I immediately closed my eyes and prayed. Within two steps, my nose began to run like a faucet and my eyes were burning even though they were clamped shut. I was half walking and half stumbling. We all were. I just knew I didn't want to fall down in there. I continued the march and eventually came out on the other end. Once outside I opened my eyes and saw my classmates doubled over in pain, still spitting with their noses running profusely. It was disgusting. We were all in the same bad shape. There was an instructor holding a water hose, and each of us grabbed and yanked for the hose and then just doused ourselves with the water to try and stop the effects of the gas. I could hear instructors yelling for us to walk around and "let the air hit you" after we were hosed down. The pain and discomfort were tremendous, but we had made it. We were finally ready to graduate.

I completed my training and was assigned to Southwest (S/W) Division as a Police Officer I, or P-1. It was my first of three choices submitted. I was elated. I lived very near Southwest Division and knew the geography quite well. Probation was going to be a snap.

# TEN:
# MY ROOKIE YEAR

January 1981. As a new probationary police officer (P-1)—or rookie as we were more commonly called—your input was rarely sought, and participation in a conversation with the other training officers was nonexistent. Your desires were of no import to anyone other than yourself. So actually having a say in my first division of assignment and then receiving my number-one choice was amazing. I could not have been happier being assigned to Southwest (S/W), which was located on the corner of Martin Luther King Boulevard and Denker Avenue.

That's pretty much where my happiness ended.

I arrived at the police station only to learn that I had been assigned to the AM watch—that is, the overnight shift. Oh, great. It was early 1981 and winter. This was also the rainy season. I would rather be hungry than cold, and here I was assigned to the morning watch. Then, to top it off, my TOs were two veteran white males. Both of my TOs drove around all night with both driver and passenger windows rolled completely down. Who does this? Are you kidding me? All night, even when they drove code-3, with their police car's red lights and siren activated, they drove extra fast, with the windows down .I thought I was going to freeze to death. During the early-morning hours, there were few cars on the street. Okay, somebody must be messing with me, I thought. This is a setup. They want to see if I can hang.

I was assigned to the basic A-car (two-officer unit) responsible for patrolling an area located on the western border of Southwest Division known as "The Jungle." According to Wikipedia, The Jungle was located in a part of the city known as Baldwin Hills; named for the famous 19th century horse racing and land development pioneer Elias J. 'Lucky' Baldwin. The Baldwin Hills was also the site for the very first Olympic Village ever built, for the 1932 Los Angeles Summer Olympic Games. This Olympic village was demolished after the summer games. Baldwin Hills was sometimes referred to as "Black Beverly Hills" based on the many wealthy Black residents, among which were professionals, athletes, politicians and entertainers. The Jungle was so named because of its lush landscaping, since the mid-1980s the city has promoted the use of the name "Baldwin Village". The Jungle is a densely populated area composed of nothing but apartment complex after apartment complex. This was a fairly rough area during the 1980s and the years that followed. Also located within the Jungle was a particularly notorious section referred to as "Sherm Alley." The term "Sherm" was short for Sherman cigarettes, a brand used by drug dealers. The Sherman cigarette would be saturated with the chemical phencyclidine (PCP) aka angel dust and sold. Sherm Alley received its name because of the rampant PCP sales and use n this short stretch of alley behind some of the apartment complexes. By the 1990s the area had become a low-income, predominantly black and latino neighborhood, its glass portals gated and once sparkling swimming pools filled in with concrete. The patrol division that served this area would become my home for the next twelve months.

I didn't know any of the officers assigned to Southwest Division. This meant that my time spent driving around with my TOs could be very isolating. Code-7 was often miserable. Most of my TOs had little to say to me and often spoke of things that I did not find the least bit interesting. I was, after all, a young, black, twenty-two-year-old female working with bunch of old white coots. There were, however, several black police officers working at Southwest Division; there was a lieutenant, a sergeant-II, P-3s, and P-3+1s. The majority of the black officers were assigned to either day watch or PM watch. I couldn't wait to have one of those guys as my TO. I was happy to see them. There's nothing like interacting with your own kind; I just needed to be patient. While on probation, I expected a partner change to occur approximately every three or four months. This was done to expose the rookie to a variety of training styles and also give the P-1 an opportunity to patrol in different areas of the division.

My first few nights out in the field on patrol were mostly uneventful. As a P-1, it was understood that you would be the passenger. As the passenger officer, it was my responsibility to maintain the DFAR—Daily Field Activity Report. The DFAR documented all of our activity and calls for service handled during our shift. Probationers were not allowed to drive. Kind of funny, I know; it's almost like we were babies or something—I mean, after all, I drove myself to and from work each day. Why couldn't I drive a police car? I was trusted to carry a gun.

There were a lot of silly little rules like that on the LAPD. You know—the proud LAPD tradition; most of this was just plain crap. Male P-1s could not grow a mustache until their TO told them that it was permissible. P-1s wore a different type of leather gun belt and long-sleeve uniform shirt. Back then, the P-1s were issued a .38 caliber revolver with a four-inch barrel. The old-timers carried a .38 with a six-inch barrel in a special holster called a "clamshell." The clamshell was cool—it had a button on it that you could just touch, and the holster would spring open. You could draw and point like the cowboys did in the old western movies. I must admit, I liked the look. Once off probation I would have a "clamshell."

As soon as my TO said I could, I dumped that ugly-ass "bruce brown" leather belt for a more stylish "sam brown" belt. I imagine that it was those little subtleties that made LAPD officers look so sharp in their uniforms. But it was also just another way of singling a P-1 out as a rookie. Citizens could definitely tell the difference. The short-sleeve uniform shirt had to be "earned"—this was very subjective and the topic of much discussion. Every P-1 yearned for the day when he or she could switch to a short-sleeve shirt. Since you don't get that white stripe on your bottom of a long-sleeve shirt until you have five years on the job, a "slick sleeve" was a sure sign of a green officer. "Slick sleeve" meant there was no insignia on your shirt sleeve. The rules were the rules, and we were not allowed to question them. A lot of the black TOs didn't play those games: they allowed their P-1s to wear what made them comfortable, and then dare a white officer to meddle in their business. The black TOs treated P-1s the same, no matter their ethnicity. That was cool. I liked the black officers' swagger.

One of the many things I learned from just sitting and listening to others' conversations was that many of the white patrol officers really did not think women had a right to be on the department. Most opined that the only reason women applied for the job was to promote to a detective position inside and/or find a husband. I heard this repeated often. I was determined that I would not be lumped into that category. I made up my mind that I was going to be tactically strong even if I wasn't physically strong. I wanted to remain in patrol for as long as possible; "building pogues"—no matter the rank— did not garner much respect among the patrol officers. A building pogue is an officer spent more time in an administrative assignment than a field assignment.

I kept my mouth shut and did as I was told—that was the rookie way. I stayed in long sleeves, which was what I needed during the cold early-morning hours. No big deal. Working with the two veteran morning watch officers was not so bad. You ever see someone and draw an immediate conclusion about their personality type, and then later find that you were so far off the mark? Well, that's what happened with my first TOs. I thought they were going to be two old, racist "white boys" who were gearing up to give me nothing but grief. I could not have been more wrong. I learned so much about the duties of a patrol officer working with those two. There were some department traditions that they upheld—like not allowing me to drive and eating where they wanted every night. We had lunch at the restaurant inside the bowling alley on Crenshaw near Jefferson every single night without fail. It was okay, the food was good and the menu was pretty big. The waitresses were very nice. They knew my partners by their first names. They always made sure we were taken care of and our food portions were larger than the other customers. I enjoyed working with them and wasn't ready for a partner change when the time came.

I quickly became acclimated to my surroundings. I kept busy, and we handled a lot of different types of calls for service, most required a subsequent police report to document what had happened. By the time I finished my time on morning watch with these officers, I could write any report completely and concisely. I had even been given the opportunity to drive a few times. My probationary evaluations were exemplary and, at times, glowing. I learned a lot about patrol working with those two. They were nothing like I had expected: yes, they were "hard-charges," and yes, they had me hopping from radio call to radio call. When my time with these TOs ended, I had been involved in a vehicular pursuit both as driver and passenger officer as well a couple of combative situations in the field where I had to deploy the department-approved chokehold to subdue a suspect. I had also completed a variety of crime and arrest reports.

I was ready to transfer to another watch. I had a good foundation from which to build. Day watch, here I came.

# ELEVEN:
# S/W DAY WATCH

Being assigned to day watch with the blessing and adoration of the diehard morning-watch TOs gave me a little bit of an edge. Those two were known to be no-nonsense, kick-ass-and-take-names kind of cops. If they said you were decent, that's all a P-1 needed to move on. So far, so good.

I was assigned another pair of male TOs: one white and the other Hispanic. There were very few female officers in the division period so forget about having a female training officer. We did have a black female lieutenant who worked Southwest. She had just been promoted to lieutenant shortly after I arrived. In 1981, she became the first black woman in the history of the LAPD to be promoted to the rank of lieutenant. My two new TOs were a little more laid-back than my first TOs. I guess the word had gotten out that I could handle myself, so the day watch commander had settled on this pairing for my next assignment. Now I was starting to interact with the black TOs that I had previously only seen in passing. On a few instances, when both of my regularly assigned TOs were on a RDO (regular day off), I was lucky enough to partner up with one of the black TOs. Heaven.

Things seemed to be going pretty well—that is, until I met with my immediate supervisor, a white male who had been on the department about five years. He had just recently been promoted to Sergeant I. I guess he decided to make a name for himself by making me his first project. As my patrol sergeant, he was responsible for monitoring my performance in the field on radio calls and reviewing my completed crime reports. In other words, he "rolled on my calls" to watch me interact with the public and then later documented his observations. Every patrol sergeant was assigned a "den" of officers that he was responsible for supervising. If in the field you had a problem with a citizen or suspect and needed a supervisor to either defuse the situation or provide an explanation, your den sergeant would be the first to respond.

One day, my sergeant met up with me for a little conversation. He wanted to feel me out, I guess. He asked what I type of work I had done before I joined the department, where I grew up, blah blah blah. This guy was in fairly decent physical shape. He thought more highly of his physique than I did, but at any rate, he wanted to talk to me about my ability to handle myself in an altercation. He expressed concern that as a female officer, I might not have the upper-body strength to get the job done and "back" my partner in a fight. I was listened to this guy and wondered if he was serious. He went on to tell me that he wanted to put together training routine for me and that I needed to lift weights to increase my upper-body strength. Okay, I thought. I was a bit of a tomboy. I grew up in the 77th. I used to fight on the bus to and from high school. Cool. I can do this.

At that time, the weights and stationary bicycles were located in the men's locker room. There were so few female officers assigned to Southwest, I guess it never occurred to anyone that maybe the exercise equipment should be in a communal area accessible to both sexes. My sergeant eventually escorted me to the second floor of the police station where the men's locker room was located. It was a fairly large locker room. There were the standard U-shaped rows of lockers with wooden benches placed between them. The exercise equipment consisted of approximately two or three stationary bicycles and dumbbells that had been placed directly adjacent to the tall lockers. There was a bathroom area and nearby showers. My sergeant told me that a curtain of some sort would be erected to section off the restroom/showers and locker portion from the area where the exercise equipment was located so that I could come in and work out whenever I wanted.

The female officers locker room was located on the first floor, which was tiny and cramped; an apparent afterthought, as more women joined the LAPD. In the early '80s, I was one of two female police officers who worked uniform patrol; others would join me in the months to follow. There were several policewomen assigned to Southwest, some of whom were not "field certified," which meant that they could not work in patrol. These ladies worked the front desk or in the detective unit. They also wore the police skirt. Some of these policewomen opted to return to the police academy for retraining and "field certification." At that point their designation changed from policewoman to police officer, and so did the uniform. No more skirts.

I agreed to work out with my sergeant during my code-7, as I didn't feel I could opt out of this foolishness. My TO at the time had recently lost a lot of weight and was trying to maintain a healthy lifestyle, so he chose to ride the stationary bike during code-7. My new TO was a very nice man and we got along really well. He introduced me to the game of racquetball. There were racquetball courts in some of the fire stations in our division, so we would go there and play a game or two during our lunchtime. I was down for whatever. I was trying to get off probation.

In February 1981, a month after I had started working patrol at Southwest, our recruit class was called back to the police academy to participate in our official graduation exercise. The Academy training was previously lasted for six months, but for some reason our class had been cut short by one month, and we were sent out to the patrol divisions to start probation a month early. Since our graduating class was so small, only twenty-eight recruits, the department combined our ceremony with the 10-80 class. There were twice as many recruits in that class as were in ours.

Soon the pomp and circumstance of graduation was over, and I was back at Southwest to resume my probationary period. Over the next few days, I met my sergeant in the men's locker room to lift weights at his direction over several days. One day, my TO pulled me aside and told me that our sergeant had been saying some pretty nasty things about my presence in the men's locker room. I guess some of the black officers heard the negative remarks also. My sergeant went around the police station and asked both black and white officers how they felt about me being in their locker room. Then he said, "If she wants to be in the men's locker room, she needs to grow a pair." The black officers didn't like the comment. Word eventually made its way to the watch commander. I was called in by one of my other supervisors and asked how I felt about my sergeant's comment. Of course, I told them that I didn't appreciate what this sergeant was saying behind my back, especially since he had almost mandated that I go to the locker room to lift weights.

Within a few days of my interview, my sergeant was administratively transferred to the Harbor Division in San Pedro, California, about twenty-five miles away from Southwest. The command staff at Southwest didn't wait for the new deployment period (DP) to move this guy—it was immediate. (DP is the twenty-eight-day calendar used in place of a normal thirty-one-day calendar month.) The fact that his transfer happened mid-DP was significant. In my young-on-the-job state of mind, I could not appreciate how big of a deal this really was. I would soon find out.

The backlash against me was immediate. A few of the white P-3s and P-2s in the division were pissed off at me. I was blamed for the sergeant's transfer. The "good old boy system" was in full effect. This had never happened before—division supervisors acting to protect a P-1. Understand, this was a different time, and women were just starting to flood patrol. I guess the other supervisors wanted to send a message to the guys not to mess with the females. Well, they hadn't done me any favors with that little move. I assumed that if any of the male officers had a problem, they should talk to our supervisors. And, if they did, my supervisors would have "my back." Boy was I wrong.

I had become the subject of "water cooler" gossip around the station. Word was quickly spreading that this lowly P-1 had been responsible for getting a sergeant transferred out of the division. Many of the white P-2s and P-3s who had spoken to me before the sergeant's transfer were no longer speaking to me. I would get the "stank eye" when I was in the station. I didn't complain; I suffered in silence. I had not expected this response. I needed to shut my mouth and figure out what the hell was going on. I had to "go along to get along." I didn't understand the LAPD culture, but I was sure learning. The department would find many more opportunities to help me learn this lesson.

What I was beginning to notice was the fact that none of my supervisors made an affirmative effort to put an end to the isolation and gossip. Understanding and consoling only came from the black officers assigned to Southwest. Richard, Harry, Joe—thank you. (If I missed anyone, please forgive me.)

I continued with my training on day watch. Day watch was not quite as busy as PM watch, but my partners managed to get me involved in a lot. There were was one particular incident that stands out as funny now, but it was not at the time. My partner and I had responded to a "hot shot" radio call of a "naked—415 man." Well, when other officers would hear calls like this broadcast on the radio, they understood the potential for use of force and would immediately broadcast that they were "backing." On the LAPD, we never wanted a fight to be fair. It was always better to outnumber the opposition. Plus, somewhere in the radio transmission, the dispatcher broadcast that the suspect was possibly under the influence of PCP. Well, if he was butt-naked in the middle of the day, I'd say he was under the influence of something.

It was a hot summer day. My partner and I arrived on scene first. Just as we pulled up, I saw a black guy, approximately five-eight, maybe 160 pounds, completely naked. He looked in our direction, jumped into a trash dumpster, and lowered the lid. I could not believe what I had just seen. My partner and I exited our vehicle and decided to await responding units. Once we had additional back-up units on the scene, we decided to confront this guy—who was still hiding in the trash container. We needed to get his naked ass out of the dumpster and handcuffed. I assumed he heard the many voices outside of the container, and as we neared the top and got ready to lift the lid, he sprang out like a damn jack-in-the-box. When he did that, the fight was on. He was flailing his arms wildly. Each of us was trying to grab one and control his movements. Two of the male officers managed to get an arm and yanked him out of the dumpster. This guy was still flopping around like a fish out of water. He was thin but as strong as an ox. I had never encountered such a thing. We were having a helluva time controlling this guy. There were about six of us now on this guy, each trying to hold and restrict the movement of a limb. The guy was wide-eyed and crazed, looking quickly left and right. It was hot outside, and he was sweating profusely. He felt like what I imagine a greased pig would feel like if you were trying to grab one. He was sweaty and slippery.

This continued for a while. We were trying to get this guy into custody and without hurting him. It was obvious he was either mental or drugged or both. As the only female officer on the scene, I was acutely aware of his exposed man parts and was trying not to injure him in that area. This thing was taking longer than I thought it should, but eventually we got him cuffed and placed in the back of one of the police cars. After things calmed down, my TO kind of patted me on the back and told me that I had handled the situation just fine. He said he knew I had his back and he was not concerned. As a P-1 his words were reassuring. I knew that the other officers would be asking him later, "How did she do?" My TO was respected among his peers, and his words had weight.

I was doing fairly well on probation, so my TO arranged for me to participate in a ride-along with the air unit. I drove downtown and met the officers who were assigned to the air ship (helicopter). I partnered with them on PM watch. They told me that I could hang out for a couple of hours and then they would bring me back down. I was bummed—I wanted to ride eight hours in that helicopter. Once we got going, it was fun to see the city from the sky. This was my first helicopter ride. I became physically ill almost immediately. Both of the officers were very nice. They offered to let me play with their "night sun." That's the really bright light they used to illuminate an area for the street officers when they are in a vehicular or foot pursuit. We eventually responded to a call of a missing adult in Wilshire Division. The officers checked the area where an elderly man with dementia had last been seen. The officers placed the air unit in an auto-rotation mode as we searched. It wasn't long before I asked for a vomit bag. I never did throw up—but, man, was I sick. I asked how much longer it would be before they could take me back. They laughed because we had only been in the air for about thirty minutes. Unfortunately, I had to tough it out until we completed the call. When we were able to "clear" the area, I pleaded to go back to my car. They obliged. All in all, I enjoyed the experience. I just wished I hadn't been so sick.

I was nearing the halfway point in my probationary training. I had been at Southwest now for approximately six months. Time to see what I was really made of. I was reassigned to the PM watch and a new P-3 training officer, another white male.

# TWELVE:
# CATCHING BAD GUYS

I was now starting to look like a real-deal police officer. My old training officers on day watch allowed me to start wearing a short-sleeve uniform shirt. I even purchased, with their blessing, the type of utility belt worn by the veteran officers. I had been driving the police car on a regular basis in the field, and my reports were well written. My probationary evaluations were complimentary and supported by numerous commendations for outstanding work in patrol. One of my most notable commendations was for the observation and capture of a serial rapist who had been plaguing Southwest Division around USC.

While assigned to day watch, my partner and I had been driving around very early during our shift (which stated with a 0600 roll call), when I spotted a vehicle that matched information given to me by a rape victim a few days prior. Our victim had been kidnapped and savagely raped by an unknown male black who drove a somewhat unique looking vehicle. We had been given partial license plate information by our victim, and as fate would have it, that car was now stopped directly in front of our black-and-white police vehicle at a red tri-light signal. I shouted out to my training officer that the car in front of ours was the one described by our victim. I was the passenger officer at the time and immediately began to broadcast our location, direction of travel, and the vehicle information to communications/9-1-1 dispatcher. I also requested a backup as we were anticipating a traffic stop.

My partner and I discussed the tactics we were going to deploy when we finally made contact with the suspect. We agreed to play it real low-key and act as though this was nothing more than an ordinary traffic stop for a minor vehicle code violation. We could hear on the police radio that officers were on alert and were en route to our location. As the backup officers continued to broadcast their location, we knew that at least two black-and-white units were within close proximity. My partner activated the overhead lights on our vehicle and initiated a traffic stop. We both exited the police vehicle, and my partner engaged the driver. My partner remained calm and soft-spoken so as not to alarm the suspect. My partner asked the suspect to exit the vehicle. Once the suspect was on the sidewalk, my partner told him that he was going to place him in handcuffs for his safety and ours as we continued to further investigate "something" about either him or his car. The suspect pretended to not be the rapist we were looking for, and we pretended to not know his true identity.

Once the suspect was safely handcuffed, I approached the car and looked inside. The suspect had tinted windows on his vehicle, which obscured our view of the interior initially. I immediately noticed several things that were very unique to the commission of rapes and had been described perfectly by our victim. The electric window controls had been covered with silver duct tape. A large object, hanging from his rear view mirror, had been described by our victim. I also noticed that there was a towel in the back seat—something the victim stated had been placed over her head once she had been coerced into the car. It was obvious—he was our guy.

As other officers began to arrive at the scene and assist us, we had the vehicle towed and the suspect transported to the police station. Just prior to placing the suspect in the back of the police unit, he asked me why he was going to jail. I informed the suspect that he was being arrested on suspicion of rape. The suspect looked at me with a harshly contorted face and refuted the allegation. I then leaned in and told the suspect that I knew he had committed a series of rapes in the area. I advised the suspect that his last victim had been acutely observant and provided a lot of details about the inside of his car and the location he had transported her to for the actual rape, which was an abandoned apartment carport. I gave the suspect a knowing smile, and just before I closed the rear door of the police car, I provided him with a detail regarding his last victim that he had not known: she was a transgender female. Our victim had had a sexual reassignment. She had been born a man.

I never understood if that had anything to do with the fact that she was so detailed and precise in her observations during the entire ordeal, but she provided key details that led to the rapist's final capture.. She even remembered a portion of his license plate. None of the other victims had been as descriptive as my victim. The suspect looked up at me wide-eyed and angrily shouted, "What do you mean, it was a man?" The suspect quickly caught himself and said nothing more during the ride to Southwest police station.

Our victim in this case was a very attractive female. I knew the rapist would not be able to discern which of the numerous victims that would ultimately show up to court was the transgender. There was nothing unusual about our victim. Obviously—because the suspect had repeatedly raped her in the back seat of his Monte Carlo without realizing she was transgender. Even the medical doctor who had treated her and obtained evidence needed for our rape kit stated that our victim had had an excellent doctor, because he wasn't sure at first that she had had reassignment surgery. When the medical doctor notified us of this fact, he wanted to know why we hadn't told him prior to his examination. We could only reply we that said nothing because we had no idea of our victim's sexual orientation.

The arrest of the thirty-one-year-old suspect, who was an out-of-work landscaper and former Pasadena fireman, was reported in the Herald Examiner newspaper. According to the article, the suspect was found guilty of twenty-one felony counts, including gang-rape, armed robbery, kidnapping, and forced oral copulation against four women. The Los Angeles Municipal Court Commissioner presiding over the case described the suspect as an "extreme danger to society" who left two of his victims psychologically dead. He was sentenced to what was believed to be the longest penalty handed out for rape in the county of Los Angeles at that time: 114 years. He would not be eligible for parole for seventy-six years.

I was so happy to get this bad guy off the streets. In September 1981, I received a commendation from my captain, which read in part: "You are to be commended for attention to duty, teamwork, and perseverance resulting in the arrest and conviction of this dangerous menace to the female populous of Southwest Area." This was not my first commendation for outstanding police work.

Because there were so few black female police officers assigned to S/W at the time, I was asked to participate in undercover narcotics and vice operations. I received written commendations from my patrol lieutenant for an undercover operation that I had conducted with the vice unit. The commendation read in part, "She entered an after-hours club, where illegal sales of alcohol beverages and gambling were being conducted. She was successful in gaining entry and conducting an investigation. She displayed initiative, confidence, and an aggressiveness in her role as an undercover officer. She gathered valuable evidence and information that subsequently led to the arrests of nineteen persons for illegal sales of alcohol and gambling. She is to be commended for a job well done."

I was also commended by the vice lieutenant for that same operation. He wrote, "Hamilton has been loaned to vice on three occasions…and displayed alertness, enthusiasm, and good judgment in carrying out her assignment. She performed in an excellent manner and through her initiative was able to obtain necessary suspect identification and record violations. For a young officer, she displays confidence that is generally inherent in a more seasoned officer. Vice supervisors were very pleased with her work."

My field performance as a probationary officer was improving, and I was attracting the attention of command staff. On November 23, 1981, my captain commended me again, this time for being the "highest achiever in the area of radio calls.

It is through hard work and dedication such as yours that Southwest Field Services is able to combat the ever-increasing criminal problems of the area. You are also commended for being the overall top producer. I commend you for your effort and outstanding achievement."

In February 1982, I was again commended by my commanding officer for my "attention to duty, observations, and alertness which furthered the objectives of the LAPD and contributed to the success of the Narcotics Task Force Operation in Southwest Area." It was not uncommon for other units to ask to "borrow" a patrol officer for a particular operation, sometimes narcotics and other times vice. I quickly learned that being undercover and buying narcotics was not my cup of tea. First of all, these drug dealers would look at me and tell immediately that I was not a "strawberry," which was the term used back then for women who traded their body for drugs. I had to learn to be a good "mess talker" to convince them that I was not the police. I didn't like it. It seemed way too dangerous. Now, vice was a whole 'other story. I loved playing the part of a street-walking prostitute.

I was feeling pretty good about my ability to perform the duties of a Los Angeles police officer effectively. However, all of these commendations were not enough to stem the tide of "haters." I had to work side by side with these asses for eight hours a day; most of the time, they wouldn't talk to me for the entire shift.

I needed an outlet. My best friend Joni from DOJ was having her own issues with the California Highway Patrol (CHP). She had successfully entered their academy and graduated. After six months of training in Sacramento, she was now assigned to the downtown CHP office.

We decided we wanted to let our hair down. We knew about a nightspot, which was located inside the Ramada Inn named Contempos. Contempos was in Culver City, near the Fox Hills Mall. Contempos was all the rage. We checked it out and true enough—it was the place to be. There would be long lines of folks waiting to get inside to party. We had to line up in the beginning with the masses. After shutting the place down weekend after weekend and becoming friends with the DJ, we could just walk up to the front of the line and go right inside. Joni and I still marvel to this day how we would close the joint at 2 a.m. and then roll call at 6 a.m. the next morning. I was familiar with the term "a regular," but I never expected to become one. I knew almost everybody who was inside the club most nights. I would party with other young black police officers from the LAPD and even a few firefighters at all of the local joints that were hopping at the time. We viewed ourselves as a "buppie"; society's term back then for a young, upwardly mobile, black professional.

# THIRTEEN: WRIST LOCKS AND TWIST LOCKS

I moved on to PM watch and a new TO. This time I was assigned to work with an Asian training officer who had just been promoted to P-3. He had five years on the job, just like my old sergeant. I don't know what it is about being newly promoted, but it seems to bring out the worst in an officer. More importantly, I didn't know why I kept getting assigned to work with these fools.

Our first few days and weeks together were mostly uneventful. I was handling many of the calls for service; I talked to the reporting person, documented any crime reported while on scene, and then finished up our DFAR to end the night.

One particular night, my TO and I had been very busy. We had responded to a number of radio calls, many of which necessitated the completion of a report. One was a rape investigation. Most officers hated to get a rape investigation, because they generally took a long time to handle. The victim had to be interviewed, transported to the hospital for medical treatment, and then back to the police station to write up the report. Being one of only a few females in the field, most of the male officers would request my presence if they received a rape call. The way it would work was the assigned male officer would ask the female victim (all while nodding his head in the affirmative) if she preferred to speak with a female officer. Of course, most women felt more comfortable recounting the events of a rape to a female officer. I didn't mind. It was all in eight hours. I was happy to assist.

I had become a pretty good writer. My reports were always well written and thorough. I could complete most crime reports in little or no time with very little correction by my TO. My TO and I had a bunch of reports that we needed to finish. We decided to go back to the station to avoid any overtime. We had been so busy there had not been an opportunity to request code-7 or even grab a quick bite to eat. As my TO drove back to S/W, I asked if he would stop at a fast-food joint so I could grab a burger. You would have thought I had asked him for a lung or something. My TO totally ignored my question and just kept driving. I watched him drive past one hamburger joint after another. He never said a word. Soon I found myself back at the police station. Well, I knew that there was a Taco Bell across the street, so I thought I'd just walk over there and get something to take back to the station.

Once inside the police station, he disappeared, and I entered the report-writing room, which was located near the back door on the west side of the station. This was a small room that the officers utilized to complete their reports and sometimes just to take a quick break from patrol. I had at least two or three lengthy reports to complete, and I knew that we would not leave the station again for the night. It was going to take me the remainder of the shift to complete the reports and get them approved by the watch commander. By the time I finished, it would be time to go home. So I asked my TO if I could walk across the street to the Taco Bell before I started to write. My TO looked at me with a crazed look and flatly stated, "No." I asked why not, and he seemed to become immediately enraged. He told me that as a probationer, he didn't care if I had anything to eat during the night. He said as far as he was concerned, probationers could eat from the station's vending machine or go hungry. He told me that I was not to go get anything to eat and that I should just work on my reports. Well, I was hungry and beginning to get a slight headache. I was going to listen to my stomach and not his dumb ass. After his mandate, he disappeared again. I walked over to Taco Bell. I returned to the station a short time later with my food and began writing my reports. Shortly after I returned, my TO entered the room and saw me eating. He knew that I had walked across the street to Taco Bell.

He immediately—in front of about six or seven white officers of varying ranks—began talking to me in a tone that I found to be very condescending as he berated me for not following his order. These white officers did nothing and said nothing to my TO. There was one other P-2 in the report-writing room at the time, a black guy who was assigned to OSB–CRASH (Operations South Bureau–Community Resources Against Street Hoodlums). I pretended my TO was not talking to me and kept writing my report and eating my food. He stormed out of the room and then quickly returned. He demanded that I stop writing and go down the hallway to see the watch commander. I looked at him and asked why. He snapped, "Because I said so." I continued to write my report. I stopped chewing long enough to tell him that I didn't have anything I wanted or needed to say to the watch commander. It was apparent to me that my TO was becoming increasingly angry and agitated. He then stated, "If you don't get up and go down to see the watch commander, I will pick your little ass up like a suspect and drag you down there." I was in total disbelief. I thought, "This dude has lost it. And, I am not the one. I am a grown-ass woman, and I don't take orders from you." So I responded, "I'm not going anywhere, and if you want me to go, that's exactly what you will have to do." On that dare, my TO approached me, grabbed the hand that I was using to write, knocked my pen out of it, and placed me in a pain compliance hold (twist lock–wrist lock). The twisting motion of my wrist caused enough pain to make me rise to my feet. Once I was standing, my TO grabbed the butt of my service weapon with his other hand. Now we were in a damn struggle in the report-writing room. The other officers in the room were just looking. My TO was getting more physical with me, and now I was yelling for him to let go of my gun. It was at this point that the CRASH officer intervened and grabbed my TO by the arm. He told him to let me go. The CRASH officer was a large man. He spoke in a tone that let my TO know he meant it, and bad things would happen to him if he continued to jerk me around. My TO released his grip and stormed out of the report-writing room. (RS—I love you, RIP.)

A few moments later, the on-duty watch commander, a black

lieutenant, came into the report-writing room and beckoned for me to come with him. I followed the lieutenant down the hall into a nearby office. He started off by saying that my TO had told him that we were having some sort of conflict. My lieutenant told me that he wanted "this to stop" and that we were to "knock it off."

I looked at my lieutenant and told him that I was not going to go back out into the field with my TO. I told my lieutenant that he had placed me in a pain-compliance hold. I told him that if my TO was bold enough to do that to me at the station around other police officers, I could not trust him alone in the field. My lieutenant stepped out of the room and returned a few seconds later with my TO. My lieutenant reiterated what I had just described and asked my TO if it was true. When my TO admitted that he had grabbed me, my lieutenant's response was to split us up immediately—my TO went to the front desk, and I went to the hospital.

As the night progressed, word of the "incident" was spreading. Black officers were coming to me and asking me if the rumors were true. Many of the black P-3s told me I should file a personnel complaint against my TO. They told me in no uncertain terms that what he did was—in their opinion—totally unnecessary and they dared him to do something like that to one of them. Of course, he wouldn't. My TO was a slight Asian man, approximately five foot seven and 160 pounds at the time. He wouldn't grab any of those black TOs because they were men—real men—and would beat his ass. But grabbing a thin framed black female who only weighed 118 pounds—well now, that he could do.

All that pulling and snatching made my wrist swell. I told my lieutenant, and he had a sergeant transport me to the hospital for medical treatment. I was eventually placed on light-duty status by an ER doctor due to a wrist sprain. My TO found himself the subject of a personnel complaint: a 181. Back in the day, 1.81 was the number on the form used to document the alleged misconduct—hence the name "181." During the administrative process, my TO had been found guilty of what amounted to police misconduct and given a five-day suspension without pay for grabbing me. His buddies (fellow officers) were not very happy with me after the suspension.

Ding. Ding. Ding. Round 2. You cannot believe how pissed off the white officers were with me this time. It would appear that I am "Super Probationer." I had "taken down two of their fellow police officers." None of the white officers were bothered by the fact that an officer would grab another officer, in the police station, no less. Many of the white officers believed that I should have been fired, including my TO. None of that mattered to me. I felt no responsibility for the five-day suspension my TO received. I didn't know it at the time, but I later discovered that a certain black commander at the time, had heard about the twist-lock incident and may have had a hand in the penalty given. He was the father of my tenth-grade classmate who had died of bone cancer. Her father had risen through the ranks of the LAPD rather quickly and was now a commander; he was the youngest, in terms of seniority, black male to attain that rank in the history of the LAPD at that time. Our paths crossed quite often throughout my career. He was assigned to the South Bureau. Southwest Division was one of the four patrol divisions under the purview of South Bureau command staff. In my, young on the job mind, I didn't fully understand or appreciate his prominence on the department.

Any of the white officers who may have been inclined to have anything to say to me before this latest incident surely were not speaking to me now. Even the other probationers were giving me a wide berth. I was sure that their TOs had told them that I was bad news and to stay away from me. The isolation began in earnest. This was just one of the many ways white officers retaliated when they believed a black officer, particularly a black female, didn't belong on the LAPD. There was a contingent of black P-3s who were supportive, but they were not always around. And as a P-1, I could only hang with them so much. I didn't feel like I could seek shelter from them 24/7. I had to stand on my own. I was used to doing that. I was good at doing that.

Soon, rumors floated around the station that I could not be trusted, and officers better "watch their back" around me. This was the jacket that officers gave you when they didn't like you: "She won't back you." This label made my life pretty miserable around the police station.

My turtle shell was forming. But I had to ask myself—where was my black lieutenant while all of this talk was going on? Why didn't he step in and make those white officers stop talking about me? Why didn't he make a PSA during roll call and say that grabbing a partner officer is unacceptable—for any reason? My lieutenant had to know what was being said. There were no secrets on the LAPD. He was the one who had initiated the personnel complaint. His silence was tacit approval of the way those white officers were treating me—even though he knew that my TO was dead wrong. He surely had heard the comments in the hallway, in their locker room, and in the parking lot. But I had to go along to get along. I was still on probation. I had better shut my mouth. I had better not complain.

I was still a little confused at this point. I had some of the more outspoken black training officers telling me that I should sue my TO and the department for the way I had been treated. Conversely, I had my black lieutenant, who was in my young-on-the-job eyes akin to Oz, telling me that I should "not cut [your] nose to spite your face." He said, "You have your whole career ahead of you. Put this thing behind you, and go on about your business. Don't try and sue the officer." My lieutenant assured me that this would be the end. He promised me that things would be better, even though he never really explained what would make it better. It was over. Nothing else was supposed to happen. I believed and trusted my lieutenant because he was black. He wouldn't lie to me, right? After all, he was a high-ranking officer on the LAPD and just so happened to look like me. He must have known something that I didn't. The department decided my TO was wrong and chose to discipline him for grabbing me—end of story. Right? That's how things happened in a "fair world." I would later learn that LAPD didn't play "fair."

That little five-day suspension did little to derail my TO's career. He continued to work in all the right places and moved up the LAPD ladder, eventually attaining the rank of lieutenant. I guarantee you if a black officer grabbed a white female, promotion would not have been an issue because a black officer would have been fired. I bet my asian TO never had to explain during an LAPD promotional interview why he had been suspended for five-days back in 1981. I know those white captains and commanders saw the suspension in his personnel package which they reviewed during the interview process. It is funny how the powers that be will look the other way when it suits them. Sometimes bad acts are not so bad. Sometimes physical violence or force used by an LAPD officer against certain segments of our society are tolerated; you know like minorities and the disabled. That's the two-tiered internal system within the LAPD. I know black officers personally, who could not explain away minor misconduct that the department found them guilty of committing during an internal investigation. They would forever more need to explain how and why they had become the subject of an internal affairs investigation. Almost like that scene in the movie Shawshank Redemption" when Morgan Freeman's character kept asking and begging for an early release only to be told by the parole board that he was unfit for release. Converse that with my training officer who seemingly just sailed through the LAPD system. Well, some years later, in an off-duty incident, he shot his finger off. Nice things happen to nice people.

# FOURTEEN: THE HOUSE NEGRO

This would probably be a good time to tell you about a phenomenon that is well-known by black people in general and specifically by black officers on the LAPD. It is seldom discussed in mixed company; the house Negro. Here's how the house Negro comports him/herself. The LAPD house Negro will try and convince an unsophisticated audience that the department is a utopia; a place where everyone is treated equally. A house Negro will falsely report, during a press conference, in the presence of the Chief of Police that racism does not exist on the Los Angeles Police Department, at all – anywhere. The LAPD house Negro believes that the LAPD does not see color. The LAPD is a microcosm of society, made up of people with different beliefs, biases and perceptions; so absolutely racism exists on the LAPD even if minutely.

The LAPD house Negro is overly concerned with the manner in which and the frequency that they interact with the field Negro. The LAPD field Negro is generally viewed as a rebel-rouser; Someone who can't be trusted; someone who won't "back you". The house Negro can't be seen by the gate keeper helping or unnecessarily fraternizing with the field Negro lest they commit career suicide.

The house Negro will refuse to lend a hand of support if asked. The house Negro feign help and then make a quick left turn out of sight, leaving you looking back only to see that you are alone.

Being fairly tender in age and tenure on the department I was unfamiliar with the house Negro. I don't believe I had ever seen one. I didn't immediately recognize my black lieutenant at Southwest as a house Negro. This was, after all, my first experience with the LAPD House Negro. I am now able to spot that dog a mile away. After my training officer grabbed me in the police station and I reported the incident to a lieutenant, who happened to be black like me, I trusted his counsel. My lieutenant told me not to "cut my nose to spite my face," When he told me to "just put this behind you" and everything will be okay, I really believed that everything would be okay. It was all a lie. My lieutenant acted in the best interest of the gate keeper. He knew full well that the LAPD propaganda machine was warming up.

Every black officer on the LAPD understands that if you choose to display a spine there will be a price to pay. One then needs to make a choice; dignity or rank. It is difficult to maintain and achieve both. Not impossible – just difficult. If you don't think and act like the department tells you to think and act, and, oh yeah, "bleed blue" retaliation will follow. The department will teach you through a series of events; suspensions, an inability to acquire coveted assignments or promote and ultimately termination—that there are definite consequences for your choices. It is unwritten and unspoken, but true nonetheless. As a black officer on the LAPD, you better go along to get along.

I'd seen what happened to the more outspoken black officers on the LAPD. I challenge anyone to point to a black police officer then or now on the LAPD, who used their spine for its intended purpose- that is to stand up straight and not choose the path of least resistance with a rank higher than that of captain of police. They don't exist. Most officers who have stepped from behind the LAPD curtain to speak truthfully about abuses and corruption and flat out lying by the department have generally held a rank of sergeant or police officer. I have never personally seen a lieutenant and certainly not a captain on the Los Angeles Police Department speak in anything other than glowing terms as it related to the practices and policies of the LAPD. It doesn't happen. It won't happen. Certainly by the time an officer is granted access to the good old boys/girls club for command staff officers, indoctrination is complete. One must question why and how it is that high ranking police command staff on the LAPD never seem to witness or even hear about the types of abuses that sergeants and police officers see. Are all LAPD command staff officers ostriches?

Those of us on the department understood that this type of activity would be tantamount to career suicide. Many of the black training officers I worked with at Southwest Division in the early 1980s surely understood this. They didn't take any mess off the white officers. Consequently, the white officers gave the black officers a wide berth. Either by their own choice or as a victim of their own outspoken-ness, most of those black officers never promoted to a rank higher than that of police officer III or police officer 3+1.

This was also true of a black lieutenant who had been assigned Operation South Bureau (OSB) CRASH (Community Resources Against Street Hoodlums) during the late seventies – early eighties. I heard him described by the black officers as a "man's man". This lieutenant seemed to have the ability to challenge LAPD authority based on the rules the department had set forth. He managed to run and supervise a specialized unit with limited resources and yet his unit and officers remained productive.

During his tenure at OSB, some of the white police officers in other divisions referred to OSB CRASH as OJB CRASH. OJB was the acronym for the Oscar Joel Bryant Association. Oscar Joel Bryant was believed to be the first black police officers killed in the line of duty in 1968 and this association was created in his memory. I never had great aspirations of promoting on the LAPD. I was happy to have a stable, well paid position so I was willing to speak my mind at the risk of remaining a police officer for my entire career. I managed to remain true to myself, diligent and dedicated to the whole "protect and serve" mantra and obtained my highest rank which was that of police sergeant. Of course, the house Negro enjoyed the prestige of being the first black this or that and having buildings and freeway ramps named in their honor; but to what end?

This is not exclusive to the LAPD but indicative of how many blacks will contort and conform to be included in the "ruling class."

# FIFTEEN: LAPD THE MACHINE

There was a process for promotion. There was a process for handling administrative investigations of alleged police misconduct. The department was adept at manipulating these processes for its benefit.

When you sat before an oral board on the LAPD, it usually consisted of a captain or higher. The department first required that you pass a written test and then an oral interview is granted before a board of command staff officers. Then, the department ranks and lists the applicants in groups from which available positions are filled. The fact that your name appeared on a promotional list was no assurance that you would be "selected" when your group was made available for selection. The department could, at will, "skip" over you and promote someone who actually had a lower score or rank in your group. This was when things became subjective.

Once you joined the department, you started to hear the same refrain repeated over and over around the police station: "P-2 for life." "P-2 for life" refers to that special breed of officer who had no desire to promote, either because they had been beaten down by the department and they recognized they would go no higher, or they were comfortable in their current assignment and understood that the pay was the same whether you were in the kit room, sitting at the front desk, or working the U-boat (the report car). However, the department seemed to infer that there was dishonor associated with being a "P-2 for life," so sergeants and the like were constantly pushing and prodding officers to promote, promote, promote. You didn't want to be a "P-2 for life." The more coveted assignments required that you were at least a P-3, so promote we did.

In pursuing this carrot, the coveted assignment that the department dangled in front of you, an officer learns that with promotion came expectation. The department required and almost demanded that you demonstrate your willingness to misuse and mistreat a fellow officer, and if you did, you would be rewarded with the grand prize—promotion.

As a young officer, you were told that there were certain assignments that, if successfully completed, would ensure that next rung in your promotional ladder. A tour through the "Building" was one such assignment. The "Building" referred to an administrative assignment in Parker Center, like the Office of Operations, where completed a lot of writing, or one of the many detective divisions, like Bunco Forgery Division, Abused Child Unit, etc. These assignments were expected to help an officer become a better report writer—a much sought-after commodity if you later promoted to sergeant, lieutenant, or captain.

The other "must do" was a tour through Internal Affairs (IA). An officer, having attained the rank of either detective or sergeant, who is assigned to internal affairs division, had the responsibility of investigating police misconduct. The IA investigator performed the duties of a "prosecutor" or advocate representing the department at an administrative hearing or Board of Rights (BOR).

This too was unspoken but known to be true. Do well during your loan to Internal Affairs; that is be petty, dishonest and overzealous in sustaining allegations of misconduct and you are guaranteed a permanent position in the unit and future promotional opportunities. This will become clearer later-on.

Now, that is not to say that all IA investigators are cutthroats. I knew a few and later became the victim of two of the internal affairs variety of house Negro. I worked "on loan" to IA as a sergeant and was trained in the art of mistreating another police officer. I just chose not to conduct myself in that way. When I was assigned to IA, I treated my accused officers the same way I did the public as a patrol officer: I was fair and honest. The facts were the facts. Let the chips fall where they may. I was not willing to sell my soul to the devil. I appreciated my "loan" to Internal Affairs, but I was not offered a permanent assignment even though I was given a high-profile case to investigate which involved a white LAPD officer who was accused of misconduct which involved the shooting & subsequent death of a black LAPD officer.

# SIXTEEN: MR. CLEAN

I am back at Southwest, and my TO had just been suspended for five days, without pay, for grabbing me. Time for another partner change. My new TO, another white male, told me that he was aware of my "history" and said he did not anticipate us having any "problems."

There was something weird about my new TO. I had seen him around the station and found him to be odd. I couldn't put my finger on what made him appear so peculiar. His posture was perfect; he was always immaculate; his uniform was perfect, right down to the crease in his shirt. His shoes were spit-shined to the point where they looked like patent leather rather than regular leather.

Right after roll call each and every day, we would meet at the gas pumps in the back of Southwest police station. I had previously stopped by the kit room and checked out our shotgun and car for the night. That was a task relegated to the rookies. You never saw any of the veteran officers in line to get equipment. The "boots" (rookies) were made to do that.

On our first night working together, I met my new TO at the gas pumps with arms loaded full of new ticket books, my flashlight and baton, a shotgun, and whatever else I needed to have in my arsenal for the evening. As I approached my TO, who was waiting for me and cleaning his prescription glasses while he looked in my direction, he very matter-of-factly and without hesitation and asked me, "Where's my coffee?" I looked around, thinking maybe there was someone else behind me that I couldn't see; surely he wasn't talking to me. I soon realized that he and I were the only two standing there. He repeated his question. I started placing the items in my arms inside the police car and told him in no uncertain terms that I did not have his coffee, nor did I intend to procure any coffee for him. He gave me this stern look as if to infer that I must be mistaken and that my previous TOs had shirked their responsibility by not making sure I understood that getting his first cup of the shift was also my job. Oh boy, this was going to be bad.

We (I) finished getting the car ready for the night's patrol, which also included washing the black-and-white (by hand) inside and out. Finally, we left the station. I soon found out my TO was some kind of a germ-a-phobe. We started every night together with me (and him a little bit), washing, wiping, and sanitizing the car's interior, the steering wheel, the leather arm supports on the door, and anything else that could into contact with his skin. It was incredible. It would take us about thirty minutes to clean the car to his satisfaction before we could depart the station parking lot. It was commonly known and widely accepted that he would task his "boot" with performing this nightly ritual—and so I/we did.

After doing my best "Mr. Clean" interpretation, we immediately went to a nearby Winchell's. For what? Yep, coffee and donuts. It was there that he gave me my marching orders for the evening. This would take an additional fifteen to thirty minutes, an inordinate amount of time in my opinion. We "briefed" about how things were to be handled in the field as we dealt with the public that night and debriefed the previous night's events. It was maddening. This continued for the next six months. I came to understand his idiosyncrasies and just dealt with them.

Everyone at Southwest knew this guy was a nut job—the officers, the sergeants, the lieutenants, and, I am sure, even the captains. For all of his craziness, he was allowed to carry on and eventually promoted to P-3+1. A P-3+1 is supposed to be the liaison between the department and the community. This officer worked very closely with the community—almost as if he belonged to the citizens who lived within his basic A-car area. When a citizen had a problem, he would be their first line of contact. It's amazing that the department would promote this guy to be that first line of contact for the predominantly black Jungle. I mean, there were no white areas in Southwest Division, but the Jungle was gang-entrenched, FOI filled, and where some of the more economically challenged residents lived. FOI is the acronym used for Fruit of Islam; the all-male paramilitary wing of the Nation of Islam (NOI).

Just as everyone knew this guy was weird, everyone knew he really didn't like blacks. Oh yeah, he pretended to and said all of the right things—especially, I'm sure, in that oral interview with the captain who promoted him to P3+1. But truth be told, I believed he hated blacks. Weird thing is, he bragged about the fact that he "dated" black women; mostly those who lived in the Jungle. I picture some down-on-her luck female who was not very discerning.

This guy sickened me. I still had a few more months before my probation ended and I needed to get beyond him. I had to listen to him tell me about his weekends with his side piece. He was married. Like a lot of police officers, had a chick "on the side." The male officers had a term they used for the time spent with the "other woman"—code-X. That's when you told your wife or main girlfriend a lie—like you are working overtime or have to go to court—but in reality you are with the other woman. This guy professed to be much in demand. I couldn't see it. I was like, whatever. At some point he asked me to join him for a weekend motorcycle ride. I respectfully declined. I'd sooner eat my own colon.

Anyway, it was easier to smile and nod, in an attempt to get along with this guy. He was a real piece of work. When he wasn't sharing the sordid details of his many conquests with black women, he was bringing me up to speed on his knowledge of and great working relations he enjoyed with the FOI. Many of its members resided in and "protected" the Jungle. There would be nightly confrontations between my TO and me and the "brothers" from the FOI. According to the FOI, their community didn't trust the police patrolling their neighborhood, and the FOI believed they did a better job of protecting their community.

Of course, that was silly, because when people had a legitimate need, they still called the real police. We would respond, and then the FOI would appear. Depending upon which of the brothers were on "patrol" at the time, the encounter could be either non-confrontational or downright combative. I watched as my partner interacted with these men, and I could tell that they had no respect for him and were just itching for a fight. There was one "captain" in particular who was more amenable to speaking and working with us when we responded to radio calls in the area. He was able to calm the younger, more agitated brothers when he showed up.

I pretty much had to go along and stand by as my TO conversed with this group. I was in a very precarious predicament. I was, after all, black. This group hated the police. I was the police. Clearly, I was not making any friends with this group. I did my job when called into the area. I maintained a professional demeanor when dealing with the FOI, and I did not take their verbal attacks personally. I understood—but I still had a job to do; sometimes that meant arresting someone they didn't think I had the authority to arrest. It was very contentious at times.

This continued for several months—this back-and-forth, love-hate relationship we shared. While assigned to morning watch I had seen military style squads of FOI forming in the area near Nicolet and Pinafore. They jogged through the to a nearby park, where they participated in floor exercises, and then they returned to their apartments. My TOs on morning watch never messed with them, so I had had no contact with them until I started working with the germ nut.

I tolerated the germ nut, and he tolerated me. I had just a couple of months left, and probation would be over. I spent my final DP assigned to STORM. The officers assigned to this unit were either P-2s or P-1s nearing the end probation and had demonstrated their ability to work as an "L" car—a one-officer report unit.

On February 6, 1982, the sergeant-II AWC (assistant watch commander) issued my final probationary report. He wrote, "This concludes Hamilton's probationary period. She has demonstrated through job performance that she is very competent at handling the duties and responsibilities of a police officer. She has worked with minimum supervision. Her productivity is high and the quality of her reports is superior. Hamilton's demeanor and appearance are always professional. She exhibits confidence when making decisions. I am more than pleased to have her work for me."

Yay! Off probation. I would transfer to a new division as a P-2 and start anew.

So I thought.

# SEVENTEEN: THE B-WAGON

The transfer was out, and I was on it. The department again gave me the opportunity to provide three choices for a new division of assignment upon promotion to Police Officer II or P-2. I requested Central Division, which is part of Central Bureau. Central Division is located in the heart of skid row in downtown Los Angeles. I had negotiated the mean streets of South Central, and I was ready for something really different in a new bureau. I had made it off probation. I was excited. The department promoted me to the rank of P-2. This promotion is the only one that the department "gives" an officer. Every promotion after this became a competition. Going forward, I would be required to participate in a written test followed by an oral interview.

Being a newly promoted officer in a new division, I was lucky to be assigned to day watch, but I was given a crappy assignment. I was assigned to work what was called the "B-Wagon." I was assigned along with another officer who was one of those "P-2 for life" guys; he had been around the LAPD for a while but was "burnt out" and, by LAPD standards, lazy. This officer had been assigned to the B-Wagon forever, and he seemed content. The B-Wagon was a large navy blue panel truck with seats affixed to each side on the interior. There were no handcuffs connected to the bench, so any arrestee placed inside the wagon was able to move about the cabin freely. Our job was to drive around all day. When the foot-beat officers came upon a drunken homeless person whom they wanted removed from the streets or storefronts (because they were either a nuisance or an eyesore), we were called. Back then, being drunk in public wasn't considered a crime. We responded to a call, placed the drunk in the back of the B-Wagon, and continue to drive around until we had a "full load." Then we made a deposit at Jail Division, which was located in the back of Parker Center on

Alameda between 1st and Temple Streets. This would be the sum total of our day. We would stop only for code-7.

This was a less than desirable assignment to say the least. No one wanted to do this. We had to search the drunks for contraband and weapons before we placed them inside the B-Wagon. Most of the homeless people were harmless, inebriated, smelly, and often uncooperative due to their state of intoxication. They could become argumentative and combative once in the back with the other homeless people we picked up along the way, so we needed to make sure everyone was safe as best we could. Some of them had even urinated or defecated on themselves before our arrival, so searching them was most unpleasant. It was downright awful.

The B-Wagon was generally the first assignment for all newcomers to Central division, so I did my time without too much complaining. There were times when the guys in the back would start to cause trouble. As we drove around downtown, we could hear arguing and cursing. The first time this happened, my "P-2 for life" partner said, "Watch this." He sped up and then stopped suddenly. You could tell that whatever had been going on had stopped, and now the angry shouts were directed at my partner as the quick stop had thrown them onto the floor of the B-Wagon. My partner thought this was hilarious. It did quiet everybody down for a while.

They were the usual suspects. We would see the same people day in and day out. Jail Division kept them until they sobered up, and like homing pigeons, once released, the homeless would go right back to the same area they had been removed from earlier in the shift. Sometimes we would pick the same person up multiple times in a shift. I thought I was going to be able to put all this big-time south-end training I had received to good use, and I found myself relegated to picking up homeless people like a trash collector.

A few of these people I found had really interesting backgrounds.

I talked to those who were willing and able to articulate how they came to be homeless. I encountered the brother of a famous Hollywood actor who had been a long time skid row resident. Allegedly, his famous brother knew he lived on skid row but this guy preferred skid row over a safer environment living with his family. I also met a purported medical professional who landed on skid row after a nasty divorce. But for the grace of God, there go I.

I remember one young man in particular who I came to know very well. He was new to skid row. I hadn't seen him before. What I noticed right away was how clean he appeared. He wore a nice sweater, with a funny pattern and a snowman, the kind someone would give as a Christmas present. He too was drunk, but he was always pleasant and agreeable. Then one day, as he stepped into the back of the B-Wagon, I noticed that he had a big hole in the back of his sweater. I hadn't seen him for a while, so I asked him about the hole. He told me that he had been stabbed in the back one night while he slept on the streets. He said the person who stabbed him also cut his pockets open and stolen all of his money. I felt bad for him. He didn't seem like the type who would end up homeless. He was too young. He must have fallen on hard times and just decided not to ask his parents for help. One day, just as he appeared, he disappeared. I never saw him again. I often wondered what happened to him. I hoped he was okay. There were a few incidents and encounters on the job that have had a lasting impression on me, and he was one.

I continued in this assignment for approximately two more months, and then, finally, I was assigned to a foot beat with a couple of old salts. This was the term I used for disagreeable, crotchety old white men. These guys were burnt out too, but I could tell by their swagger that they thought they were "somebody." They were both P-3s, and all they did all day was walk around the area of Main Street and Los Angeles Street between 4th and 6th Streets and meet with the business owners in their area. They would flirt with women coming downtown to shop in the garment district and get cozy with the various restaurant owners, who would let them eat for free during code-7. The restaurant owners seemed to enjoy having the police in their establishment; at least they never had to worry about a robbery if the police were there. The downtown cops loved to get free stuff, so it was a win-win situation. Clifton's Cafeteria on Broadway and 7th Street was a favorite.

I was happy to be off the B-Wagon, so I was ready to make the best of this "new start" that my former lieutenant, the house Negro, had told me about. It wasn't long after I had started working with these two white officers that I began to notice during code-7 that the topic of conversation never included me. No one ever asked me about my days off, my family, or what I liked or disliked. As a matter of fact, it quickly became obvious that my partners and the other white male officers who joined us for lunch seemed to purposefully exclude me from the discussion. They talked about things that were of no interest or import to me, and after a while, I just thought "oh well." I couldn't make them include me in their conversation. Who could I tell that I felt mistreated? I had to go along to get along. This was a new division and supposed to be a new start. This was far from that new start promised.

One day during code-7, one of my partners started asking me questions about my time at Southwest as a probationer. He tried to make his questions appear innocent and non-probing, but I later found out that the white officers had been talking about me behind my back. My old partner on the B-Wagon, being a white male, was sometimes privy to their discussions. They were very comfortable speaking bluntly around each other, never stopping to be sure of their audience. So, word got back to me, and I found out that Central patrol was no different than Southwest patrol.

Actually, my "P-2 for life" partner explained a little factoid to me—he told me that several officers from Southwest had called ahead once my name was on the transfer. The Southwest officers shared stories about me with the Central officers; false stories, but stories none the less. Cops love to spread a good rumor, so these rumors spread like wild fire. P-2 For Life had heard the officers from Southwest division "wanted them to know what they were getting." P-2 For Life also told me that Central officers had been told that I was a Muslim, a plant, that I couldn't be trusted, and they should "watch their back around me."

It all made sense now. I understood why I had been assigned to the B-Wagon when I first transferred into Central. I understood why the jackasses on the foot beat treated me so poorly during code-7 every day. I understood why many of the white male officers were monosyllabic in their communications with me. I could not believe this crap. This was Southwest all over again, and again I was the only black female who worked patrol in Central. Funny that none of the Southwest officers mentioned my exemplary probationary evaluations and commendations when they spoke of my time at Southwest. I guess good news doesn't tell so well.

Central had a black captain in charge of the division. I had never seen one of these. Wow. Impressive. He seemed somewhat preoccupied. Whenever I saw him in the hallways he hardly even acknowledged my presence. He pranced and preened like a pretty peacock. I must admit, he was a sharp dresser. His shirts were obviously tailored and almost hugged him. He had a nice physique; for an older man who was graying around his small Afro. I imagined some might found him attractive but there was an arrogance about him. I didn't like his bedside manner. He seemed full of himself. One day, he found the need to have a conversation with me but it was nothing like I expected. I expected him to welcome me to his division and then maybe offer some advice that a young black female might find useful as I travelled through this LAPD wilderness. I thought maybe he had heard how the white officers had been talked about me in and around the police station. Instead, he wanted to talk to me about my fingernails. Damn house Negro.

He called me into his office and asked to see my fingernails. I extended my hands. He looked at the length of my nails and asked me how long? I told him that I didn't really know, but if I had to guess, probably an inch or two. Well, he told me that I needed to cut my nails; they were too long. What? Really? I respectfully told him that I was not going to cut my nails and asked him if there was any policy that prohibited me from having nails this length. He looked at me in amazement but had to respond, "No." He asked me what would happen if I broke a nail while in the field. I told him that I would grow another one. This continued for a few moments. I had made up my mind that as long as there was no policy against me having long fingernails, I was not cutting them. That was that. He dismissed me. Not one word about the gossip.

Sometime during the next few weeks, I ran into a young black P-2 who was also assigned to Central patrol. I had not seen him before. We struck up a conversation and when I saw him around the station a few days later we arranged to have code-7 together when time permitted. I spoke to him about the problems I was having and the way I was being treated by the white officers. He listened intently but had little input and certainly offered no assistance. I knew he had only a few years more than I did on the job, but I thought he could offer something by way of what I should do. I never asked him to say anything to those white officers, and he never did. He did, however, pull me to the side one day when we were both in the station and told me that a few of the white officers had pulled him aside and gave him the "skinny" on who he was associating with. He basically told me in so many words that the white officers had given him a bit of advice: if he wanted to do well (i.e., promote) on this plantation—I mean, department —he might want to rethink his acquaintances. When I asked him if he was going to stop meeting me for code-7, he looked me straight in the eye and said, "Yes. I don't need any trouble." He said that someone had shown him a copy of our MDT (car computer) transmissions and knew that we were using the MDT to communicate during our shift. He abruptly stopped meeting me for code-7 and stopped chatting with me. Really? Another house Negro. He was the only other officer in patrol at the time that I felt a kinship toward. Man, I couldn't believe this. What happened to that fresh start? Guess he needed to go along to get along.

So now I have come to know that there were varying ranks of the house Negro, much like ranks of police officer—I, II, or III. You have the house Negro who will look you in the eye and tell you something that he knows is in the best interest of the department and not you (the individual officer), and then there is the silent house Negro: the one that just flat-out won't help or speak out. This house Negro is like a weed on the department— it just keeps sprouting up in different places. Where's my round-up" weed be gone? House Negroes come in all ranks I see.

This P-2 house Negro was true to his word—he remained quiet, listened to those white officers, and stayed the hell away from my black ass. Guess it worked—he later went on to enjoy all those coveted assignments in specialized units like vice and detectives, and he worked in administrative assignments in the Building and the Bureau. The department kept its word to him too—he eventually became a deputy chief. Now, that's not to say he wasn't a good guy. He was much beloved on the department by most of the blacks for his accomplishments— but at what price?

According to the department, he did some really great things on behalf of the LAPD for the community, particularly in the south end of the city. One question we can never really know the answer to is, "What was his motivation?" Was it self-serving? He obviously was well compensated by the department and qualified for sure—but what I do know is this: he spent long hours in the trenches in one of the bureaus with the highest rates of violent crime. He often responded to high profile shooting incidents during early-morning hours, only to follow up with his regular duties as a command staff officer in the Bureau. He had become the face of the department at significant incidents in South Bureau. Seemingly all of the high ranking blacks were assigned to South Bureau and South Bureau only - a seemingly department sanctioned type of institutionalized segregation I am not certain if there has ever been a black officer prominently placed in West or Valley Bureaus. These areas tend to be more affluent and predominantly white. Interesting. It is my belief that with an assignment in South Bureau where crime is rampant and relentless, the stress on a commander or deputy chief is enormous. His untimely death, at the age of fifty-three tends to support my premise. It's hard out here for a house Negro. Well, the department and city did name a freeway off ramp in his honor.

# EIGHTEEN: THE LAPD CULTURE

I had been on the department for nearly two years. I knew about the payday drink fest that went on, but I didn't want to get caught up. LAPD paychecks were issued every other Wednesday, and that was the time that most of the white officers (and a few black officers) would find themselves at the Elysian Park Academy Lounge. The officers would show up like clockwork, and so would the civilian females looking to "hook up" with a cop. The officers would socialize and drink (to excess) with women to whom they were not married, mostly. It was common knowledge that this went on and was much anticipated. I knew about this even before I became an officer. I worked with a lady at DOJ who was married to an LAPD officer and she told us all about it. Joni and I went with her to the academy lounge a couple of times to see what it was all about. The police academy lounge was not the only drinking spot that LAPD officers were known to frequent. There was another joint located in Rampart Division called the "Short Stop." This was another majority white officer hang out. The black officers on the LAPD spent their time off duty at a restaurant by day club by night on 11th and Olive in downtown L.A. called Lil J's. The L.A. County's black deputy sheriffs and marshals frequented a Chinese restaurant around North Broadway and Sunset. It's funny how every law enforcement group found a place where they could go and discreetly meet women, tell lies and drink to excess. The owners all knew that these were off duty cops but looked the other way when the night was over and scores of police officers stumbled out into the streets to their cars. It was a restaurant by day and a dance/bar situation by night. I was not much of a drinker, so neither really appealed to me. I had been to Lil J's a few times during my career, but I did not want to get a reputation for being a "punch board"—the term I heard officers use when referring to a promiscuous female. As a female officer, you were one of two things: a witch or a slut. I found myself in the "witch" pool. A witch was usually the way officers referred to a female officer that they didn't like for whatever reason. Maybe you rebuked their advances or spoke your mind—I did both.

When I first graduated from the police academy, many black officers "hit" on me, but most were, in my opinion too old for me. The younger, twenty-something blacks came later after the department launched a recruitment campaign in Detroit, New York and other previously ignored cities. Since there were so few black females in the police academy during my time as a recruit, I naturally gravitated to the first black I saw. She was in the 10-80 class. There were about four or five black females in that class. This one young lady and I became inseparable. She became my partner in crime during my visits to Lil J's . Since it was a cop hang out, my neighborhood friend Jan was not so interested in going. I saved Jan for the non-cop spots. Eventually, Jan moved away to Texas, where she grew up, in an attempt to get away from a jealous and physically abusive boyfriend. She met and married a local and stayed to start a family. We stayed in telephone contact. I did have a chance to visit her one summer. We tried not to let geography come between us.

The male training officers seemed to expect that drinking would be a regular part of the "learning" experience and therefore a requirement. As you might imagine, there were many officers involved in DUIs, bar fights, and the like. I am sure that this also led to an increased divorce rate among LAPD officers. I heard stories of officers being stopped by other LAPD officers as they left the Short Stop and the Academy Lounge and then driven home in their personal vehicle while the partner uniformed officer followed so as not to get the inebriated officers into trouble with the department. That was how the old LAPD worked.

But there's another side to police culture. One that is not so unique to the LAPD.

That side I am often asked about when something awful happens in black and brown communities. The other side of the blue wall. That place were unseemly things only gets talked about in quiet corners of dark rooms.

To help the reader understand police culture I will explain it from an insider's perspective. My introduction to police culture came when I entered the LAPD police academy. Much like the military, the LAPD tried to break me down to purportedly later build me up.

It was my belief that my experiences were not unique to the LAPD and it is not my intention to infer that this was an "all" and "every" type of situation. I have also affirmed that it is my belief that most police officers conduct themselves professionally, appropriately and are well intended in the discharge of their duties. Those officers amongst us who have given this occupation a bad name are in the minority.

So, as you think about police interactions that you may have been personally involved in or heard about from a friend or family member be mindful that every police chief was once a police officer. And know that there are some racist cops on police departments who do well, promote and become racist police chiefs. Like Frank Nucera, Jr., fired chief of the Bordentown Township Police Department.

According to the Washington Post, On November 1, 2017, Nucera, chief from a small New Jersey township was arrested on federal hate crime and civil rights charges for what authorities described as a pattern of racist comments and behavior. Institutionalized racism sometimes starts at the top.

So, when you see a police chief who has responded to questions during a press conference and has justified a use of force, remember he was once a cop too. And when that chief starts clutching their pearls and suggesting that somehow the community got it wrong and just didn't understand the dangers associated with police work, remember he was once a cop. Just because that person holds the rank of police chief or commissioner does not mean that they won't lie. Rank does not necessarily preclude an individual from being intellectually dishonest. It is unreasonable and unlikely to assert that every single police shooting that has occurred was justified. There were certainly times when the force was excessive and unnecessary.

Certainly, there are times when deadly force must be used. It is an unfortunate circumstance of law enforcement. I do not celebrate the loss of life- on either side. I do not condone violence by the police and I do not condone violence against the police.

It seems to me that most police chiefs' first instinctive response is to protect his agency. I have never in the history of ever, heard a police chief admit that one of their officers violated policy or training protocols when they used deadly force- as a first resort rather than a last resort. These chiefs could always be heard saying, "let's wait until the investigation is over." Or when the investigation has been completed, "the officer feared for their safety."

In that February 2015 speech, by former FBI Director James Comey with regard to one of his stated hard truths about law enforcement personnel he opined, "Many of us develop different flavors of cynicism that we work hard to resist because they can be lazy mental shortcuts... Something happens to people of good will working in that environment. After years of police work, officers often can't help but be influenced by the cynicism they feel." Comey went on to state, that law enforcement officers "...must better understand the people we serve and protect—by trying to know, deep in our gut, what it feels like to be a law-abiding young black man walking on the street and encountering law enforcement. We must understand how that young man may see us. We must resist the lazy shortcuts of cynicism and approach him with respect and decency."

It is for this reason that I say it is way past time that police departments start doing a better job with psychological testing of its employees. These agencies and communities would be better served if there were constant psychological re-evaluations to ensure that officers are mentally fit to serve. An officer who is fearful of a black person just because is problematic. These officers should be identified and helped over to an occupation that better suits their skill set. Officers who become enraged when a suspect fails to comply or attempts to evade arrest should be removed from the force. You don't get to shoot someone because the run. Suspects trying to avoid jail, by any means necessary is inherent to the job.

I am clear that not every person who wants to become a police officer should in fact become a police officer. If the mere presence of a black man is frightening; and scares you more than anything ever in your life (as in the stated case of former officer Betty Shelby who shot and killed Terence Crutcher) then this is not the job for you.

As I neared the end of my recruit training, I understood that I had to now survive the twelve-month field assignment that followed graduation. This was going to be critical. That is, critical to my very existence. It is important for the reader to understand that as a rookie or probationary police officer I was considered an at-will employee and could be fired very easily. That meant, that my training officer literally held my life in his hands. My training officer was the one who was responsible for evaluating my field performance as a rookie and thereby the gate-keeper to my permanent employee status.

Once I finally graduated from the LAPD academy, I was singularly focused on getting off probation. I had come too far to allow anything or anyone to get in my way.

Surviving the police culture was a never-ending process. Failure to perform in the field as expected was grounds for termination if properly documented by a training officer. So, if a probationary officer was assigned a training officer who may "bend the rules" a bit; as a rookie you better keep your mouth shout as a means of survival. If as a rookie, your shown the "wrong way to police" by a training officer, something that may be contrary to academy training, you keep quiet as matter of survival. If a citizen who is deemed to be "different" or an "other" and is treated poorly or unjustly by an errant officer and a partner officer or supervisor acquiesced the misconduct- as a rookie you better keep your mouth shut.

Maybe that "different" did not deserve to be treated with dignity. So, for these hypothetical officers, it became easier and easier to be disrespectful; to get physical right from the start of an encounter; and to lie on an arrest report because a "different" made you mad. Because that "different" was unrelatable. Because there was no distinguishable commonality between the officers and the "different." It appeared as if the most obvious common bond of all was non-existent in the minds of these officers; humanity. At the end of the day aren't we all the same being? Human.

Sadly, unfortunately the answer is, "No." In the fatal police shooting death of Philando Castile, a police officer fired seven rounds into Castile's car, during a traffic stop. At the time the officer fired those shots, a small child sat strapped in her car seat in the back-passenger area of the car. Clearly that officer did not see that small, little black girl as someone that could have been his daughter, sister or niece. As a mother first and a sergeant second, it appeared to me that Jeronimo Yanez did not view this black family as being much like his own. I believe that former officer Jeronimo Yanez failed to recognize their shared humanity.

When two Baton Rouge, Louisiana police officers struggled with and straddled Alton Sterling who had been accused of selling CDs on the street the officers body cam recording seemed to indicate everything but a shared humanity. The recording showed one of the officers as he straddled Sterling shout if he

[Sterling] continued to move the officer would "fucking shoot." The officer made good on his promise. Where was their shared humanity?

As this police culture, this good ole boy system is laid out before the public's eyes via police dash cam recordings the focus becomes clearer.

I think a lot of cops are nothing more than sheeple. What else could it be? How then can a group of so-called, well trained police officers stand around and watch one of their own choke someone to death or beat the crap out of another without intervening? Not one amongst them was willing to step in and say, "Hey! That's enough." I'll tell you why. Because many of these white officers working in minority communities can not relate to that minority community. They don't see our children, our husbands and our mothers as their own. During former FBI Director James Comey's February 2015 speech, he opined, "We simply must find ways to see each other more clearly."

So now, racial profiling, harsh language and excessive force has become standard operating procedure (SOP); lessons that were taught, learned then passed on from officer to officer.

Being new to the culture, needing the job, mouths slam shut. That officer must now hope that a new partner or reassignment will happen before becoming ensnared in misconduct.

So now the hypothetical officer has made it off probation. Whew! No more keeping your mouth shut, right? Well, now, the officer has just teamed-up with a new partner; an officer who newly transferred into the division and has about three years more in seniority.

This new partner was from the "bend the rule" crowd; he too had been trained by one of those ole school, crotchety, kick-ass take names training officers. What do you do? Do you can stand on your principals and report your new partner the first time you see him commit misconduct? Or, do you keep quiet and look the other way; pretend as thought you hadn't noticed. After all, it was not a big deal; no one was really hurt by your partner's actions. By doing nothing, you have just bought into the police culture. You have just slid behind the blue line. You are now one of them.

This was the path of least resistance. This was much easier, for some, than falling prey to the pack. The pack of errant police officers who can make someone's life miserable if they don't go along to get along.

An officer who stood on principal and the side of right by reporting police misconduct ran the risk of being ostracized by the "bend the rule" crowd; given a "jacket" or "label" signifying that the officer could not be trusted. Being ostracized would be a small price to pay; a delayed response by back up when requested, could get an officer hurt or even killed. It's the culture.

There were other consequences; undesirable details and work shifts. The inability to promote through the ranks could be a consequence as well. For an officer who finally made it off graveyard with an assignment that afforded weekends off the penalty for speaking out was too big a price to pay.

What do you do? Do you report the misconduct to your supervisor? Oh, wait, the sergeant was part of the wolf pack. There is no safe zone for whistle blowers on police departments. Reporting misconduct while knowing that peer and supervisory support is non-existent becomes improbable.

It is the police culture; the desire to fit in; the conditioning that determines which path an officer will take. This is your livelihood. I can tell you from first-hand experience that there is no such thing as whistle-blower protection.

I reported misconduct at LAPD's so-called "safe-place". By the time I had returned to my division of assignment, word had already spread that I had filed a complaint. So, when I am asked, "why don't the good officers report the bad ones?" It's the culture.

# NINETEEN: SUMMER, DOWNTOWN LA

I continued to work different foot-beat patrols with a garden variety of white asses. I vividly remember during the hot summer months, we would get radio calls for a "death investigation" at the hotels used as residences by many of the transients who had saved up enough money to get off the streets for month or two.

My very first death investigation was awful. A gentleman had not been seen for several days. When my partner and I arrived at the hotel, we were met by the hotel manager. He said there was a terrible smell coming from this guy's room. I already knew this was not going to be good. But, I was, after all, a P-2 now. I could handle this call. So we approached the door to the room, and my partner took out a cigar and lit it. I was not sure what to expect, so I started breathing out of my mouth. I couldn't smell anything, but I was starting to get a weird and funky taste in my mouth. This was bad.

We entered the hotel room. I was behind my partner. He tried to make me enter the room first, but I refused. I flat-out told him that I had a problem with dead bodies. The manager was directly behind me and watching this back-and-forth between my partner and me.

There was a body lying on the bed, bloated and discolored. The skin on the body raised approximately ten or twelve inches, and I could see liquid between his translucent skin and his muscle tissue. Oh no. We backed out after confirming the obvious— this guy was dead. We then notified the coroner and waited. The coroner investigator arrived. He was alone. He told us that he would need some help lifting this guy onto his gurney but warned us that his skin might pop once we touched him. Oh hell, no. I'm not touching this guy. I told my partner he was on his own with this one. I was not helping to lift this guy off the bed and have him explode all over me. I took several steps back. They eventually lifted the deceased, and he didn't pop, but he did ooze a little liquid. I knew I had to get out of Central Patrol. I could not handle another death investigation—especially during the summer.

The piss-poor treatment continued; the white officers working Central patrol didn't want to interact with me. I endured. I heard of an upcoming opening in Central Traffic Division. CTD was located in the same police station as Central patrol. Their office was right down the hall from the patrol watch commander. CTD was considered a specialized unit. An officer had to "interview" for an assignment—even a P-2. CTD consisted of police officers responsible for accident investigations (AI) and motorcycle officers responsible for traffic enforcement. More importantly, CTD ran a lot of "L" cars, or one-officer units. This was just what I needed: an assignment where I could work alone and not have to contend with the day-to-day crap that was going on in Central patrol.

I knew the black lieutenant who worked CTD; he coincidently was a personal friend of my parents. I would see him from time to time when I was in Central Station. I approached him and asked him about the position, and he told me to apply. I applied, thinking that this was so cool. I had a friendly in CTD. I was sure to get this position.

The schedule for interviews was posted, and the family friend saw me and pulled me to the side, stating he wanted to talk to me. There's about to be another house Negro sighting, I thought. This black lieutenant told me that since he knew my parents, he recused himself from the interview process. He didn't want any of the (white) officers involved in the process to find out that he knew my parents and accuse him of favoritism in selecting me. What the hell. Are you kidding me? I could not believe he just said that. How many times did white supervisors participate in the selection process of other white officers that they knew, directly or indirectly, and later pick that person for the position without a care in the world? I could not believe that this dude would be so damn scared. What the hell was he afraid of? Hell, he was already a lieutenant on the department. He certainly knew at the time, although I did not, that he would promote no higher than lieutenant. One thing about the LAPD; you don't get to have secrets. Police officers love spreading other officers' business.

I had been on the department only a few months, but I knew his sordid history. It seemed that this guy had a thing for transvestites. He had been "popped" several times off-duty with a skid-row transvestite in his personal car. He even got caught getting head from one. Back then, the department handled discipline a little differently—especially if you were a higher rank. We all knew that. So he got a slap on the wrist and kept his job. Maybe that's why he was so damn squeamish about drawing attention to himself. Naw, that wasn't it, because he continued to pick up transvestites until finally the department had to tell him to find a new church home and be fired or he was allowed to retire in lieu of termination. That was something that was reserved for command staff if they "got caught dirty." A command staff officer would be allowed to quietly, during the hours of darkness complete the forms necessary to retire. You just heard they did something and then –poof!! They were gone. I had my own name for it—I called it leaving the department "under a cloud of mystery and suspicion."

I interviewed for the AI investigator assignment and was selected anyway. I really didn't need any help from that ole house Negro. I was selected because I was qualified and had earned the selection.

# TWENTY: CENTRAL TRAFFIC DIVISION (CTD)

As a new officer to the division, I was assigned to a P-3 on day watch. All new accident investigators (AI) were assigned to a senior officer at first. Of course, I was assigned to another white male. LAPD was mostly white, and the traffic divisions were just about all white. Every bureau had a traffic division—i.e., South Traffic, Valley Traffic, Central Traffic, and West Traffic.

I think it is important to say that my experience with this P-3 was great. Obviously, not every white male on the LAPD was an ass, but the jerks were plentiful. This P-3 remained someone whom I considered to be a friend throughout my career. He was very patient and an excellent teacher, just what I needed.

Our very first call happened to be a fatal, solo-car T/C (traffic collision) in Northeast Division in the Hyperion Tunnel. Working CTD meant that our area included all five divisions within Central Bureau: Central, Newton, Rampart, Hollenbeck, and Northeast. This was a lot of territory. I was assigned to the T-car (traffic car) in Northeast Division; however, I could roam freely in any of the other divisions as long as I handled any calls for service in my assigned area. This meant code-7 was going to be amazing; I had so many different restaurants to pick from. When I worked patrol, I had to remain in my division of assignment for code 7; variety was not something I enjoyed. There was actually policy about leaving your division to eat and if the officers from that division saw your police car in their area, they would confront you. Some officers didn't like it when you ate at their "pop" spots. (The restaurants that served free or discounted food.) This was going to be great. See ya, patrol.

My partner asked me if I wanted to handle this call. He told me that since it was my first day, I might as well get my feet wet, so to speak, with a fatal. Cops have a twisted sense of what I guess is black or gallows humor. Anyway, I was there to learn, so why not? Let's go.

My partner and I handled many T/Cs over the next few weeks and months. I learned how to administer the field sobriety test (FST) to suspected drunk drivers and then document my findings in the arrest report. I investigated a myriad of misdemeanor and felony traffic related crimes. I had three months to learn as much as I could, and then I would be required to take a test. As a new AI, I was referred to as a "pinkie." That just meant that I was on "probation" and assigned to work with a more experienced AI until I could pass the "pink" test. Once I passed the pink test I was able to work alone as an "L" car.

I was able to "get off the pink" the first time around. I had become proficient in the investigation of traffic collisions as well as traffic and DUI enforcement. I was ready to go out and be an "L" car, which was why I transferred to traffic in the first place. I enjoyed working with my TO. He was good people. We continued to back each other in the field and have code-7 together when time permitted. If I had questions on a complex T/C, he was always available to help. He would assist me with setting up road flares on some of my calls and cleared intersections of traffic debris. I liked working with him.

It was now time for me to rotate over to PM watch. On the night shift, there were no one-officer units, due to tactical considerations. I again had to partner with another officer. Great. I was assigned to a radio car with two white male officers, both P-2s. So now, everything was equal. These officers had more time on the job than I did, but we were all P-2s.

I didn't seem to be having some of the same issues working CTD that I did in patrol. At least, not at first. I found myself again the only black female assigned to CTD, just like Southwest and Central. Heck, I was the only female, period, in CTD. I would get an occasional stare and whisper when I traversed the halls of

Central Station, but I didn't care. I came to work, did my job, and went home. I was having a good time, though. I was making decent money and my bill situation was improving, so I decided to treat myself to a new car. I bought a black convertible Corvette with glass T-tops. I even had a vanity plate.

I was enjoying my newfound freedom on the job, and life was good. None of the other officers was messing with me, and my supervisors left me alone. I did a good job, handled my calls, and issued the required number of traffic tickets daily to keep the sergeants off my back. Even so, there were a couple of officers, both in AI and certainly on motors, who would give me a sideways glance from time to time. Again, I didn't care. You are not the boss of me, I would think. I had earned my first hash mark on my uniform sleeve. I had over five years with the department. I no longer tolerated any crap off these white boys.

I was reassigned to PM watch; this happened regularly. I had new partners; both were P-2s, and we were getting along well. One of my partners in particular was very welcoming and inclusive. He and I became fast friends. He even invited me and my boyfriend at the time to his home. Once, he invited us to go to the mountains, where his family had a cabin. We spent the weekend four-wheeling. It was a good time. That was really a switch. I had never had a white partner quite like this one.

He had a ferret that he brought along on the trip. I had never seen a ferret before. It was so cute and behaved just like a cat. I had so much fun playing with his ferret that I decided I wanted one. Then I found out that they were illegal in California—so that was that. Didn't want anything illegal, right? Not looking for any trouble. We continued to work together, and our families spent time together away from the job.

The three of us remained assigned to the same AI unit for several months. Then, one day, the quiet partner didn't report to work. It was quite the scandal—he had been arrested. It was shocking. He was arrested for stealing yachts initially, and then later he was charged with murder. I had no idea. He was so quiet at work.

Not long after that, my other partner was arrested too. They were both very good friends away from the job—so much so that the partner (who I had gone to the mountains with) was accused of being involved in the whole stolen-yacht situation with the quiet one. I was really sad to lose him as a regular partner. Both were eventually fired and the quiet one went to prison.

Back to day watch and my beloved "L" car.

# TWENTY-ONE: MOTOR SCHOOL

Time was moving on, and I was excelling in my position as an accident investigator. My traffic captain loved my work ethic; my sergeants and lieutenant alike were happy with my job performance in CTD. I received numerous commendations for outstanding police work as an accident investigator. My evaluation issued in September 1986 stated in part, "Her enthusiastic approach to field investigation has added to her development as an accident investigation officer. She can handle complex field investigations with minimum supervision."

I also attended the department's Advanced Officer School during this time. My supervisor wrote that I "should apply myself to the task and compete favorably for promotion." I was even commended one deployment period for issuing the most traffic citations in the entire division, more than even the motorcycle officers. I loved to issue traffic citations. I really did. Don't judge me.

During my assignment at CTD, I also received additional training and a certification as a Drug Recognition Expert (DRE). I attended a department-sponsored class and then spent several hours over many weeks observing arrestees who were transported to Jail Division and required additional evaluation prior to being booked. The officer who trained me was at the time the department's only DRE, and I was part of the first group of officers who also received this training.

Since I enjoyed traffic enforcement so much, the next logical step was to participate in the interview process to become a motorcycle officer. LAPD didn't have any females assigned to "motors" at that time; I would be the first. Yeah, right.

I purchased a motorcycle and began practicing on the weekends with some of my black male police officer friends, who were also applying for a position as a motor-cop. We would meet up at Rio Hondo College, where a cone pattern had been set up in one of the college's parking lots by some of the white officers, who used this location to practice. We would place large orange cones on the painted spots and then very, very slowly maneuver our motorcycles in, out, and around the varying patterns. The department's motorcycle officers drove Kawasaki 1000s, which were pretty big bikes when fully loaded. The key to getting a passing grade through the course was to demonstrate that you could maneuver at idle speed through the cones. If you dropped the bike, there was a technique for lifting it up off the ground. It had little to do with upper-body strength. I wanted to try it. I not only practiced on the motorcycle, but I also spent a lot of time in the gym, lifting weights.

I had no problem scoring high on the interview portion of the test. I had recent commendations in my personnel file, as well as a performance evaluation dated February 1987, which stated that my "productivity level had been among the highest on the watch. She has an awareness of her part in attaining the objectives set forth by the Department Battle Plan and strives to impact the traffic-related front by handling a maximum number of calls for service and concentrating traffic-enforcement effort on accident-causing violations. Her continued level of productivity is exemplary to her peers and makes her a valued asset to the division. [She] is obviously intelligent and articulate and an officer who could compete well for promotion with a little more attention to detail in conforming to Department regulations on grooming."

My failure to conform to grooming regulations had to do with the on-again, off-again battle I waged with the department over the length of my fingernails. I continued to refuse to cut my nails. Many of the white officers didn't like them. I was repeatedly told to cut my fingernails, and my response was always the same: "Is there any policy that states I must?" It was not policy, so I refused to shorten my nails. I guess since the department wasn't used to dealing with women in the field, it had never been an issue. That is, until I came along. I pride myself in being singly and totally responsible for the department adopting a policy on the length of officers' fingernails. Eventually, they came up with a policy, and I was forced to comply. Well, I was a trailblazer, huh?

I interviewed and was placed on the list to attend motor school. I actually placed high enough on the list to attend the very first motor school offered for that group of officers. The list would not expire for two years, at which point if an officer was not selected to attend, he or she would have to re-interview.

Not my concern. I was in the first class. My friends, with whom I had been practicing, were also in this first class. Motor school consisted of one week of actual riding on the motorcycle, and the second week was all classroom. At the end of the two weeks, if you were successful, you were given a department-issued motorcycle to take home. You would then drive your motor to and from work daily.

I was elated. I was about to make history—becoming not only the first female in the history of the LAPD, but the first black female, on a motor.

The first two days of motor school were uneventful. By the end of the third day, I was still holding my own. I guess it was at this point that the white instructors realized they had only two more days to make me "wash out," so they needed to get busy. We would play follow-the-leader on the motorcycles. The instructors started taking us on paths that were somewhat off the normal course through rough, dirt hills and debris. Everyone was having difficulty but none more than me. I kept dropping my bike and of course had to pick it up each time. I didn't complain. I would just get right back on the bike and get back in line. This continued right through lunch. As we broke for lunch, one of the white instructors came up to me and told me that he was afraid I might hurt myself. He thought it best if I dropped out of the course. I didn't seem to have much of a choice; he didn't appear to be asking me as much as he was telling me that this was my last day. I was devastated.

They sent me home. Later that evening, I received a telephone call from one of the other black officers who I had practiced with and who was still part of the class. He told me that as soon as they returned from lunch, they just started riding around in circles. Al said it was obvious to him that the instructors had intentionally taken the group through a difficult part of the course to flunk me, and when that had been accomplished; they were riding around like children on tricycles. Damn it—they got me. How could I prove that they intentionally placed obstacles in my way to prevent me from being the department's first? Oh well, I still had a job, right? I returned to CTD and resumed my duties as an AI investigator.

A year later, there was another date scheduled for interviews for motor-school candidates. Another opportunity, so I thought – silly me. This time around, there was a white sergeant working in motors who was married to a female officer on the LAPD. She worked in another traffic division, but she was rumored to be a pretty good motorcycle rider and "destined to be the first for LAPD." I heard the rumors, but I planned to take the interview again anyway. I should have known the deck was stacked: we were the only two female applicants. After the interview process, she placed within the first group to be selected to attend motor school. Surprise, surprise. I heard from some of my coworkers that her interview consisted of "weather talk" and discussion about what she would do as the very history maker that she was about to become. The rest of us were put through the rigors of having to respond to legitimate tactical and traffic-related questions during our respective interviews.

As you probably already know, she passed motor school with flying colors and was indeed the first female in the history of the department to graduate and be assigned a motorcycle.

I was not surprised—disappointed, but not surprised. I just

continued on in my assignment as an AI officer, doing what I had been doing all along. The list that I had been placed on eventually expired. I knew that I would not put myself through that ridiculousness again. I would do all of my police work in a car.

Then, one day, I got a call from one of my sergeants, who told me that for some unknown reason, the list for motor school had been reactivated, and there was going to be a motor class starting in two days. My sergeant wanted to know if I was interested in attending. I thought about it for a minute and started to say "hell no." Then I concluded that I would not make it that easy for the department to dismiss me, so I said yes.

I knew in my heart of hearts that I was not nearly as prepared physically as I had been for my first motor school. I no longer owned a motorcycle, and I was not lifting weights like I had been previously. But I was going to give motor school the old college try.

The very first day of motor school, I was selecting a bike and getting ready to line up with the rest of the officers when I noticed that the police chief was on the grounds. I guess he had decided to stick his head in our class to let the instructors know he was watching. After all, he was the first black chief who had come up through the ranks of the LAPD, and I would be the first black female on motors if I made it through the training course. I appreciated his presence. He didn't say anything to me, but he did give me a nod and a smile before he departed.

The course was the same. The instructors were very helpful in the demonstrations. They even asked me, "How can I help you?" when I struggled on a particular cone pattern. They offered pointers on how I should position and point the front wheel when negotiating the cone pattern, but I was struggling. I kept dropping the bike and knocking over cones while going through the various patterns at idle speed. Finally, they told me that the class was ready to move on to another area and that

I was not going to be able to continue with the training. It was time for me to go. I knew it. I just had no intention of quitting. I wanted them to tell me I was done. They did so on my third day.

# TWENTY-TWO:
# WHEN SUPERVISORS
# ACQUIESCE

I was still having a good time in CTD, I was really enjoying the job. This was to be short-lived. It turned out that there was an officer assigned to the PM watch who had decided to make me his project. He was a P-2 like me, but I found that he was monitoring my activities, both on the job and off. One day I entered the CTD office, and I overheard this P-2 talking to some other male officers. In the midst of their conversation, I heard him say my father's name. My dad has a real unusual name, so I knew when I heard it that he was up to no good. I was certain he had uttered my dad's name. I didn't say anything, because I didn't talk to them and they didn't talk to me. Later that night, I was approached by a field sergeant. He was new to the division, and he wanted to talk to me.

This sergeant was a bit of a jokester and a real character. He told me, "You know, one of these white boys has a hard-on for you." I was confused by his comment, but I asked who and how did he know that. He gave me this sly grin and then he handed me my vanity plate from my Corvette. He told me that the P-2 who I had overheard speaking my father's name had given him my license plate earlier during our shift. The P-2 had handed the sergeant the plate and told him that he had "found it" in the parking structure and recognized it as belonging to me. Well, I knew that was a lie, but I didn't interrupt. The sergeant went on to say that the P-2 told him, "Oh, by the way, I ran her plate, and it's registered to ____." He gave my father's name. Well, it was true—my Corvette was registered in my father's name. I guess the P-2 found it odd that I would be driving a car not registered in my name. The sergeant handed me the license plate and told me not to worry about that P-2. He said he was a dick and whatever he was trying to start, he (the sergeant) wasn't biting.

I was so pissed off that this ass had tampered with my car, but I couldn't really prove that he had—what I did know was my license plate was attached to my car with four screws, so if three had come off, wouldn't my plate have been dangling? I would have noticed that. He was full of it, but I had no proof. However, the sergeant recognized his story as questionable, but he did not feel compelled to tell that officer to knock it off. Again, I have no proof of that either, other than this guy continued to mess with me with no fear of reprisal by the department. I knew I needed to keep my eye on this guy from now on—him and all of the other white males working CTD.

This sergeant, my supervisor, clearly knew that the P-2 was targeting me for no other reason than the color of my skin—yet he failed to intervene. The sergeant allowed it. He acquiesced to misconduct—something the department would hammer an officer for doing. Everyone in CTD knew that this P-2 had a problem with blacks, on and off the department. This would later come back to bite him in the ass.

The job was messed-up, but my personal life was about to take a turn for the better. One day I was driving around in the area of Crenshaw and Vernon when I happened to stop to gas my car. I saw these two guys also getting gas. The passenger looked in my direction, exited the car, and came over to introduce himself. He was very complimentary and immediately asked me out on a date. He then followed up with an "I'm going to marry you." I was like, "Yeah, right."

Well, he did just that—we had a whirlwind relationship that ended up in a Vegas wedding chapel. Shortly after we were married, we were expecting. This was cool, because my pregnancy gave me a break from the jackasses in traffic. I could no longer work the field, so I was reassigned to the Accident Investigation Follow-Up Unit (AIFU) within CTD. The officers assigned to AIFU were veteran AI officers who handled the follow-up on traffic investigations that involved an arrest or maybe a hit-and-run with a vehicle description.

I spent my time at a desk, moving paper around. It was cool. My son, Darnell, was born, and I remained off work for about three months. Not long after I returned to work, my husband was involved in a traffic collision—it was a fatal, head-on collision with another driver. Damn, damn. I was a twenty-eight-year-old widow—wow.

# TWENTY-THREE: TUNA CLIPPER

I went back to work as an Accident Investigation (AI) officer. I continued to receive commendation after commendation for doing a job well done.

A new officer transferred to the division—a white female. It was nice to have another woman in the division. They partnered us together. I was her training officer and helped her get off the pink. That was the term used for newly assigned officers to the traffic unit who had yet to learn the proper way in which to write and investigate a traffic collision.

We worked together for about a year, and we had a blast. We got along so well. We were both mothers of young sons and loved the soap operas. We spent nearly the entire eight-hour shift talking incessantly. I found out that she was married to a young police officer—her academy classmate. He was assigned to Hollywood Division and going to school at night to become an attorney. We had such a good time together— we stopped chatting only long enough to handle our traffic calls, and then we were right back at it. When it came time to go home, we didn't want to part company because we were not finished talking. I loved working with her. I did say that she was white, right? On the LAPD—as in life—there were good white people and bad white people. I was happy to have known and worked with a couple of the good ones.

She and I worked the Rampart T-Car. One day we were assigned a radio call that involved a serious accident. A young mother had been crossing the street while holding her small son by the hand. A drunk driver hit them as they crossed the street, critically injured the young mother and fatally injured the small child. When my partner and I arrived on the scene, the pair had already been transported by ambulance to the hospital. Citizens were holding the driver so he could not leave.

It was so sad to see the aftermath of this accident. As a parent, I could really empathize with this family. Eventually, my partner and I responded to the hospital. Once there, we met the husband/father, who had just arrived at the hospital. His young wife was off to surgery, and he was inquiring about his son. We told him to have a seat and we would locate his child. The hospital staff advised us that the child had been pronounced dead on arrival (DOA). The dad was in the lobby area, clutching a Bible and anxiously awaited our return. We suspected that he would want to see his child's body once we told him what happened, and we wanted to be there with him when he entered the room where his little son now lay, dead. There had been no time to request additional family members to join him.

So, my partner and I slowly escorted the dad into the hospital room and stood off to the side to allow him a moment to grieve his loss. Within a matter of seconds, my partner and I were both wiping our eyes as we watched the man openly weep. We stayed with him for some time and then escorted him back out of the room. We did what we could to comfort him, but now his attention was diverted to his wife. He needed to get to her side. This was another of those moments that haunts me. After we left the hospital, my partner and I had a funny moment: not in the sense of funny-ha-ha, but funny because here we were— the big-city police, supposed to be there to help, and we both fell apart in the face of this tragedy. Thankfully, neither of us had become jaded by the job, we maintained our humanity. We later arrested and booked the suspect for vehicular manslaughter.

The males in our division soon realized we were having too much fun. Time to mix it up. Word got back to us that the male officers were referring to us as the "Tuna Clipper." That same sergeant who had given my license plate back in the prior incident was the one who told me. I was not sure why he told me, really. It wasn't like he had planned to put a stop to it; rather, I think he wanted to see our response. As a matter of fact, there were a couple of occasions during roll call, when this sergeant, our supervisor, would refer to our unit as the "Tuna

Clipper" rather than the T-car or traffic. All the male officers thought this was so funny—the room would erupt in laughter, the sergeant included.

I am certain that these men would not have found this situation so amusing if it were happening to their wives, sisters, or daughters. My turtle shell was doing its job—but I didn't like it. Who would I tell? My sergeant was the one making the crass joke. I had learned from my Southwest days that it was best to keep quiet. I had to "pick and choose my battles."

It is for this reason that I have great empathy and compassion for the countless women in the current #MeToo movement. I guess I could come forward now, some three decades later to complain about the mistreatment and sexual harassment we received at the hands of our peers and supervisors; but why?

Folks would wonder, "Why now?" While I don't view what happened to me as criminal it sure was demeaning and demoralizing. But I survived. And I stand with and support any woman who wants to come forward and speak their truth no matter the time delay.

My female partner's husband eventually finished law school, and with that they both quit the LAPD and left the state. I sure hated to see her leave.

I was back to working with all white male officers again. CTD was a small unit, and the pairings were pretty much static. Most of the white officers were not interested in partnering up with me. There were times when I would be assigned a male partner, and he would not even talk to me during our entire shift. The only words exchanged between us were the starting and ending mileage of our police car, information I needed for my DFAR. I had to really turtle up to get through this.

There were moments of levity when I was assigned to CTD. I didn't like most of the officers I was around, but I did enjoy watching them get into trouble for the stupid stuff they did. There was this Hispanic sergeant in the division with me. He really didn't mess with me. I was assigned to him once or twice when he was my "den" sergeant. He was an odd egg. He kind of reminded me of a Latino Groucho Marx. He smoked a cigar and always held it a peculiar way in his mouth. Later, I found out why.

This sergeant, while working AM (morning) watch, got his ass in a snare. Turned out that a local area transvestite—most of the guys called them "dragons," short for drag queen—came into the patrol desk to file a complaint.

The story went like this: the transvestite said that an unknown uniformed officer had been coming to his apartment almost nightly and shining a light at his bedroom window, which faced the street. This was a signal for the transvestite to come downstairs. The transvestite was at first willing, but now he no longer wanted to play this game. He felt compelled and unable to put a stop to the officer's demand for oral sex. The transvestite did not know the officer's name but described his police car as a plain vehicle, like the ones detectives normally drove. The patrol watch commander was confused, because all uniformed patrol officers assigned to Central division drove marked black-and-white police vehicles. The patrol supervisors did a little research and quickly determined that the offending officer was actually a sergeant assigned to CTD. The traffic sergeant would get the keys to one of the plain vehicles used by the AIFU traffic detectives who worked day watch. When the sergeant had finished his business with the transvestite, he returned to Central station, parked the plain vehicle, and then entered his assigned black-and-white to patrol around as if nothing had happened.

One of the benefits of working a specialized unit like CTD was the minimal supervision. We rarely saw a supervisor in the field once we left the station. As long as you handled the radio calls in your assigned area the supervisors left you alone. This was also true of the sergeants; no one looked over their shoulder either.

Well, the jig was up. The transvestite wanted no more of this. The sergeant was relieved of duty, and we never saw him again. I don't know if he was terminated or allowed to retire in lieu of termination.

In September 1994, I received word from Momma Lyndee that my dear friend, Jan had passed away. Jan had just given birth to her third child about a year prior and then unexpectedly diagnosed with colon cancer. Even in her own sickness Jan flew to California to support me in the loss of my mother. She died within a few short months of that diagnosis. She left to cherish her memories three beautiful children, Justin, Jakeya and Jamaal. They are now all grown up. Geography and life has made it difficult to stay on top of significant events in their lives but this is a testament to unwavering support and love. (I'm always here for you.)

# TWENTY-FOUR: BANDIT TOW TRUCKS

There was so much foolishness going on in CTD during that time. We just had two officers arrested for yacht theft and murder; then, a few short months later, another one of the white officers was arrested for confronting couples parked in and around Elysian Park late at night and making the male leave the area while he groped the female. This occurred in Rampart Division, the couples were mostly young latinos. I guess the officer never expected that one of them would actually report his activity. I am, certain that he picked on this group because he believed that there were undocumented and made easy prey. They were able to obtain his vehicle license plate number and used that information to help identify the errant officer. The couple had actually chased the officer through Elysian park and had written down the license plate of his black-and-white twice before they backed off. Now picture this: the officer makes the male walk away while the officer stays with the female, who in this case was seated in a van with the side door open. The young man reported that he did walk away but watched from a distance, and he could see that the uniformed officer was reaching into the van up to his elbows. The young man could not describe what he was doing with his hands, because they were deep inside the van. What the young woman would later tell her boyfriend was that the uniformed officer was groping and fondling her breasts. When the officer finished assaulting this young woman, he returned to his black-and-white and left the area. Well, as soon as the officer entered his police car, the young man quickly entered his van. The officer noticed that the van was now following him and began to increase his speed to the point that that citizen was actually in pursuit of the officer. Crazy but true. Once the patrol supervisor was given the "shop number" of the black-and-white, they were able to determine which officer had checked it out. It was a CTD officer. We were shocked to find out who the officer was that had been assaulting the women. He was quiet and unassuming.

At least one thing was universal: if you did something stupid, the officers didn't have a problem making you the brunt of their jokes. When everyone found out who had been charged with assaulting females in the park, they came up with a name for his activity. The officers would kind of do a football end-zone dance with their arms and hands extended straight out in front of them and then make a pinching motion with their fingers while moving their feet back and forth—and the "Dupont Shuffle" was born.

This was the dumbest, dirtiest bunch of cops I had ever seen. These guys were involved in more than a little bit of mischief— yet they still found time to mess with me. Remember the fool who had taken my license plate off my Corvette? His name was Douglas Iverson. Well, this ass liked to go to the mountains with his family when he was off-duty. On one of his weekend trips, he was involved in a traffic accident. The agency investigating the accident found several LAPD handheld radios in his personal vehicle and notified the department. (Officers were not allowed to take city equipment home.) These handheld radios—or rovers, as we called them—had been reported missing by the kit room officer during a routine inventory check. They had been missing for several months, maybe even a couple of years. Supposedly, Iverson, wanted to make sure he had the ability to reach a LAPD dispatcher if he ever had any problems while camping in remote areas. Officer Douglas Iverson received a slap on the wrist for this misconduct by way of a transfer from CTD to STD (South Traffic Division.) He would live to re-offend. His next offense was one the department could not overlook nor defend.

Officer Iverson seemed to have a real and uncontrollable dislike for black people. Not only did he mess with me, but he was constantly harassing with the black guys who drove tow trucks. He seemed to take great pleasure in writing them traffic tickets whenever they showed up at traffic accident scenes. Many of these tow truck drivers had scanners in their trucks, and when they heard a police call that involved a traffic collision, they would "roll" to see if they could get permission to tow the wrecked vehicle before the police arrived. Generally, once the traffic investigators arrived, the Official Police Garage (OPG) tow truck would be called in to remove the vehicles if they had been disabled. The majority of these "bandit" tow truck drivers, as they were referred to, were black.

Now, if I know this guy did not like black people, then it's safe to assume others knew this too: the officers, sergeants, lieutenants, and captains for whom he worked. Why would the department transfer him to a division in South Central LA? South Traffic Division was located in the Crenshaw Mall on King Boulevard in Southwest Division. I am certain he was happy to go to the south end of the city so he could screw with the black tow truck drivers and any other black person he encountered. Iverson had been allowed by the LAPD to conduct himself in this manner for years. He didn't hide his racial bias—no need to; no supervisors ever checked him.

It was also widely known by officers that the citizens in certain parts of the city just wouldn't put up with foolishness. The more affluent the area, the more likely a supervisor would get a call if an officer was even perceived to misbehave. Profanity directed at a citizen, perceived rude behavior, or even just doing your job was often met with a series of "whys" and "what for."

I worked the west side of town. I had citizens call the police station to complain about the noise one of our air ships (police helicopter) was making. It was a sad reality that the disenfranchised, poorer population had also learned to go along to get along. I have heard many black citizens say that LAPD "won't do anything, so why bother making a complaint." So officers like this one were allowed to roam freely about the city, leaving a path of death and destruction in their path, literally.

Remember, this P-2 had harassed black tow truck drivers

relentlessly while assigned to CTD. Do you think there may be one or two black tow truck drivers responding to traffic accident calls in the south end?

This officer would get so irate when the black civilian tow drivers would come on scene that he cited them. There was an obscure section in the California Vehicle Code that prohibited the "bandit" towing activity. Of course, the tow truck drivers hated this P-2 because they were trying to make money, and he was costing them money. This officer had no "off switch."

While working in 77th Division, in the area of Crenshaw and Florence, Iverson eventually involved himself in something he should not have and ended up killing a tow truck driver.

According to the 1992 Los Angeles Times article, "Iverson and his partner had spotted John L. Daniels, Jr., filling up his truck at a gas station. Because the vehicle had earlier been impounded, the officers pulled in to check Daniels' towing license. Iverson contended that he fired his weapon because he feared Daniels would run down pedestrians after the tow truck driver ignored an order to remain at the scene and began driving away. Witnesses reported Daniels was no threat." This was classic Doug Iverson. He took things personal. It would appear that Iverson was pissed off that Daniels had managed to get his tow truck out of impound and was back on the streets. Iverson decided to create "probable cause" to initiate a traffic stop on Daniels for a second time in the same day. Who does this? Someone who is obsessed. It was unfortunate that Iverson's partner that day didn't have the intestinal fortitude to tell Iverson to "let it go." I had heard of the same behavior by Iverson when I worked with him at Central Traffic. Why on earth would the department transfer a guy like Iverson to south central Los Angeles when he had demonstrated on more than one occasion his hatred for blacks.

In 1995, Chief Willie Williams fired Iverson after a BOR determined that he was guilty of drawing and firing his firearm in violation of department policy as well as using bad judgment during the traffic stop of John Daniels.

There was a definite divide amongst officers on the LAPD during the many Iverson trials. The Los Angeles Police Protective League (LAPPL), which was comprised of all ethnicities but really catered to the white officers stood firmly in the Iverson camp.

As reported in the Los Angeles Times, in March 1995, "the Los Angeles Police Protective League's decision this week to finance Officer Douglas J. Iversen's civil court appeal of his firing was met with sharp negative reaction from the head of an association of African American police officers." Oscar Joel Bryant Association (OJB)

"Sgt. Leonard Ross, president of the Oscar Joel Bryant Foundation, said Police Chief Willie L. Williams "made the proper decision" in firing Iversen for shooting an unarmed tow truck driver. Williams' decision was made at the recommendation of a three-captain Board of Rights hearing panel.

'While Iversen is entitled to support, he had his day in court,' Ross said. He had that representation. At what point do they (the league) determine that an officer has broken the law or done something wrong?

In the wake of Iversen's termination, then "Protective League President Cliff Ruff announced that his union would fund an appeal by Iversen claiming the veteran officer's termination set a bad precedent. 'Previously, officers haven't been terminated for out-of-policy shootings or (for) drawing of weapons,' Ruff said."

The Board of Rights found Iversen guilty of drawing and discharging a firearm in violation of department policy in the shooting of John L. Daniels in a Southwest Los Angeles gas station near a flash point of the 1992 riots, which had occurred several weeks earlier."

There were two more murder trials, and I think the jury was "hung" in both. I was called to testify in the second trial about my knowledge of Iverson's propensity to harass the tow truck drivers during his time at CTD. I was more than happy to assist—I'm just sorry that Mr. Daniels's family didn't get the justice they deserved.

This attitude toward black citizens in general was common. I recognized that many white officers assumed that every black male was either on "parole" or "probation"; every black male was either a gang member or an affiliate of a gang. Probable cause, or "PC," was often manufactured, and racial profiling was real. I've been the victim of racial profiling. Once the errant officer found out I was the police, attitudes changed and I was allowed to continue on with my day. Of course no citation was issued because no infraction had occurred. I had the benefit of knowing exactly what PC is and what PC isn't.

It is for this reason and countless others that I constantly remind my four young sons to be careful when dealing with any police officer. I understand the damage an overzealous police officer can inflict on an unsophisticated young black man. I don't want my sons or anyone else's to be another Mr. Daniels: a black man who simply "dared" to be.

# TWENTY-FIVE:
# I KNOW THEY'RE DATING

I continued to bounce around from partner to partner until a young black male P-2 transferred into CTD. We were very close in age. My supervisors recognized that I was a very patient training officer with the new accident investigators, and I was given the charge of helping this new officer get off the pink.

Yay! Finally, someone who looked like me. We started working together, and it was reminiscent of my working with the female officer. This P-2 and I were having such a good time. I trained him on day watch, and then we put in to go to PM watch together. We both received the watch change together. Our first night together, we met our new "den" sergeant, a male Hispanic who was new to the CTD.

Right after roll call, we were downstairs in Central station in the CTD office when the sergeant pulled us both aside and told us to "get him on the radio for a meet in the field once we had our cup." Neither of us thought much of his request, as he was going to be responsible for supervising our field activities. We assumed he wanted to tell us what he expected from us in the field.

This sergeant was older than the both of us—we were in our late twenties, and he appeared to be in his mid-thirties. When we made it out to the field we broadcast a location over "simplex," a radio frequency only he could hear, and asked him to meet us. He did. What he said to us was shocking and disturbing.

The sergeant, who was an obvious Latino, told us that several of the white officers had been talking after roll call. This group included police officers and supervisors. The sergeant said that someone in the group (he didn't mention his rank) stated that my partner and I were "dating." The officers all affirmed this to be true. They stated that they had no proof but "just knew it had to be true because blacks can't keep their hands off each other." Now, this sergeant certainly didn't share our ethnicity—but he was a minority. I never understood what made these white officers so comfortable that they felt that could speak this way in his presence since he was newly assigned to CTD and not personally known by them. The sergeant told us that the comments had offended him, and he wanted us to know what was being said and that we needed to "watch our backs."

When we parted company with the sergeant, we were upset, of course, but we knew that the assertion was false. We decided that we would do our job—which was what we did while assigned to day watch. We allowed our work ethic to speak for us. We were consistently highest in recap among the AI officers in nearly every measurable category: accident reports, arrest reports for DUI, and citations issued. None of those white officers could touch our performance. We were again commended repeatedly by the commanding officer. We continued to work together on PM watch and then, at some point, we were reassigned back to day watch and each to our own "L" car.

One would wonder why my sergeant didn't report what had occurred to a higher authority. It was the LAPD code of silence at work. My sergeant didn't really want to get involved. The sergeant didn't tell anyone other than the two who were the most powerless to do anything about it other than "to know." He was a young, up-and-coming sergeant. I'm sure he had aspirations of promotion—like we all did. He knew he needed to go along to get along. He had to listen to those disparaging comments being made about us and laugh and grin with the white boys making the comments and not piss them off.

The department reinforced the keep quiet lesson over and over again. There were many stories of officers who had crossed the thin blue line and spoke out against injustice and harassment on the LAPD only to later become the subject of retaliations by command staff. Then there were the officers who just spoke truthfully about an event they witnessed and also discovered the LAPD backhand. They spoke of betrayal, disbelief and then depression. That is what happened of you bled blue. There are those skeptics who refuse to believe the stats. But I know of at least one individual who suffered greatly at the hands of the LAPD.

My black partner and I continued to assist each other on accident investigations and have code-7 together. I was really getting tired of the whispers, lies, and just bad treatment. Of course, there were moments when I could glean a little happiness. There were brief respites. But this stuff takes a toll on you, and I did not want to explode.

Thankfully, all of my detractors were below the rank of P-3 and had no real effect on the job assignments I sought. My sergeants, lieutenants, and captain absolutely loved me. I had been in CTD for five years, and it was time for a change.

I heard that there were openings for P-2s in Operations South Bureau–CRASH (Community Resources Against Street Hoodlums) unit. It was time to go back to the south end. This was during the time that the police chief was deploying officers on something called the "Hammer Task Force," which dealt with the rising gang violence in the south end of the city. "South end" was the term used to describe the part of the city that included 77th Division, S/W Division, Southeast Division, and the Harbor Division down in San Pedro, California—basically everything south of the Santa Monica Freeway. I applied and was selected as a CRASH officer.

# TWENTY-SIX:
# LET THE GOOD TIMES ROLL

When I arrived at OSB–CRASH, I was a tenured officer. I had nine years on the job. I had spent all nine of those years in patrol or "the field." You see, I was really a field Negro; proud to be one. Because I had spent my entire career in patrol-related assignments, I had the immediate respect of my peers; this was a first.

One of the other reasons I enjoyed working patrol was because I felt I had greater impact, in terms of how folks were being treated in my community when the police engaged them. I continue to believe that change on any police department will come from the inside. If you don't like what's going on in your community – join the PD.

It's no secret that organizations who mean us no good are infiltrating police departments across the nation. There is documented evidence that the KKK is making its presence known and felt. When I hear millennials say eff-the police, I shake my head. That's exactly what some would want young black men and women to say and feel about becoming a police officer. You can't stop an out of control, drunk with power officer from coming into your community and murdering your brothers, fathers and sisters from the sidelines.

There not many times that I had to intervene, because white officers knew up front I would not tolerate mistreatment and abuse but on a few occasions I worked with white partners who wanted to sit a black man on the curb during a traffic stop. My response was, "oh no, we don't do that." I have always conducted myself with the mind sett hat on any given day the person being detained or arrested could have been a family member. No need to be disrespectful.

OSB–CRASH was a much sought-after assignment. This would

surely lead to a promotion to P-3. Plus, there were a lot of blacks working in OSB. The black officers were the only ones who could effectively work with the growing gang population in S/W, 77th, S/E, and the Harbor. I mean, any ethic group could make an arrest, but that was only part of what was crucial to being an effective CRASH investigator. We had to develop a rapport with the gangsters if we wanted to solve homicides and shootings.

As a CRASH officer, we would alternate from plain clothes details to uniformed assignments. This was great. I was assigned to partner with a veteran CRASH officer. He looked black, but he was from Panama. He was a bad boy. He had been in the military, the Navy SEALs. He was an imposing figure: large in stature with a heart just as big. Everyone called him simply "T."

There were other black officers assigned to CRASH who I had come to know from having worked with them in other divisions The same black officer who rescued me from that asshole of a TO when he grabbed me back at Southwest Division when I was on probation now also worked CRASH. There were many young black P-2s and P-3s assigned to patrol and several more assigned to work plain clothes and uniformed detective details. Even our lieutenant was black. He was what they called "an old SWAT dog." That meant he had previously been assigned to the Special Weapons and Tactics team (S.W.A.T.). He was real laid-back. He allowed us to go out and do police work without all the back-office drama. It was great. I was in hog heaven. No pun intended

Working with this group of officers was the most fun I had ever had on the department. I am not at liberty to discuss a lot of what went on in the field. I'm not sure about the statute of limitations regarding perceived misconduct, but suffice it to say, we had a blast. That was why I joined the LAPD.

There were several project complexes or low income residential areas within the south end, and many of the gangsters lived there. Most of the black officers were only a few years older than many of the gang members; so we could relate to their plight although we did not agree with their activity. It was just a good time to be a police officer.

A thirty-something, black sergeant transferred into the CRASH unit. We used to call him Papa Smurf. He, too, was a former SWAT dog. He was what most officers call a "kick ass and take names" kind of officer. He was a policeman's supervisor, which meant he always supported his patrol officers. If there was ever a citizen complaint about something an officer did in the field, you wanted Papa Smurf to come to your supervisor request.

We soon had a supervision change. The black lieutenant transferred out, and a white lieutenant transferred in as the officer-in-charge of the CRASH unit. We had been having so much fun working the gang unit, and this supervision change initially gave us reason to pause. This was truly a life-altering moment in my career. This new lieutenant would first become my adversary, then later an ally, an advocate, my biggest supporter, and most importantly, my friend. I don't have the words to express what he meant to me as a person and an officer. What I can say is that when he passed away in 2007, I was deeply saddened. I do, however, to this day remain eternally grateful to Commander James Tatreau for his unwavering courage and willingness to stand up for me and with me when no one else had the guts.

# TWENTY-SEVEN: ROLLING 60'S

I had been in CRASH for a several months now. My training officer and I had been involved in some very complex gang investigations. One such investigation sent us out of state to Ohio. We had to accompany two young female witnesses to a gang murder back to Los Angeles for the trial of a local gang member. During this time a crips faction known as the Rolling 60s and a blood gang known as Van Ness Gangsters were in an all-out war. There were shootings almost daily and at least one murder a week.

There was a shooting that involved the death of a Crip gang member, and we were certain that the Blood gang member arrested by CRASH officers would be tried in court and found guilty of the crime. I had been in the courtroom during his trial, and listened to witnesses who testified. I also had an opportunity to observe the accused shooter. I found the arrogance and lack of remorse on the part of the gangster defendant to be shocking. His demeanor and posture while seated in the court was enough to make you want to jump over the railing and choke the crap out of him. I imagined how the family of the victim felt, having to sit in silence, knowing their loved one had been senselessly killed by this individual who is seated just inches away. The trial lasted only a few days, same as most of these cases, because the witnesses didn't want to get involved, either because of the victim gang's desire for street justice or the stone-cold fear of retaliation.

The defendant at some point in the trial, through his attorney offered, what I believed to be, a bogus alibi. He said he was out of the state at the time of the shooting. He even produced a bus ticket from Greyhound to support his claim. He beat the charge; not guilty.

Shameful. How could this be? Well, you know karma is a

mutha—two weeks later, my partner and I responded to a radio call of a gang shooting on 54th and Van Ness in 77th division. It appeared that one of our gangsters had been killed on the steps of an apartment building on the corner. When we arrived, we approached the body, which was on the ground, covered with a sheet. The paramedics had just arrived on scene a few moments before we had and pronounced this guy dead. It turned out that this was the same guy who had beaten that murder charge a few weeks prior. Wow. Maybe if he had been found guilty, he would have still been alive—in jail, but alive.

The violence went on for a long time. There was a Rolling 60s gang member who the CRASH unit knew well. The "60s" referred to a neighborhood where the street numbers were between sixty and sixty-nine. That was how many of the Crip gangs identified themselves: 60s, 40s, 90s, etc. The Bloods used a little different in choosing gang names.

This gangster was a little guy in stature, barely five-four and thin, but he was certainly violent. He was believed to be responsible for a number of drive-by shootings, but no one was willing to testify against him—so he walked. Then one day, the world righted itself. He was out on his bicycle riding around his 'hood, and a rival gang member drove by and shot him. He had been what the gangsters referred to an as "OG" original gangster and their leader.

When his gang laid him to rest, you would have thought he was a head of state. There were a line of powder-blue limousines that stacked up for at least a block along the curb in front of the funeral home on Crenshaw Boulevard. During the service, I was secreted with a couple of other CRASH officers, behind a curtain in what would normally be the family viewing area. Other plain clothes CRASH officers were positioned just outside the mortuary in and around the parking lot and adjacent side streets. We were visible in an attempt to make prevent a rival blood gang from disrupting the service, as they were known to do. The mortuary was a stone's throw from Blood territory in the Jungle.

The funeral went off without a hitch until the very end when two females started a near riot when they began cursing, pushing, and shoving each other while standing at the casket. I guess both thought she was his only woman. All I could think of was, oh no, this curtain is going to come down, and they are going to see us back here and then start fighting with us. Several of the OG (original gangster) members stood sentry next to the open casket. The OGs wore powder blue tuxedos and matching patent leather shoes. Suddenly, during the parting view, there was a ruckus. Two females were yelling and swearing at each other. Two of the tuxedoed gangsters stepped between the combatants. One of the young girls yelled, "Get her out of here—get her out of here." I assumed she was the mother of his children and therefore outranked the other female, who was then led away. I had never seen anything quite like this; fighting at a funeral.

The viewing continued. I watched the gangsters file past his casket; some were crying and some threw up their gang sign as they passed the body. The deceased was dressed in what I like to call "full gang regalia." The deceased wore all blue clothing, a blue hat, and a pair of dark sunglasses. There was a large blue floral arrangement with his gang name/moniker, in blue carnations, prominently displayed next to his casket.

The procession from the mortuary to the cemetery blocked traffic for several minutes as the cars slowly snaked down Crenshaw Boulevard to Inglewood Park Cemetery. Many of them were standing up and sticking their heads and upper bodies out of the open rooftops of the limos and the low-rider cars that they rode in. It was crazy to see. They were yelling gang chants and throwing up signs with their hands indicating their hood.

A few of the CRASH officers celebrated his death. I had a hard time with that philosophy—after all, this was someone's son.

I don't remember his exact age at the time of his death, but I am certain he was under the age of twenty-five. We had a white sergeant who supervised a group of officers assigned to CRASH, but actually worked an undercover robbery detail. The sergeant encouraged his group of officers to wear something red to the funeral. All of the CRASH officers wore plain clothes with a raid jacket that said "Police" on the back. But a few of the officers had placed a red bandana, identical to the ones worn by the bloods obviously placed somewhere on their body. You can imagine that seeing police officers wearing red at the funeral for a crip sent the gang members into frenzy. Some of them made their displeasure known during the funeral; others waited and called the CRASH office the next day to complain. Their complaints fell on deaf ears.

OSB CRASH now consisted of about 60 police officers; mostly black. I was lucky enough to get assigned to a gang car with two other black officers who were also young P2s like me. We became the three amigos. BADDAB aka They Physical Thang and Dre. Then there were the other "usual suspects" Grape Ape; Sport; Officer Friendly; the Ultimate-Male-n-The-Flesh-Baby; the Corvette Brothers, whom my mother named because of their cars, and the 700 Club. All characters in their own right, but the 700 Club deserve a special mention. These two guys each claimed to have slept with seven hundred women—thus the name. Both of them were in their early twenties, so I am not sure if that claim was even mathematically possible. My all-time favorite addition to the CRASH unit was Hobo Cop. This guy would come to work missing one piece of equipment or uniform almost daily. I heard how he would go around asking to borrow a uniform shirt, socks, tie and even a gun because he didn't have his department issued weapon. He would sometimes look inside unlocked lockers to scavenger hunt for uniform pieces. He once borrowed the name plate from another officer which he wore on his uniform the entire shift.

It never mattered to Hobo Cop if the uniform pants were too short or too baggy for his thin frame. He would just laugh it off in his good natured way with that half-smile he always maintained, as he blamed his wife for whatever item he was missing. Hobo Cop could never remember to bring the things he needed for work each day but he always made sure he had his daily vitamin regimen.

I was having so much fun working CRASH in the south end of the city. By early 1988, then police chief Darryl Gates started weekend sweeps of gang members in an operation dubbed, The Hammer. Large groups of police officers, with riot gear in hand, would converge in the parking lots at the Los Angeles Memorial Coliseum and adjacent Sports Arena on King Boulevard near Exposition Park. We would eventually partner up to work this joint task force which was designed to arrest as many gangsters and their associates as possible. Officers from all over the city would be assigned to work this detail. Most of us would arrive well in advance of our roll call or start time and visit with one another before we would partner up and hit the streets. During one such event, a group of CRASH officers had been standing around talking when a patrol officer from 77th division came over to say hello. I noticed as he approached us he was wearing his LAPD issued ballistic helmet with the face shield raised up over his forehead. Why he had his helmet on I don't know. But as he neared our group, Grape Ape yelled out, "Hey Oscar! What you been doing, eating pussy in that helmet?" Everybody within ear shot instantly doubled over in laughter. All eyes were now on this guy's face shield. It was noticeably yellow and scratched. Don't ask me how that happened. But the visual was hilarious. Grape Ape was a fool.

There were many instances of foolishness going on in the CRASH unit. We lost a few officers due to administrative transfers and a few more to firings. Sport was eventually fired for taking his badge off his uniform shirt and removing his gun belt after a gangster told him he wasn't such a bad guy without that gun and badge. So, Sport took it off and challenged the gangster to fight in the middle of the projects. Word got back to a supervisor. Then there were the "jump-ins". I am not sure when this "tradition" started in the CRASH unit, but the "OG" officers would "jump-in" the new gang officers, much like the gangsters in the street. We eventually learned a new word: hazing.

Several of the male officers assigned to CRASH were a bit too heavy-handed in one of their "initiations." Officer Friendly who stood about 6'3 and weighed about 240 pounds and muscular; Grape Ape who was about 6'4 and 340 pounds, and the Ultimate Male who was the runt of the group along with several other CRASH officers became involved in an incident with a patrol officer at Southeast station. The OGs were in the midst of a jump-in on a CRASH officer when this patrol officer said something that caused the group to focus their attention towards him. A few punches later, this officer had sustained bruised ribs, or maybe it was his liver or kidney. I'm not sure which. But he had to go to the emergency room. At first he tried not to "give it up," but he was doubled over in pain when the group that had been hammering him finally stopped. He was in so much pain that he couldn't finish putting on his uniform. He had to say something. There was a big personnel investigation into the mater. None of the officers involved wanted to cross that thin blue line and rat out another but word eventually made it back to a supervisor that Grape Ape, for sure, was involved. The department instituted a "no hazing" policy.

This was just one of the many incidents which involved Grape Ape. A story circulated that Grape Ape had stopped a group of gangsters who had been playing loud music; you know the blaring sounds that came from a 1980s boom box. Grape Ape approached the group along with his partner and asked, "Whose box is this?" Of course, none of the gangsters answered and after he asked a few more times they all replied, "not mine." So, Grape Ape announced that since the boom box didn't belong to anyone he would "send it sailing into the air" and that's just what he did. Grape Ape grabbed the boom box and threw it like a hand grenade. He and his partner wondered how long it would take for that "beef" (personnel complaint) to make its way to the CRASH officer; but it never did.

Grape Ape worked a lot of "off duty" jobs. That's the term we use for security jobs that officers work on their time off from the department. Some of us worked at the local movie theatre, or at concerts and sporting events sanctioned by the department. One day, Grape Ape had been assigned to a security post at a local hospital where he was supposed to monitor a gangster who was being hospitalized prior to being booked into jail for whatever injuries he had sustained during his arrest. This gangster had been in the hospital for a few days and Grape Ape relieved the previous officer on duty. Well, after three days of watching Grape Ape fall asleep during his shift, the gangster made a break. The gangster later told officers after he was captured that every time Grape Ape fell asleep he would make noise to see how loud he could get before Grape Ape would awaken. On the fourth day when the Grape Ape fell asleep and the gangster felt confident that he was in a deep sleep he began to make noise again. When Grape Ape didn't awaken, the gangster removed the hand cuff key from the sleeping officer's gun belt and freed himself. The gangster then removed Grape Ape's weapon from his holster and hid it in the room so that when he did awaken, he would need to first look for and find his weapon before he looked for the escaped prisoner. Of course, when we heard about this latest caper, we thought it was hilarious; Mostly, because Grape Ape didn't get hurt. However, the supervisors were not amused. The gangster was eventually located and returned to his hospital room, with a different officer watching this time. Grape Ape earned a division change. We were going to miss his antics.

This chapter is dedicated to the memory of my much beloved partner and cherished friend, one of the three amigos - gone way too soon.

ANDRE (Dre) Gawain DAWSON
Sunrise January 13, 1958 - Sunset February 10, 2018

Got but never forgotten...

# TWENTY-EIGHT: HOLY CRAP

I was having the time of my life. This CRASH detail was the bomb. That is, until I came to work one day after my hair had been rinsed in a burgundy cellophane. During this time, a lot of black women wore "cellophanes." It was a temporary dye that would lessen in intensity with each subsequent wash. Cellophanes came in a variety of "rinses," like burgundy, blue, brown, and black. Of course, me being me, I chose burgundy.

When I walked into the back door of the CRASH office on 103rd and Central, all of the officers were assembling for roll call. My white male sergeant looked in my direction and just yelled as loud as he could, "Holy crap!" Of course, everyone in the room stopped what they were doing to see what had caused him to respond in such a loud and raucous manner. I knew exactly. It was my hair color. I ignored the stares and the sergeant's look of "what the… " and proceeded to my seat and sat down.

He didn't say anything to me. He went on about his duty as watch commander and began to call roll. He called the partner assignments, and by the time he had finished, my name had not been called. My regular partner was there; I was sitting within close proximity to him, so I didn't understand why he called a different officer's name to work with my partner that night. After roll call ended, I approached the sergeant and asked him why he had not called my name. He responded that I would be working the desk. He said he was not going to let me go out into the field with my hair "looking like that." I didn't know exactly what "that" was, so I asked. He said that I could not go out into the public with my hair that color, and I would remain assigned to the desk inside the CRASH office until I changed the color of my hair.

I worked the desk that night, but the next day I was going straight to the lieutenant. I was beyond pissed. This was not fair.

When I arrived at the CRASH office the next day, my lieutenant was there. I went straight to his office. I should have known he already knew what I wanted to talk about. He listened to my side of the story and then informed me that the sergeant had a right to make that call, and he supported his position. I could not believe my ears.

We talked a bit more about this situation, and he did not budge. Well, he left me no recourse but to file an employee grievance, and I told him that's exactly what I was going to do. My lieutenant told me, "Go ahead, girl." It wasn't so much what he had said as how he said it. Understand, I didn't like what he had said at all. He called me "girl." I asked him, "Did you just call me girl?" He replied, "Yes, grieve that, too."

Oh, now my blood was boiling. I wanted to sock him in his throat. I felt certain he was being racist. Why else would he add the whole "girl" thing? It was akin to a white man calling a black man "boy" in my mind.

# TWENTY-NINE: GET OVER IT

Sure that I was on solid footing, I followed all of the rules. I filed a department grievance against my sergeant for refusing to allow me to work in the field with my hair a color that in his subjective opinion was an embarrassment to the department. My personnel action was summarily denied. I appealed the department's decision. White female offices were allowed to dye their hair any color they desired—streak it, lighten it, bleach it—and there were no repercussions. I tint my hair with a temporary rinse, and I'm told I am an embarrassment. This decision was again upheld at the final appellate level. I had to return to the CRASH office and stand before my lieutenant with my tail between my legs. I had been absolutely sure I would win this fight.

I should have known something was up because before the battle had even begun in earnest, my lieutenant coyly warned me, "Don't be mad if I win." He said he wanted me to come back to work and continue to do my job in the same manner that I had prior to my decision to file the grievance. I sharply responded, "No problem." He then followed up with a sly, "And if you win—I won't be mad either."

He knew I would lose. He knew what I did not—the LAPD's system. He knew that each successive level would "back" the lower level's decision. That's the LAPD way. My lieutenant knew that the final decision regarding my appeal was going to be made by someone who was in the "command staff club for men." He knew that all he had to do was pick up the telephone. He eventually explained to me that on the "telephone" was where decisions were made. My lieutenant had done this dance before. He picked up that phone and called his captain or commander-buddy upon whose desk my grievance had landed and told him how he wanted my grievance resolved. This thing had gone back and forth for so long that my hair had actually grown out and the burgundy color was no longer detectible. But I fought on—it was the principle.

I had to meet in person and discuss the grievance with the command staff officer responsible for adjudicating the matter. I was not expecting the person handling my grievance to be none other than the unicorn, my old captain from Central patrol. The same captain, Mr. House Negro, with the tailored-to-fit perfectly shirts, the one who had tried unsuccessfully to force me to cut my fingernails back in the early '80s. So I guess I should not have been surprised when my grievance was denied.

When I next spoke with my lieutenant, he gave me a kind of "told-you-so" look. I was pissed all over again. But then he told me to close the door to his office. We had a frank discussion about the inner workings of the LAPD. My lieutenant first told me that he liked my spirit; I reminded him a lot of himself as a young man. However, he told me, "The LAPD is a machine. It will eat you up and spit you out. You are just a cog in this system. Pick and choose your battles carefully." The only other thing that he wanted to know was if I was going to honor my promise to continue to work hard in the field and remain a productive and professional officer. I gave my word—and I kept it. He would later become my biggest supporter.

The CRASH unit had almost doubled in size. We had one group of officers assigned to gang suppression and another group assigned to a newly created robbery suppression detail (RAD). It appeared that there had been a spike in robberies in the south end, and a decision had been made to utilize CRASH officers to combat the problem. As a result of the numerous officers added to our ranks, there were also additional sergeants and one other lieutenant added to the unit.

In addition to garnering the attention of that field sergeant who didn't like my hair, there was an officer who I later found out had been paying me particular attention. He was a young P-2, newly off probation and a recent transfer into CRASH. I heard from a fellow CRASH officer that the P-2 had a crush on me and thought I was pretty. An introduction was later made. We eventually worked as partners when our regularly assigned partners were on a day off. We struck up a friendship—and then one thing led to another.

It wasn't long before we were dating. We kept that information a secret for as long as we could from our fellow officers, but I guess people noticed how we looked at one another or how we engaged each other during code-7. Eventually we admitted to a few of our closest peers that we were dating, but we did not want our supervisors to know, none of them.

We would spend long hours on the telephone after working PM watch, sometimes till two or three in the morning. We were inseparable off duty. Remember, I had been previously married but recently widowed. My husband had been killed in a head-on car collision. I was left with two small children. My baby was just a toddler when his dad was killed. All I could think of was the fact that I was again a single mom, this time with two small children, and for sure, my husband was not returning.

I gave the young P-2 a second look. He was not really my type—a bit shorter than I liked but he was handsome [to me] and of course had a good job with a pension and drove a nice car. Those were all things on my list of must-haves. I had a theory: equal to or more than. Well, I owned a home in Altadena, and he rented. I needed him to be a property owner before we could take the next logical step. I eventually persuaded him to purchase a little piece of property. Now, we could do this matrimony thing.

During our brief engagement, that newly transferred in lieutenant discovered that we were dating. He was a short, little man, but he grew five or six inches each time he put on his LAPD uniform. This lieutenant reminded me of the kind of person who used to get his ass kicked as a kid, and now that he was a big-city cop, he liked to throw his weight around. This lieutenant went out of his way to let us know that he was running the CRASH plantation and had decided that one or both of us needed to find a new "church home." He inferred that our relationship was nothing more than a seedy little affair, and because of it, we were now going to be forced out of the unit. He repeatedly told us that he did not want us working CRASH. I believed his angst had little to do with our dating and more to do with the fact that he didn't like blacks and this was a way for him to "stick it to us". I have no proof that he was racist; it was just his way and condescending tone when he interacted with you. It was very different from the way he dealt with the white officers in CRASH.

Well, although he was a lieutenant, he was not the officer in charge (OIC) of the CRASH unit. That designation remained with the other white lieutenant, against whom I had filed the grievance regarding my hair color. The OIC and I had become fast friends since our little falling-out. I went to him to discuss the impending transfer. My lieutenant told me not to worry about it. He told me that neither of us had to worry about being transferred out of the unit. He said that he was happy with our job performance as gang suppression officers, and that was all that mattered. He assured me he would handle the little guy. The OIC had met and married a female officer on the LAPD and he did not have any heartburn about the two of us working the CRASH unit.

A couple of days later, my lieutenant pulled me aside and told me that the problem had been solved. We both continued in our assignment. Well, the next time I saw the little guy, I think I was about five or six inches taller. I gave him a sly grin and a knowing nod. His face flushed with each encounter, but he stayed out of my way.

I thanked my lieutenant. This was when I first realized that he had a lot of clout on the LAPD. I would see over and over that he pretty much did what he believed to be the right thing on behalf of his officers with absolutely no regard for what others thought, particularly the brass. He was becoming my BFF.

I eventually married my coworker. We stayed in CRASH but did not work the same patrol unit going forward. The little guy left us alone.

The department posted notification of a promotional exam for P-3s. My lieutenant pulled me aside and told me that I should take the test. He told me that it was time for me to get serious about my career and promote. I took the promotional exam and placed high enough on the list of potential candidates for P-3 that I was in contention for selection early in the life of the list.

My lieutenant was aware of my placement on the list and told me that he knew a female captain who was in charge of the patrol side of the house at Pacific Division. My lieutenant told me to apply for a P-3 position in Pacific. He told me that he would call his friend—the captain—and tell her that I was going to interview. Wow. First this guy and I have a big fight about hair color, and now he was my biggest supporter. Who knew?

I think what made our CRASH lieutenant so cool was the fact that he could relate to black people and was comfortable around us, and not in a phony, pretend kind of way. He was genuine. He had played on the department's mostly black basketball team in the '70s. You could just tell he was real comfortable around black people.

I interviewed for the P-3 position at Pacific. I received a call within a couple of days after my interview from the female captain. She told me that I had been chosen and would be on the next transfer. Amazing. I was so excited. I was headed to West Bureau to work patrol. I knew that the officers already assigned to Pacific would be looking at me sideways, but I didn't care. I had ten years on the job, and all of it in patrol. I had credibility. I was also confident in my abilities to be an asset to the department. I looked forward to training probationary officers. And another thing—I knew what type of training officer I would not be.

Shortly after I arrived at Pacific Division, a few of the other CRASH officers from OSB transferred in as new P-3s. They also got the home-hookup from our CRASH lieutenant. One thing about my lieutenant, if he liked you – he liked you; no matter your ethnicity. He promoted whomever he wanted and took those he trusted with him when he transferred to another division. He did not care what anyone had to say; his spine was straight.

# THIRTY:
# LA RIOTS, YOU KILLED MY BROTHER

Nineteen ninety-two. The LAPD was in the midst of a real situation. Three white police officers and one white sergeant had been found "not guilty" of beating a black motorist, Rodney King. The natives were restless.

Everyone knows how this story ended, but what a lot of people don't know is that there had been a "come to Jesus" meeting between one of LAPD's finest, Fred Nichols, and the department. You see, Nichols was a prominently positioned sergeant on the department. He had been called to testify at the trial of the white officers regarding the department's policy on the use of force. Sergeant Nichols was a spokesperson for the department and a use-of-force expert assigned to the training division at the police academy.

Sergeant Nichols testified under oath truthfully because that's what police officers were trained to do. He stated publically, what everyone on the department knew to be true: "excessive force" had been used by the white officers. Oh, did I mention that Sergeant Nichols was black? He used his spine for its intended purpose. He paid a price for that decision.

Sergeant Nichols was black, but unfortunately he bled blue. He worked some great assignments around the department, many specialized units. I assume he probably socialized off-duty with some of those white officers who also bled blue. I believe he played on the department's tennis team; if not the team, he certainly was a regular fixture at the Academy tennis courts. He had bought into that "good old boy" system. He was one of "them." He was even married to one of "them." Well, that is, until he testified truthfully against (four of) "them." By all accounts, he had arrived, so to speak.

The LAPD opened up a can of "whup-ass" (figuratively) on him. The backlash was immediate, unrelenting, and, in Sergeant Nichols's mind, retaliatory. The first act of vengeance came in the form of reassignment from his coveted expert position to a "lesser" post. He was no longer the department's spokesperson on use of force. He was a "captain without a ship," so to speak. According to an article in the LA Times, "this was the third time that the department's high command had been accused of punishing supervisors who spoke out against the LAPD..." The department did what the LAPD always did—denied it. The department tried to convince the public and those of us on the department that Sergeant Nichols' transfer had nothing to do with his testimony at the Rodney King Trial and was coincidental. The LAPD has no problem tapping a black officer on the shoulder and, almost in a whisper, reminding you that you are STILL black. We let you on our department, place a few select ones in pretend positions of importance but if you anger me, I will give you a spanking of epic proportions. The department never has and never will admit wrong doing. They don't want to open up the city's wallet. That only happens when a court intervenes and forces the department/city to pay for abuses.

The LAPD had a plausible explanation for Sergeant Nichols's reassignment—but the timing, well, that was uncanny. Nonetheless, the LAPD machine plowed on, as if to say, "Never mind, you little man—we have work to do; never mind that you were a good and loyal officer; never mind that you performed your duties in an exemplary and dignified manner for the citizens of Los Angeles; never mind that you worked in specialized units. Sergeant Nichols—you crossed the department, and now you will pay." This was LAPD-101.

Sergeant Nichols, in an interview with the Times, reported that he "suffered severe stress-related problems, including anxiety, insomnia, and vomiting, since he was...removed." He said, "I can't work, I can't sleep. There's not one minute that I don't think about it. Sixteen years of working in specialized units, doing my tasks, and now, because I'm honest and fair, they do this to me. What career do I have left? It's gone. If you make waves in this department, it becomes close to impossible to ever promote again."

For those who wonder out loud why officers don't just "go get another job," the answer is that LAPD will make sure that there is no other job. Understand that there are real consequences for officers who find themselves in the LAPD's crosshairs. Bleed blue if you want to—the LAPD will watch your blue blood run down the street and into the gutter.

This unfortunate tortured soul endured the humiliation heaped on him by the department for as long as he could stand it, and then one day he snapped. LAPD Sergeant Fred Nichols checked himself into a hotel, placed a shotgun to his head, and pulled the trigger. I am sorry that he bought into the LAPD culture. I'm sorry that he let his position seemingly define him as a man. I'm sorry that he didn't realize that there is life after LAPD. I am proof.

I am not speaking in the abstract. I knew him. I worked for him. He was the sergeant, affectionately known as "Papa Smurf" when I was assigned to OSB–CRASH. He was dedicated, smart, tactically strong, sharp in his uniform appearance, and had a beautiful spirit. The LAPD pushed him over the edge.

Thankfully, Sergeant Nichols didn't create a manifesto and seek revenge on those who he felt had wronged him. He suffered in silence. He didn't take on the LAPD machine. He didn't spend the next five years after being stripped of his coveted assignment waging an unsuccessful battle against the department in an attempt to be returned to the prestigious positions that he had worked so hard to attain. He didn't appeal the department's decision to "reassign" him with any appellate court, only to have that body side with the LAPD. He didn't leave the department and seek other employment. He already knew there would be no other employment. He wouldn't give the department the satisfaction of grinding him down to a nub like the LAPD had done to so many others before him—nope. Fred Nichols just blew the top of his head off. He deprived his wife and children of his presence in their lives. Sergeant Nichols had been beaten and betrayed by the very LAPD that he loved so much—the LAPD that he proudly represented as its use-of-force expert, the LAPD where he spent many hours of overtime working away from his family. The LAPD spanked him for being honest, the same way the LAPD spanked Christopher Dorner for his honesty. According to Dorner's published manifesto, Dorner believed that the LAPD retaliated against him ten months after he reported misconduct he witnessed by his white female training officer. Dorner was sent to a board of rights hearing where he was alleged to have lied, even though the victim of the misconduct testified at his BOR. Dorner was found guilty and terminated in February 2008. Dorner cited a conflict of interest in the make-up of his BOR panel because one of the captains was a "personal friend" of his female training officer and the department advocate from internal affairs was purported to also be a "friend" and former partner of the female training officer he accused of misconduct when she kicked a suspect in the head. Both of these individuals were allowed by the LAPD to remain in their respective positions in the administrative hearing. Years after the LAPD terminated him, Dorner was discharged from the military; something he obviously believed LAPD caused. Two days after his discharge, he went on a murderous rampage seeking revenge against those LAPD employees he blamed for his firing. He eventually killed two family members of an LAPD captain involved in his BOR and subsequent firing. Dorner also fatally wounded two police officers and injured three other police officers from surrounding agencies who became involved in his manhunt. Dorner was eventually cornered and killed, about a week later, in an abandoned mountain cabin in San Bernardino, California. I do not condone his actions, but I understand how the LAPD can grind you down and cause an otherwise rational thinking person to snap in the midst of seemingly insurmountable despair.

When word spread of Sergeant Nichols's untimely death, of course the black officers wanted to do what we could to outwardly express our love for our fallen "brutha." We knew there would be no high-profile police funeral. There would be no missing-man formation flown by the air units, no riderless horse, no bagpipes, and no folded American flag presented to his widow by the police chief. But we wanted to attend his private "garden variety" funeral and wear our Class A uniforms as a show of respect. We wanted to let his extended family know that we hurt too.

Several of us asked if wearing the police uniform would be permissible—because, realize, an officer can't wear the LAPD uniform unless it's sanctioned. An LAPD officer can't just put on the department uniform and say and act any way he or she desired. This required approval by the chief of police. You know, like the kind of approval a sergeant might need before attending a press conference in front of a bank of cameras and TV reporters while falsely stating to the world that racism does not exist anywhere on the department.

Well, we wanted to wear our uniforms now. We were first told that it would not be allowed. Someone must have rethought that position, because we were eventually allowed to attend Sergeant Nichols's private funeral service in our Class A (long-sleeve shirt, tie, and department hat).

Most of the uniformed officers sat together in the chapel. There seemed to be uneasiness during the service. I could not tell if our uniformed presence was appreciated by his family. It just felt odd. Then, during the two-minute remarks, a woman stood up and took her place at the podium. She identified herself as Fred's sister. She spoke fondly of her brother and the many things that she would miss now that he was gone. In concluding, Sergeant Nichols's sister, with what seemed like utter contempt, looked out and over to the pews of uniformed officers and proclaimed, "LAPD—you killed my brother." She was right. RIP Papa Smurf—gone but never forgotten.

# THIRTY-ONE:
# PACIFIC'S NOTHING LIKE THE SOUTH END

I was promoted to P-3 and assigned to morning watch, like most new officers who transfer into a new division. I hated working morning watch. It always felt cold to me, and I had a hard time staying awake. No matter how much sleep I had get before my shift started, at two o'clock a.m., my body would just shut down. That would be the time I would request code-7. At least if I was in a restaurant, I stood a chance of staying awake.

Anyway, I was the big cheese now. So I would be calling all of the shots. My probationer would have to follow my mandates. I would be fair—but we were definitely playing by my rules from now on.

I never really understood what it was about morning watch that seemed to draw the weirdest and what I viewed as racist cops. I don't know if it was because those racist cops could do more "dirt" during the hours of darkness—fewer prying eyes around to witness misconduct—but it was the so-called "ass kickers" that worked this shift.

As usual, I got the stank eye when I first arrived. Mattered not, I was the HNIC (Head Negro In Charge). My probationary partner, like all probationers, was excited and delighted to be out of the academy and doing police work. I/we had no problems. I was lucky enough to get assigned a new recruit who was academically strong and a quick learner. He was certainly teachable and trainable. What a gift. His reports were clear and concise, and he was tactically strong, for a rookie. I didn't play any of those you-can't-drive games or you-can't-wear-short-sleeves stuff that I had to endure. He was a grown-ass man, with a family, and I treated him like one.

I remained at Pacific Division for the next five years until I promoted to sergeant in 1994. One of the many amazing things I learned about working on the west side of town was the way that the department interacted with the citizens. There were some very affluent areas in Pacific. Some of the residents were very liberal in their thinking and a little eclectic in their behaviors. We even had a few celebrities who had homes near Venice Beach.

I remember being assigned to the desk, during a time I was pregnant, and there was this big commotion working its way through the doors to the police station. About the same time, unbeknownst to me, the vice officers had entered the rear of the police station with a white male in handcuffs. Once the officers had the suspect secured and cuffed to the bench in the back of the station, where all arrestees waited to be booked into the division jail, they came to the front desk area. I assume they knew what was about to happen in the lobby.

This white female came storming into the station, demanding to speak to "someone" who could tell her why her husband was arrested and transported to the station. It appeared that she followed the black-and-white to the station. One of the vice officers, a black male who I knew from OSB–CRASH, came over to me and whispered in my ear that the male suspect had approached him in one of the bathrooms at Venice Beach (notorious for lewd activity) and propositioned him. Turned out that the man had been riding his bicycle on the boardwalk with his wife and two kids and he stopped to "use the restroom." Of course, the wife and kids waited outside while he relieved himself. The next thing the wife saw was her husband being escorted out of the men's restroom in handcuffs. Naturally, she wanted to know what had happened. The officers refused to tell her that he had asked the undercover officer (UC) if he would "give him head" as he exposed himself to the officer. The UC decided he would wait and let the husband offer his own version of events to his wife. This sent her into a verbal tirade.

I could hardly contain my laughter. This lady was going berserk. She was asking for everyone from the watch commander to the chief of police to come out to the lobby and tell her why her husband was in handcuffs. No one did, despite her protestations and threats of "having our jobs."

I came to understand that in an upward socio-economic community, there were two types of enforcement: one fraught with demands and expectations from the citizens, who questioned why you were performing a particular task and followed up with, "I will call my councilman," to whom they referred to by the first name, versus those I encountered in the south end, who were either ignorant or had no expectation or idea that there was a remedy for their solution beyond that officer who they had first contacted. Residents in the south end rarely called to report suspected misconduct or lodge a verbal complaint about the manner in which an officer treated them during an arrest or an escalating situation.

In those rare instances when a citizen in South Central Los Angeles filed a verbal compliant, many of the white sergeants (the first line of supervision) would dissuade the complainant by placing a series of obstacles in their path, such as, "You need to come to the station" if transportation could be an issue, or by instructing the complainant to call another supervisor on the department, another good old boy who would ultimately minimize the officer's actions as something other than misconduct, under the pretense that the offending officer would be counseled. So many obstacles would be placed in a complainant's path until they just gave up. This kind of activity by the police was not tolerated by residents in West Bureau. They understood that the squeaky wheel got the grease. Clearly two different LAPDs existed.

# THIRTY-TWO: COME WORK FOR ME

During my five years assigned to Pacific patrol I had become one of the more tenured P-3s in patrol at that time, and the only black female P-3. There were other black female P-2s and P-1s assigned to Pacific, but I was the only training officer. I eventually applied for a senior lead position—P-3+1 but was not selected. Hmm, was that one of those LAPD coincidences. I worked for two white male captains. I continued to get outstanding performance evaluations, now tenured office but could not represent the department as a senior lead officer in the predominantly white Venice beach area. The female who previously promoted me to P-3 had transferred out; back to business as usual. The white captains did eventually promote a male black to the senior lead position; but he was one of those less outspoken types-you know.

I hadn't had any officers taking license plates off my car, but I did have a couple of patrol sergeants, young-on-the-job white boys, who decided to make me a project. I was getting pretty good at deflecting their crap by now. Bring it.

I was a firm but fair training officer with my probationers. I made sure as best I could that each probationer who moved on was tactically sound and diverse in their patrol exposures. As usual, the simple-minded white boys that supervised me could not "get" me on anything substantive, so they zeroed in on the petty.

One day, I was working with a probationary officer who was having trouble writing reports, and we had just left the police station, headed back out to the field. As we departed the station, I began discussing with my probationer areas in which I thought he could improve on his reports and ways in which to make that happen. My probationer was driving. I was passenger. We were having this back-and-forth dialogue and had only driven about two blocks from the station when I heard my sergeant ask the dispatcher over the police radio for my location.

Having heard his inquiry, I responded, "We are at the station." I knew that I was within close proximity and assumed that if my sergeant needed something, I could have my probationer turn the car around and return to the station. I thought perhaps it had something to do with the reports we had just turned in. Before he could respond and request that we return to the station, I directed my probationer to do just that. We arrived back at Pacific station within seconds, only to find my sergeant and another white male sergeant standing in the parking lot just outside the back door to the station. My sergeant looked in our direction as we entered the lot. I exited the police car and approached him. He immediately snapped, "Where were you?" I replied that we were just up the street. The jackass, I mean sergeant, continued by stating, "Well, your MDT [car computer] shows you 'at the station.'" I told him that my probationer and I had been talking, and I had not yet hit the button on my MDT, which would have changed our unit status from "station" to "clear." ("Clear" meant we were in the field and available to receive radio calls.) I went on to explain to Sergeant Jackass that obviously we had still been close, because he could see how quickly we returned when he asked communications for our location.

He immediately, in front of the other jackass sergeant, who I guess was acting as his "witness," accused me of some felonious conspiracy in not properly updating my status via the MDT. I looked at him in sheer amazement. He must be kidding, right? He then proudly advised me that he was going to "write me up" for "lying" about my location via a notice to correct deficiencies (NTC). I encouraged him to do just that. At this stage in my career, I had become pretty vocal. When I saw crap, I called it. So go ahead, give me an NTC. He did so the very next day. I signed the NTC, and he placed it into my personnel folder.

The female captain who had first selected me for the P-3

position had since moved on. A series of different male captains had taken her place, most of which had little use for me and the type of training officer I had become. Nonetheless, I persevered. I continued to do the only thing that I knew how—work hard and treat the public fairly in the discharge of my duties as a Los Angeles police officer.

I knew that I was nothing more than a serial number to the department. I was okay with that. I did what I did not because of the department, but because of Cheryl. I had a work ethic that was unparalleled. Many times officers and supervisors messed with me, hoping to catch me slipping. Well, as the saying goes, I was born at night—but not last night. I was determined not to give any of them ammunition to later use against me. I did what was expected, required, and the right thing to do.

This was never more apparent to me than when my parents passed away; my dad in 1989 and my mom in 1993. My father passed away after a lengthy illness and then my mother grieved herself to death. Thankfully, my immediate supervisor, a black lieutenant and personal friend had been very accommodating during that time. I was able to take off work as needed for the two-a-days I did at Daniel Freeman Hospital. Not once did I ever receive any acknowledgement from the command staff at Pacific when either of my parents passed away. Neither of the two captains for whom I worked sent a floral arrangement or a card expressing sympathy at the time of my losses. Nothing.

I hadn't really expected any outward expression of empathy to be shown, but I did wonder what had happened to all that "we are family" stuff the department liked to spout off when cameras were rolling. "We take care of our own"—but that didn't apply to me. When I buried my mother, there was not one command staff officer from West Bureau or Pacific Division present at her funeral. Yes, there were friends and former partners who were supportive and had kind words to later send my way, but supervision did nothing. The only command staff officer who attended my mother's funeral was my former lieutenant from

OSB–CRASH. He didn't even make a big deal about making his presence known. I just happened to look up while seated in the front row and noticed that he was in the procession of mourners for the parting view. Wow. I wasn't even working in his division at that time. I hadn't spoken to him for a couple of years. Our paths hadn't crossed. We were working two totally different bureaus. The fact that he, number one, was even aware that my mom had passed, and number two, took time to attend her memorial service, meant the world to me. He did not have to do that. But he cared. He was always willing to demonstrate to his officers that he appreciated you as a person. I didn't have a chance to acknowledge this the day of the funeral—there was just too much going on.

It was time for another department promotional exam. I decided I should take the upcoming sergeant's test. I began compiling department bulletins and special orders, and I poured over the department manual in preparation for the test. During the midst of this, I encountered my old CRASH lieutenant. I told him that I was studying for the sergeant's test. He gave me a smile and a wink as only he could and told me, "When you pass, give me a call—come work for me at Newton."

# THIRTY-THREE:
# YOU MIGHT WANT TO LEAVE
# MS. DORSEY ALONE

I passed the sergeant's test with a final score sufficient to place me fairly high on the list of officers to be chosen for promotion. Once I saw my name on the list, I called my former OSB–CRASH lieutenant, who was now the captain-I (commanding officer) in charge of patrol at Newton. As soon as there was an opening at Newton for a sergeant, he selected me to fill the position.

On November 16, 1994, I was promoted to Sergeant of Police. My very first day at Newton, I stopped to say hello to my former CRASH lieutenant. He was now the patrol captain. I thanked him for the support he had shown at the passing of my mother. I wanted him to know how much his presence at her funeral service had meant to me. He simply nodded and said, "I know."

Newton Division was located on Central and Newton Street across from the Coca-Cola building. A more modern police station was re-built in the nineties and is now located on Central and 32nd Street. I was assigned to day watch (at the old station). Newton was great. There were many of the same OSB CRASH faces now at Newton. The captain had brought them along after he transferred in; one by one when openings became available. That's how he got down. He did not have a problem taking those he trusted and liked with him wherever he was assigned. Newton was basically OSB–CRASH (North). There were old CRASH officers working both patrol and detectives at Newton. One of the assistant watch commanders (AWC) in patrol had also been the AWC in CRASH.

Everybody loved this guy. He was one of those old salts who appeared rough and gruff on the outside but was really a marshmallow on the inside. He talked a lot of mess. You know the type, television cop shows always have one in the station who swears and yells a lot at his officers. That was our AWC. But there was nothing he would not do for you when you asked. He would fuss for a bit and then give you the shirt off his back (so to speak.) He "took care" of his officers. Most police officers will understand what this means.

He definitely bled blue, but he did not take the job too serious. When it was time to take the uniform off, he was just plain ole Terry. He supervised us and he socialized with us. I didn't drink but I heard stories about the male police officers closing down local dives.

The guys would shut down a bar and then move the "party" to a nearby cul-de-sac, where a series of "shots fired calls" would generate because someone had one too many and started shooting at the street lights. I had heard stories about one of the members of the "700 Club" would allegedly throw himself on the asphalt in front of the cars when an officer would try to leave before all of the beer was gone. There were the bar fights that involved beer bottles being broken over the head of some loud and obnoxious bar patron who didn't know he had just challenged an off duty police officer to a fight. Then the damnedest thing happened: the AWC came to work with a black eye. No one ever really explained how that happened. Guess you had to be there.

My time at Newton was mostly uneventful. By now I had fifteen years on the department, all spent in patrol. No one messed with me. Well, almost no one.

We had a new female transfer into the division. She had recently promoted to lieutenant. She came from a "pogue" position. She had no "street cred," so to speak. She had been mostly in detective assignments prior to coming to Newton as the patrol lieutenant (watch commander). Other officers were already starting to talk about her in a negative way before she physically arrived. That was the LAPD way. Transfer's out—let the bad-mouthing begin.

I like to refer to this one affectionately as "the speckled-back hyena." She had barely settled into her new position before she started trying to make a name for herself—mostly on the backs of the many female officers assigned to Newton. The word on the street was she had lost a lot of weight, and I guess she thought she was cute now. She sashayed around the station and batted her lashes for the male officers and treated the females like crap. She had a litany of "dislikes" when it came to the female officers. She didn't like the color of nail polish we wore; she didn't like the hairstyles worn by some of the ladies.

My locker was closest to hers. She had to pass me to get to her locker. Every day this horse would come into the locker room and almost instinctively demand that we clear a path so she could get her wide ass through. I would never move. One day she came in and then just stopped right in front of me. She gave me this look like I should step aside purely because she was pale and privileged. I thought. I'm not moving. I stood my ground. After a few tense moments and unyielding stares, she hopped her lard ass up on the bench and then waddled past me. Aah, satisfaction. Bars or not—I wasn't moving.

She was relentless in her attacks on the females. We could only giggle and stare when we would see her seated behind the watch commander's desk with her Wilma Flintstone hairdo and big-ass bars on her shirt collar. I don't know if it was an accident or ignorance, but one day she had the larger-size bars normally worn on the uniform jacket on her uniform shirt instead of the small lieutenant bars. She looked ridiculous—but none of the females would say a word.

This harassment continued for several weeks until finally she went to our captain. He was now the Captain III at Newton; no longer in charge of just patrol, but the entire Division. He later told me the story of how she had come to him to complain about me—both the color of my fingernail polish and my hair. I had my hair styled in an "up-do"—a hair piece braided into a bun on the top of my head. I must admit it did sit pretty high, about two or three inches. I had a ponytail braided into my own hair and then wrapped it around itself to construct this "thing." Well, the speckled-back hyena had told me several times to take it down, and I refused because department policy only stated that a female officer's hair couldn't touch the shirt collar. The policy didn't say anything about height. This monkey told me that it was too high, and I couldn't get my department hat on my head. My retort was, "When do I wear a hat in the field? Exactly." So I refused. This infuriated her. As my captain told me this story, and I could tell that he enjoyed putting her in her place. He said he listened intently, and when she had finished being petty and complaining about what to do with this out-of-control patrol sergeant (me), he looked her flatly in the face and stated, "You might want to leave Ms. Dorsey alone." That was that. Take that—get back on your broom and be gone.

I continued to wear my hair as I saw fit and colored my nails with the most vibrant shade of red I could find—because red is power—and handled my business.

I always appreciate it when a jackass gets his—or her—"comeuppance." This particular comeuppance came four years after I had retired, in approximately 2004, but it was joyous nonetheless. As fate would have it, that former female lieutenant from Newton, had promoted to captain and moved on. She was married to a LAPD detective but had a little boy-toy on the side and found herself embroiled in a scandal. She and the boy-toy were alleged to have been involved in copyright infringement in a scheme to sell counterfeit and pirated movies. She was eventually arrested while on her way to a department Christmas party, driving her city issued car. The arresting officers found hundreds of DVDs in the trunk of that city vehicle. Amazing -she was always so hard on police officers she suspected of "wrong doing"; always ready to discipline someone. She used her rank to bully an officer. What a hypocrite. The Los Angeles County District Attorney filed for forty-one felony counts against her. I'm not sure if she was fired or allowed to retire in lieu of termination; she had nearly twenty-five years on the department. Too bad—too sad. Buh-bye, speckled-back hyena.

# THIRTY-FOUR:
# A TOUR THROUGH IA

While still assigned to Newton Division as a patrol sergeant, an opportunity presented itself to work on "loan" to Internal Affairs Division (IA). My captain-I had suggested that I take the "loan" assignment to broaden my supervisory experience. He was pushing me to continue up the promotional ladder. An assignment with IA was an unspoken requirement if you wanted to be a lieutenant. I did not particularly like the reputation that officers assigned to IA had but decided it was a necessary evil if I wanted to promote.

The only reason I even entertained the thought of promotion was due to the fact that a promotion meant a larger pension base. I was nearing retirement. What the hell. I had no intention of being some kind of hatchet job. I would do my job, like always, and let the chips fall where they may. No "burn 'em to learn 'em" for me. This was a phrase used by officers that meant that a supervisor would "burn" or generate negative discipline to teach an errant officer a lesson—thus the "learn."

This was a temporary assignment, aka "loan." Since I was assigned to the Central Bureau, I worked the IA unit that was located in the historic Bradbury Building in downtown Los Angeles. My first and only alleged misconduct investigation involved Frank Lyga, an on-duty white narcotics officer. While working a plain-clothes assignment, he had been accused of intentionally shooting and killing—in a case of road rage—Kevin Gaines, a black LAPD officer, who was off-duty at the time of the incident.

"There was a confrontation at a stoplight between Lyga and Gaines which resulted in a shooting.

I interviewed Officer Lyga regarding the incident and reported the facts. I did not have any preconceived assumptions regarding

Lyga, although he appeared suspicious of my involvement in the IA investigation since I too was black. I believed Lyga eventually came to realize that I was not the stereotypical IA investigator and that I would be fair. He fully cooperated with my investigation. There were three separate internal investigations.

"The Lyga shooting was eventually found to be 'in policy' and the LAPD concluded there was no racial motivation on the part of Officer Lyga.

Officer Gaines's family filed a wrongful death lawsuit against the City of Los Angeles, and the city settled for $250,000.00.

However, since some police officers are big mouths and like to tout their "accomplishments", Frank Lyga during an LAPD in-service training day spoke on the Kevin Gaines shooting many years after the fact.

"Why LAPD Detective Frank Lyga Won't Be Fired"

Reprint (in part) LA Progressive

It was reported that a Los Angeles Police Department administrative hearing known as a Board of Rights (BOR) recommended the termination of LAPD Detective Frank Lyga as a result of racist, sexist and inflammatory remarks he made last year during a joint LAPD training day. The truth is, Det. Lyga quite possibly may live to offend again; with another agency.

Det. Frank Lyga is a 28-year LAPD veteran. As such, he certainly has earned the right to retire, with a lifetime pension. As a retired LAPD sergeant, I will be the first to declare that a service pension earned should not be denied — under any circumstance. However, there should be a designation made on the bottom line of Detective Frank Lyga's retirement page to indicate that he was factually found guilty by an administrative process and should forever more bear the mark of a disgraced officer.

Det. Frank Lyga, who is white, during the training day bragged about a day back in 1997, when he shot and killed off-duty LAPD officer Kevin Gaines; a black man. Lyga told the group that he had no regrets over the murder of Gaines, saying, 'I wished I could've killed more of them.' I have been waiting to hear exactly what Lyga meant in his reference to "them". It sounded to me and a lot of other people as though he dreamed of shooting more black men. This story was first reported, after an audio tape had been obtained and delivered to political consultant.

Sadly, I don't think Lyga will be fired by LAPD's Police Chief Charlie Beck. No, Detective Lyga will grab a handful of retirement papers and run over to police headquarters where he will meet with the retirement counselor and then make his way over to the pension department well before Chief Beck can hit the "send" button his [Lyga's] termination papers.

Errant police officers who have been found guilty of serious misconduct at a BOR have routinely been allowed to leave the department, in the middle of the night, under a cloud of mystery and suspicion. This is part of the LAPD culture. This is partly what's wrong with the LAPD's disciplinary system. Only those officers connected to the right sponsors are lucky enough to slither away without a bruise to show for their transgressions. So, before Chief Beck takes his victory lap for agreeing to side with the BOR's termination decision, let me explain how the system "pretends" to work.

Lyga has three days to retire now that his BOR has concluded. So, let's say hypothetically that a chief decided to wait until the end of day three to sign on the dotted line – the officer in jeopardy could, if he acted quickly, "retire on day two." That newly retired officer is then able to ride off into the sunset.

This scenario is much like the one that played out a couple of weeks ago when the California Highway Patrol "allowed" Officer Daniel Andrew to "step down". The fact that the CHP allowed Officer Andrew to resign is an insult and punch in the face [pun intended] to everyone who witnessed the mixed martial arts-style beating Marlene Pinnock suffered at the hands of Andrew. "Former" officer Andrew possibly lives to offend again; on another police department. The distinction between "former" and "fired" is vast in the law enforcement community.

# THIRTY-FIVE:
# IT'S TIME TO GO

Nineteen ninety-two. As a result of the Rodney King aftermath, then-LAPD Police Chief Darryl Gates resigned. Willie Williams was brought in as an outsider to head the embattled department. Williams was the first black chief of police for the Los Angeles Police Department.

Williams was destined to fail. He was an outsider. He did not understand the culture of the LAPD, and there didn't seem to be anyone on the department at that time who was willing to "school" him. For instance, our uniform: he created some long dress coat that he wanted command staff officers to wear. It was rumored that he was uncomfortable about the way he looked in the LAPD uniform due to his large stature. According to rumor control, Chief Williams showed up at his very first recruit class graduation, which all chiefs presided over, wearing some kind of fancy dress shoe. Word on the street was that he and Assistant Chief Bernard Parks didn't get along. Allegedly, whenever Parks tried to explain LAPD protocol, there was immediate tension. The department was rumored to be divided into two camps as a result of their friction; one for Williams and one for Parks. Williams was a one-term chief. Parks replaced in 1997. According to the gossip mill, once Williams left Parks retaliated against everyone he believed to be in the Williams' camp. The first thing Chief Parks did was restructured the LAPD organization chart and removed the Assistant Chief (AC) classification; a position held by Ronald Banks, also a black man. AC Banks had been promoted to AC by then Chief Williams. AC Banks was a veteran with, my best guesstimate- probably thirty-something years on the LAPD. AC Banks held his title but that was all. He was immediately transferred from his high profile assignment to a lesser post. I envisioned AC Banks having been given a box of paper clips and told to go sit in a corner and count them – and then re-count them again once finished.

The only thing that spread quicker than an ember on a windy day was a good rumor around the LAPD. Allegedly, Parks wanted Banks gone. Too bad, because they seemed to have been friends from "back in the day." One thing we know on the LAPD, grudges run deep. Allegedly, when Chief Parks took command of the department, there was an absolute "bloodletting" on the sixth floor of parker Center where the top brass were assigned. AC Banks needed a new church home. In 1998, Ronald Banks became the chief of police for the City of Inglewood. Rumor had it that when the city of Inglewood called over to talk about AC Banks resume' it was reported that the "sun shined out of his ass". The department wanted to be sure he got the hell out of PAB. That must have been some kind of ringing endorsement. Why doesn't LAPD offer this kind of going-away present to its police officers when the department has had enough of you? If you are a low ranking officer on the LAPD, the department will send you away- but with a knife in your back and then watch you slowly bled out.

Due to complaints of police abuse and corruption and the Rampart CRASH debacle that involved about seventy police officers being implicated in some form of police misconduct and a subsequent federal consent decree, Chief Parks also became a one-term police chief. It is interesting to note that "the LAPD Board of Inquiry into the Rampart Area Corruption Incident released in March 2000 sanctioned Chief Parks for "not addressing structural problems within the LAPD." It is my contention that those "problems" continue—not between officers and citizens, but within the command staff in their dealings with LAPD officers. These problems are systemic and part of the LAPD culture. They've been around forever.

 He was replaced in May 2002 by William Bratton from New York.

I soon encountered another one of those moments on the department that stayed with me. I don't know if I should describe the incident as a "staying" or a "haunting" moment. I responded to a radio call along with several other officers and supervisors to a "jumper" on Central Avenue and 27th. There was a very tall building on the corner, and by the time I arrived, there were several officers on scene as well as the fire department. I noticed a young black man, approximately nineteen or twenty years old, standing on top of the building. He was looking down at the officers and fire department personnel as they arrived. One of the P-3s in Newton started to talk to the young man. The officer stood halfway up a ladder affixed to the side of the building. The young man looked wide-eyed and confused. He never said a word. As the fire department attempted to set up an inflatable bag below the building, we watched and silently prayed that he wouldn't jump. The officer continued to divert the young man's attention and attempted to get a response from him, the young man took several steps back, away from the edge of the building. I thought for a moment that he was going to walk over to the ladder and come down from the roof. Instead, he took those four or five steps backward and then just started to run. He was picking up speed as he neared the edge of the building—and he didn't stop. As he leapt into the air, you could hear audible gasps and a chorus of "oh no" as he became airborne. The young man began flailing his arms in a backward motion as if he wanted to reverse the inevitable. He was kicked his legs like a swimmer and rotated his arms wildly, and in a few short seconds, he collided with the pavement. The fire department had not been able to inflate the bag. When he hit the ground, I could hear his bones cracking and breaking. He landed in a heap. I looked away because I really didn't want to see what I had heard. I finally gathered the strength to look at the ground, and I saw this poor young man, still alive and shaking slightly. The paramedics on scene quickly approached him and began to treat him and prepare him for transport to the hospital.

It was just awful. I was the mother of a young man about that same age. All I could think was this could have been my son. His mother was going to get the notification that no family wants. I was sure she would be devastated. He didn't die—at least, not that day. I never knew what ultimately happened to that young man. I often think of him. Some events and images you just can't shake.

My time as a probationary sergeant had ended, and like all new assignments, I was now subject to "the wheel." This simply meant I had to leave Newton.

My captain-III discussed my options with me. I had never worked in Valley Bureau, and he thought this might be a good time for me to broaden my experience and go "over the hill," which is how many referred to those divisions in the San Fernando Valley. My captain told me he had a "friend" who worked North Hollywood Division. He said he would call him and put in a good word, another "phone-jack." My captain spoke to the captain-I in North Hollywood, and I was on the next transfer.

# THIRTY-SIX: I'M GOING TO KILL MYSELF

I had a good time at North Hollywood. An old partner of mine transferred in shortly after I arrived. He and I had worked together in Newton. He was now a P-3 and assigned to the desk on AM watch. I was also working AM watch. This P-3 and I were both sergeants at Newton, but the department charged him with administrative misconduct and demoted him back down to the rank of P-3 and ultimately transferred him to North Hollywood. I was happy to see him.

I would stop by the station and pick up my P-3 friend for code-7 nearly every night. We had a blast. A Thai restaurant had become our favorite hang-out spot on morning watch. I also had another former OSB–CRASH partner working North Hollywood in the vice unit. He was the lieutenant, or OIC (officer-in-charge), of the unit. When I wasn't eating with the P-3, I was with the vice lieutenant. Three senior black officers working in a predominantly white North Hollywood Division—we were having a good time, each in our own way.

Around this same time, the department had just appointed its second black chief of police. There were many officers who did not have nice things to say about Bernard Parks. It all depended on one's experience. I personally never had any problems with Chief Parks. As a matter of fact, I do believe that he quietly helped me along the way at various stages in my police career; like when my training officer at Southwest received the five-day suspension for grabbing me and then again when he showed-up at motor-school. The all-white male instructors suddenly became very helpful once Chief Parks had made his presence known. I sought his advice a time or two when I was prepared for promotional exams, and he always helped by sharing some of his experiences and trails on the department. I appreciated his counsel. I believe he was willing to extend a hand of help because I had been classmates with his daughters at St.

Michael's. So, I was happy to attend his promotional celebration when he was sworn in as our new chief.

I was back riding around alone as a supervisor on morning watch, and the off hours were killing me. I struggled through the drive home every morning and made it to about the Dodger Stadium area before I would start to get sleepy. Then it was "drive by braille" the rest of the way. I rolled over those little bumps in the road like a drunken person. I envisioned the other cars sharing the road with me breaking and changing lanes to get away from me, not knowing if I was drunk or sleepy but guessing I was going to hit them if they stayed close.

One morning I was so tired that I decided to sleep during my code-7 in my black-and-white. Most of the police stations had what was referred to as a "cot room"—yep, like it sounds: a room full of small twin-size cots. I didn't like sleeping in the cot room, because one never knew if or when the sheets on the cot had been changed. I chose the dis-comfort of my black-and-white. I don't know how long I had been asleep, but I suddenly heard the dispatcher trying to raise me over the air. I quickly answered and identified myself, at which point I heard my lieutenant chime in, "Cancel the air unit." What? Cancel the air unit? I guess I had been sleeping longer than I realized. And they were about to have an air unit fly around to locate me. This was bad. I immediately drove to the station, figuring I had some "splainin' to do."

I went right into the watch commander's office and apologized to my lieutenant. I told him that I had been asleep in my car. He told me he understood but suggested the next time I wanted to sleep I should come into the police station.

I agreed but knew I needed to get out of North Hollywood. I asked my lieutenant for a watch change, but he said that I had not spent the requisite time on the watch yet and couldn't change shifts. I tried to no avail to explain that there was going to be an opening on morning watch shortly, because I was going to kill myself trying to make the seventy-mile drive home at the end of my shift. I had to do something. This was not going to work.

I called my old captain at Newton and told him that I wanted to come home, and he said, "Come on." Back to Newton I went.

# THIRTY-SEVEN:
# HOME-SWEET-NEWTON

I was back at my beloved Newton Division. Shortly after I returned to Newton patrol, an opening in Newton Area Vice became available. This would mean a promotion from sergeant-I to sergeant-II. The captain would make the final decision from the group of sergeants who applied. I smelled a promotion party.

I interviewed for the vice sergeant position and was selected. This was the first time in the history of the LAPD that a black female had been assigned as the officer-in-charge of that division's vice unit. My captain was willing to go against the grain when he promoted me to this coveted assignment. I was certainly qualified based on my past experiences and job performance. I was articulate, presented myself well, and had obviously demonstrated that I was the best candidate. Others would disagree.

While I was assigned to vice, a new captain-I transferred into the division. He was a newly promoted captain. The new captain-I happened to be a black guy. I knew him; we had worked together when he was a sergeant in OSB–CRASH. Our paths had crossed on and off duty over the years.

My captain-III and I had a real good rapport. We talked often and candidly about the goings-on around the police station. Whenever we talked, rank was never an issue; it was always just Jim and Cheryl. My captain told me that he was "going to keep this new captain-I on a short leash," because he didn't trust him. He was right—this new captain did bear watching.

This captain-I was a real piece of work. He fashioned himself to be a real ladies' man. I remember seeing him as a frequent guest at an all-black women-in-law-enforcement group I had joined. I went to network. He went to be seen. He would stand up during the monthly meetings and announce his presence to the group, including his rank, as though it were part of his name. People like him kill me. He acted as if he were royalty. Joni, my old coworker from DOJ, had worked a couple of years with the CHP (California Highway Patrol) and made a lateral transfer back to DOJ as a special agent. We often attended those meetings together. She knew the captain-I as well, both because of his presence at the meetings and also because he happened to socialize with her partner at DOJ.

LAPD was big, but it was small at the same time. It was not uncommon to run into other blacks on the department at different functions. During a meeting of Black Women in Law Enforcement meeting, we saw another high ranking LAPD command staff officer. He was there on the prowl too. He was a bit older than we were, but that didn't stop him from asking Joni out to lunch. He handed out business cards like they were Skittles. We used to call him "Let's Do Lunch."

So my girlfriend sees the captain-I and, just being nice, said hello and engaged him in a bit of small talk. The topic of an all-black ski club came up, and Joni asked the captain-I where he went skiing, because she too was a skied. The captain-I, in his usual smug way, gave a chuckle and assured her that she "didn't ski where he skied," so he didn't bother to say. The nerve of this guy—who the hell did he think he was? Well, every dog has his day—and his was coming.

There were many times when his arrogance would be on full display. He would brag about his $35 socks and the fact that he lived in Windsor Hills. His favorite line was saying the only thing that would make his life better was if there were two of him. One of him was too much—two would make you vomit in your own mouth.

This captain-I, like a lot of guys on the LAPD, spent an inordinate amount of time in pursuit of women. Something about a man in uniform, I guess. Normally half of these guys couldn't get a woman, but when you have a good job, drive a nice car, and have medical benefits, all of a sudden you are "nice-looking." Never mind that you refuse to take full advantage of the city's dental plan and your mouth looks like a mega-mouth shark with three rows of teeth. Rumors were always going around about this captain-I and his philandering ways. Allegedly, he had been married several times, and he was on his fourth or fifth wife when he was busted on a cruise ship with a woman—not his wife. As luck would have it, his wife's good friend was also on that same ship and made a ship-to-shore call when she saw his punk ass.

He was not cured, however. The next story to be bantered about involved a weekend away and a credit-card bill sent to his home and intercepted by his wife. According to the gossip mill, the wife saw the balance due and questioned the credit card company, only to find out about hotel charges that she did not personally enjoy. That little faux-pas precipitated a visit from the county marshals, who showed up at his front door with a "time to get your stuff and move out" letter. Sucka.

For a time, allegedly, he didn't even have a personal car. The only vehicle he drove was his city-issued car. Then there were the stories about his driver's license being suspended for failure to pay child support. I don't know if any of this was true—but I guess it was fun for others to repeat. If there was one thing police officers liked doing, it was spreading someone else's business. Supposedly, the way the story went, his most recent last wife "took him to the cleaners." But rank has its privileges, and he took full advantage. He continued to pretend like he had it going on. It was not uncommon for him to pick his kid up from school and bring the child to the police station for a few hours before he drove the child home to the mother. This captain-I didn't even try to hide the fact that he was doing this on-duty and using his city car for personal use. Some nerve.

# THIRTY-EIGHT: YOU CAN'T WORK FOR ME

While still assigned to Newton vice, one of my vice officers, a young P-2, found himself the subject of a personnel complaint. He was still active military reserve and allegedly had been involved in horseplay five years earlier with other servicemen during one of his military details. Evidently, someone was holding a grudge and decided to notify the LAPD about this incident even thought it was five years old and had been adjudicated by the military. Since that time, this young officer had even been promoted in his reserve unit a few times, so clearly, this was not an issue for the military.

However, good ole LAPD seized the opportunity to mess over this guy by initiating a personnel complaint into the stale charges citing violation of LAPD police CUBO- Conduct Unbecoming of an Office and I think the department threw in a criminal element; a brandishing a weapon because gun play was involved. Due to the seriousness of the allegations of police misconduct, the young officer was sent directly to a board of rights (BOR) for adjudication rather than have the personnel matter resolved at the division level by a captain of police.. Termination was a real possibility. The timing could not have been worse. His wife was expecting their first child, and he was preparing to apply for a position as a motorcycle officer. His promotion was put on hold pending the outcome of his administrative hearing (BOR).

The P-2 was subsequently found guilty. Now came the phase at the BOR where the accused officer can offer character witnesses testimony to mitigate the penalty that the BOR considered. Also, the department advocate presents testimony from a department command staff officer as to why the officer should be terminated. The captain I from Newton Patrol showed up at the BOR on behalf of the department.

This was the same captain who had been using his city vehicle as his personal car; for child custody exchanges, dates and whatever else he deemed necessary. He was allegedly driving around in that city vehicle on a suspended driver's license when he became involved in a traffic collision in another city and disciplined by the department himself. This undesirable was the department's best pick to come into that BOR and detail why that officer should be fired for an act that happened away from the department five years earlier. Why would someone go out of his way to harm another? Are you drunk with power? I guess the urge to grind this officer down was more compelling than the captain's own humanity. Maybe he dreamt of promoting to commander.

The young P-2 was positioned squarely in his seat at the defendant's table in his BOR when the captain-I was asked by the board if he wanted to command this officer, knowing that he had been found guilty of such serious police misconduct. I'm told that it was common practice to ask this of every command staff officer who testified at a BOR. The captain-I replied, "Absolutely not." With those words spoken, the P-2 was terminated.

Several Newton officers were present to support this young P-2; they said he turned ghost-white. The chief of police was the only person who could overturn the BOR decision The chief had the authority to impose a lesser penalty. Chief Parks sided with the BOR; Even though several officers and the captain III at Newton signed a letter which begged for leniency. I was disappointed in Chief Parks for the very first time. The officer was escorted out of the building and home, supported by his peers. There was a concern that he might harm himself. The captain-I had done his job. I lost all respect—what little I had—for him. I absolutely loathed him. The captain-I seemed satisfied; the department would show its appreciation later.

I needed an outlet. I decided that I would train to compete in the Police Olympics. This was a yearly event, and all of the participants were law-enforcement officers from all over California. I had a female friend on the department who had competed in the bodybuilding competition the year before, and she inspired me to train to see what kind of shape I could attain.

I began working out at my local gym with my husband, who was an experienced weight lifter. We worked hard, and I was pleased enough with my results that I entered in the "seniors" category for the next two years during the Police Olympics (now called the Police and Fire World Games). I was forty years old at the time. I wanted to compete against females who were not on the "juice" and had been through a few things—like having kids. I didn't want to compete against female bodybuilders who were in the gym six to eight hours a day. I had a job to maintain and children to raise, and the gym was next on my list of things to do. I wanted the experience to at least be fair (in my mind).

Bodybuilding is such a selfish sport, but I immersed myself and managed to grab a gold medal in my division representing the LAPD. I was happy with the outcome.

# THIRTY-NINE:
# MY NAME IS WENDY

Things were going great at work. In the midst of it all, I managed to still find a little joy. Newton Vice was a blast. The other supervisor assigned to vice was another one of my former OSB–CRASH partners; a black officer who our former CRASH lieutenant now Newton captain had promoted into the vice unit.

As a "working" supervisor, I had the opportunity to participate in undercover. As a vice investigator, we conducted investigations into citizen complaints of gambling (in the local parks), prostitution on the streets, and "bugs in the bottle" at local bars—yes, real bugs, like fruit flies. It was a violation of the Health and Safety Code to have unsanitary conditions in a bar. Violators were easy to spot—all we had to do was enter a bar, grab a bottle, hold it up to the light, and bingo! Bugs in the bottle. Yuck. If people only knew what they were ingesting. It was our job to keep the unsuspecting public safe.

The vice unit often assisted other agencies like ABC (Alcohol Beverage Control), ATF (Alcohol, Tobacco and Firearms), and the Los Angeles County of Department of Health in joint task force operations in the furtherance of reducing crime. We also teamed up with other LAPD vice units on joint prostitution enforcement details; targeting prostitutes as well as the johns who sought their services. We operated in an undercover capacity in gentlemen's clubs, or, as the guys referred to them, "tittie bars," massage parlors, and much more. Vice was a fun assignment. As a supervisor, it was important to have a good group of officers working for you. Vice was a small unit; everyone got along well. All of my officers worked with minimal supervision, and that made my job easy. Complaints by citizens of misconduct were nonexistent in vice. No excessive force, no mouth-beefs—just hard-working officers. ("Mouth-beef" was a term that we used on the LAPD to describe a citizen complaint of rudeness by an officer.)

I remember one detail in particular when one of my officers was assigned to investigate an allegation of lewd conduct at a local massage parlor. He was sent in alone, of course, and we waited outside in the area for his notification of a violation. A violation meant that the female masseuse had attempted to give him a "hand-job" during the course of the "massage," or made an offer for some other sex act in exchange for money. So, the whole vice unit was stationed in various spots around the establishment for what seemed like an inordinate amount of time. We were actually beginning to get worried about this undercover officer's safety. Finally, out he came. We waited for him to walk back to his undercover vehicle. He transmitted over his police radio: "Did not get a violation."

Well, the other vice sergeant was in the car with me, and we immediately looked at each other as if to say "are you kidding?" My partner supervisor thought aloud, "He's lying." We left the area and met at a nearby hamburger joint to "debrief." As we looked this officer in the eye, listening to him retell the events of his undercover operation, most knew "something" happened in there, and he most certainly had to say "no violation."

There was no proof, of course, and the other sergeant and I didn't want to blow the cover of our operation as we may want to revisit the spot later—with a different operator—so we just dropped it. Zero for the city—one for the vice officer.

On the north end of Newton, there was an area that was constantly plagued by street-walking prostitutes. A few of the prostitutes were "strawberries." However, the majority of the prostitutes were drag queens (men who wear female clothing and makeup). Some of them were in various stages of gender-reassignment, and then you had what were referred to on the streets as "she-males." These were men who outwardly appeared to be females. Many had breasts and figures that resembled a woman's from the waist up—but they also had penises.

It was amazing to me how many out-of-town truck drivers would frequent this area. Understand, it wasn't like these guys were being fooled into thinking they were with a woman—they came to this area specifically looking for this particular type of prostitute. I always treated my arrestees with respect. There was never a reason not to be humane. I did find, however, that in being nice to the drag queens, many of them would talk candidly with me. They would tell me how much money they charged a john—most drag queens were able to command a higher fee than the "strawberries." Some of them explained this phenomenon to me this way: "These men like the illusion of being with a woman but want to be with a man."

There was even a large, multistory hotel where all of the drag queens seemed to live—safety in numbers, I guess. The officers referred to this building as "the compound." In the early-morning hours, usually around 2 a.m. or later, there would be a procession of drag queens exiting the building and heading over to 7th Street in the heart of skid row where they "worked." There were several bars in the area, and whenever they spotted a black-and-white, they would just slip inside the bar until the police car passed and then they went back out to stand on the street and wave the truckers down.

I had an officer working for me at this time who was Hispanic. He was an outstanding undercover officer. He had a thick accent and long hair. We used to call him "Jesus," because he looked like every picture of Jesus you ever saw propped up on a living-room mantel. He had no problem getting prostitution violations from the drag queens. Not all of the officers liked to work this detail. Many of the prostitutes attempted to grab the officers' genitals during conversation as proof, in their minds, that the officer was not a cop; thinking a cop would not be touched in this way. One of my veteran white officers, who was a good undercover, told me that whenever the drag queens placed their hands on his thigh to see how he would react, he would just "blossom like a flower." Cops are a crude, sick bunch. I needed you to get that visual.

Back to "Jesus"—during one operation, he got out on foot and started walking in the area of skid row. He was almost immediately approached by an obvious drag queen. This guy was dressed like a woman in a short black miniskirt and tight-fitting top with black clunky heels, but the problem was he was built like a side-by-side refrigerator. He was just a giant square. The undercover officers who were acting as backup in the area noticed that this "girl" looked different than most. "She" had something wrapped around her head, almost like a Muslim female; we could only see her eyes.

All of us were talking on "simplex" on our police radios so only we could hear each other, and we were just dying laughing and commenting because we all knew that "Jesus" was not having a good time with this "girl." We were watching intently for the signal that he had a violation so we could swoop in and make an arrest. There it was—he gave us the signal. Everyone jumped out of their cars and areas of concealment to converge on this "lady." As soon as the first officers made physical contact with "her," now being assisted by "Jesus," the fight was on. This damn fool suddenly became the Incredible Hulk. He made this big, sweeping movement with his arms and came completely out of his headdress. He had a full beard.

This guy was fighting like his life was in jeopardy. It took five officers to finally subdue this guy and get him handcuffed. Now, his headdress was gone—turned out it was a white short-sleeve T-shirt he had fashioned over his face to cover his beard. He had kicked off his pumps, and his stockings were torn on both knees. The other supervisor and I placed this guy in the back of one of the black-and-whites and asked him why he was fighting so: "What the hell is wrong with you?" The guy was tearful and stated that he was married and had children at home. He said he "just couldn't go to jail." OMG. Really?

Once back at the police station, the other male officers were really giving "Jesus" a hard time about his "date." The suspect had kicked off his pumps and torn his miniskirt off in an effort to keep the other male arrestees from seeing him dressed like a woman. He walked into the police station in handcuffs wearing only his white Fruit of the Loom underwear.

We asked "Jesus" about the conversation he had with this guy just prior to getting the violation. "Jesus" said that the guy told him in a very soft and demure voice that his name was "Wendy" and that he [the suspect] offered to pay the undercover officer ten dollars if the UC would allow him/her to "suck his ass." True story. And now I'm done.

# FORTY:
# BRAHMA BULLS - YOU CAN DO ANYTHING YOU WANT

The drag queens in the Newton area were not our only source of entertainment. The female prostitutes were equally funny and, in some instances, pretty tragic. There was an area near 27th Street and Central Avenue, not too far from Newton Police Station, where these older Hispanic female prostitutes worked. They were on this corner day and night.

We deployed some of the male officers to work undercover to get them off the street. We had targeted this group regularly—but they always came right back. The male officers working vice referred to them as the "Brahma Bulls." These ladies were a little older than most of the street-walking prostitutes, plus they were "big girls" or thick" or "plus-size"—whatever term you want to use. Some of these ladies were borderline obese.

We had "Jesus" out again—he was just that good. He drove up to the group of ladies and struck up a conversation. Within seconds we got the signal—a violation. The backup team was told which of the ladies in the group had solicited "Jesus," and an arrest was made.

What stunned us about this arrest was that my officers were placing handcuffs on this very elderly, frail woman who had been standing in the group of Brahma Bulls. I thought to myself—there must be some mistake here. This senior citizen was placed in the back of the police car, and I got "Jesus" on the police radio. I asked him meet us around the corner from the arrest location, out of view of the other prostitutes who were watching; we didn't want to "burn" him. My UC told me that as soon as he pulled up next to the curb, "Granny" approached him and told him that for twenty dollars he could "do whatever he wanted to do" to her. "Jesus" said he felt really bad. But he had a violation, and an arrest was made. I later learned that this senior was kind of down on her luck and in need of money urgently. She was ultimately transported to the police station and booked. I did have a conversation with her and explained the dangers involved with selling her body for money. I cautioned her and told her that she was lucky that she had stumbled across an undercover police officer and not some sick and vicious predator who may have taken that "do anything you want" literally.

The Brahma Bulls remained active on that corner, but I never saw Granny again. I hope she took my advice.

# FORTY-ONE: THINGS TAKE A TURN

I was at the point in my career where I could see the light at the end of the tunnel. I had eighteen years on the job and every intention of taking the department up on its offer of a lifetime pension at the end of twenty years with the LAPD. I was young enough that I could go out and get another job or start another career if I chose, or just do nothing.

I was beginning to choose nothing. The job was the job. I was having a good time, but I just wanted this to be over. I appreciated the LAPD for affording me the opportunity to eat meat. I managed to raise my children and did at least as much if not more for them as my parents had done for me growing up. I lived in a nice suburban neighborhood; my sons didn't have to walk around looking backward to make sure they were not to be the victim of a slow-moving vehicle about to do a drive-by. I had no complaints about the department. I met some people along the way that I will forever remember. I had enjoyed many friendships. There were also those who I would not piss on if they were on fire in the middle of Pershing Square.

I worked some pretty fun assignments. I didn't get to do all of what I wanted during my career, but I was fairly happy. My personal life was a different story. My husband, who was also an LAPD officer, and I were not getting along so well. There had been several incidents when we argued, and the situation seemed to escalate out of control. Understanding that we both carry guns, I often decided that I better remove myself from the situation and let cooler heads prevail. My husband was not always so ready to let it go. On those instances when things were really ugly, and he would do things to prevent me from leaving like hide my keys, etc., I would call the local sheriff's department for quick intervention.

I always made calling the police a last resort, because I knew that there was a possibility that one of those white boys who showed up to the house just might tell LAPD what was going on. I certainly didn't want the LAPD in my business. But I could not get my husband to knock it off and stop. He understood the ramifications if the department became involved, but alcohol makes you do stupid stuff.

Somehow the LAPD found out about the many visits to our home by the sheriff's department. LAPD could not wait to get involved in our domestic discourse. A personnel complaint was immediately initiated and my husband, who was a P-3 had been charged with misconduct.

An investigator assigned to Internal Affairs (IA) came to our home to "interview" me regarding the charges against my husband. Oh shoot, this was not what I wanted. I did not want him to get into trouble at work. I certainly didn't want him to get suspended without pay or, worse, lose his job—we were after all still together.

I answered the questions posed to me by the IA investigator, a black detective. Well, his skin was black, but not really, kind of a mocha color, but you get what I mean. He was of black heritage; it ended there. I was about to have another encounter with the nefarious house Negro. This was not your regular house Negro—he was the house Negro to the tenth power.

I continued to be interviewed and I was being truthful, because I understood the ramifications of this situation totally. During the interview, IA asked me if my husband and I had ever had an altercation. I quickly answered, "No." Obviously he did not know my husband. He was not the kind of guy you wanted to get into a fight with. There was no way, even during our many heated arguments that I would have ever struck him. Had I done that, the LAPD would have been involved a long ago, because surely there would have been a hospital trip involved for somebody.

The IA investigator then showed me a police report completed by one of the sheriff's deputies during an episode at our house. I acknowledged that the report was accurate and that I had generated the report. He asked me to explain the circumstances that had led to that report. I told him that on that date, my husband had pushed me and I had landed against a television, which had left a bruise on my upper arm. I explained to the IA officer that it was never my intention to get my husband in trouble at work—again referencing the fact that we were still together and that we had children in common. The house Negro looked at me as though he understood my dilemma but continued to take notes and offered nothing more.

It wasn't until a couple of days later that I was contacted by someone in IA and told that I too was now the subject of a personnel complaint. The house Negro had done his homework. He had contacted the sheriff's department and found out that they had records showing six responses to our home over a several-year period. The house Negro initiated a personnel complaint against me and charged me with six counts of misconduct. The house Negro alleged that I violated LAPD policy when I "unnecessarily caused the response of an outside agency" to our home. I was familiar with this policy, however, I interpreted this violation in a different way, obviously.

I could not believe the department alleged that my calling the sheriff and asking them to diffuse an argument that I had with an intoxicated person was "unnecessary", particularly when that person had access to a gun and did not allow me to leave the location. All I wanted was for the sheriff to provide me a safe avenue of escape, and prevent the possible use of a firearm by one or both of us. The department decided to "prosecute" me and send me to an administrative hearing when they knew full well that I had been the victim of domestic violence because the department was at the same exact time, pursuing my husband for the abuse. .

The house Negro also accused me of "giving false and misleading statements to [him] an Internal Affairs investigator"; a charge that could lead to my termination if sustained.

# FORTY-TWO:
# A BOR OF MY OWN

Well, well. So here I was being charged with seven counts of misconduct, one of which is a fire-able offense for me as a supervisor. As a sergeant of police, I was held to a higher standard than an officer, and this was really serious.

I asked another department employee, a male Hispanic officer and former partner from Pacific Division whom I trusted, to act as my "defense representative." We met and plotted our strategy for my pending Board of Rights. I knew this was a big deal and nothing to be taken lightly. The fact that I found myself in this predicament was not good to say the least, but I didn't even want to entertain the thought that the department would actually terminate me over this.

Well, as I prepared to save my damn job, the department geared up to stomp me out like an out-of-control blaze. A sergeant working Internal Affairs was assigned to act as the department's advocate, or prosecutor, at my BOR. He was black. This was no coincidence—of this I am certain. He was an up-and-coming house Negro bucking to make lieutenant. The department would prop his ass up as the one to go head-to-head against a black female sergeant accused of misconduct. Can't cry racism now, can you, Blackie?

He was also the exact same IA advocate the department had used to "prosecute" my husband at his BOR, which had taken place the month before. I had been forced to testify at my husband's BOR where this ass portrayed him as the devil incarnate. The advocate argued vigorously that my husband was out of control and should be fired. The BOR panel found him guilty but let him off with a suspension without pay. Then this ass turned right around the following month and now he is pretending like my husband was a saint and I was the devil. The advocate now argued at my BOR that I could not be believed and that the domestic abuse my husband had been found guilty of was really not all that bad. The male white deputy chief who chaired my BOR said to me that he did not believe that I was the victim of domestic violence because in his mind, "not a mother in the cosmos would have stayed in a relationship like that." Oh really, asshole, now you are an expert on domestic violence.

Where else is it reasonable or even allowed to force a married couple to testify against each other?

In a BOR, an officer is not allowed to make objections. You had to just sit and listen as the department and its witnesses lied. Rules of evidence normally applied during a criminal trial were none existent at an LAPD BOR. The board decided what was to be considered evidence, what was relevant, and which witnesses would be allowed to testify on an officer's behalf. An administrative BOR is a stark contrast to a criminal proceeding, where rules of law and evidence are followed. The BOR is totally arbitrary and capricious. It really is a kangaroo court.

My Board of Right panel members consisted of a male white deputy chief, who was the chairman, a male black commander, and a civilian. The civilian was nothing more than a figurehead and yielded no real power. The LAPD command staff on the BOR panel called the shots. An appointed civilian would be unable to compel a high-ranking LAPD officer to change a preconceived position as to an officer's guilt and subsequent penalty.

I had eighteen years on this funky department. Remember, when I started with the LAPD, it was a time where if I got fired for whatever reason, I would lose my pension in totality. But they couldn't fire me for asking for help when I really, really needed it—could they?

I was not happy about having my personal business out there. I certainly didn't want to disclose every single sordid detail of my married life. Well, the department was certainly doing a job on the Dorsey family. By now, my husband and I were separated and rarely spoke to each other.

My employee rep and I decided that there would need to be full disclosure as to the frequency and severity of domestic discourse in my home. I contacted a domestic violence (DV) expert to testify at my BOR regarding victimization and the cycle of violence. My rep and I already suspected that the department would try and assert that I had not been in a domestic violence situation.

As the officer "on trial" at a BOR, you don't get to do anything other than sit and take the unfair treatment that's coming.

I knew this was going to be a fight. I knew that the LAPD would not play fair. I wanted to spotlight the travesty that was about to take place on the third floor of the historic Bradbury Building in beautiful downtown Los Angeles. I wanted to have a camera crew and reporter present to document and memorialize how the Los Angeles Police Department was about to treat a female police officer who was the victim of domestic violence at the hands of her husband, another police officer. I contacted a black reporter from Channel 5 News. He was an older gentleman and had been around for a long time. We spoke about his attending my BOR. However, he would need LAPD approval. I asked the department through Press Relations to allow this reporter to document my BOR—the department denied my request. Allegedly, personnel matters were confidential. Really? This was not a personnel matter—this was my life, and the LAPD was trying to snub it out. This sure felt like an inherent flaw in the LAPD system. Liars.

The deputy chief, or chairman, pretty much ran the kangaroo court that is a BOR. Although the other sworn member held the rank of commander, I could sense that he tried to "do no harm" based on the way he presented his questions to both my husband and me. After all, I knew the commander. Most of the black officers on LAPD knew one another. We were not social friends, but I would see him out at department promotional parties or retirement parties and at eating spots for code-7. He also used to date a female friend of mine. She and I were in the police academy at the same time. We had also both participated in the pre-recruit physical training program that the department put on. This commander had been a P-3 in that unit at the time. So, I felt somewhat relieved when he did not display the same overzealousness the chairman and IA advocate had shown toward me and my husband.

My hearing was not going well during the testimony of my domestic violence expert. The chairman was very disrespectful and at times questioned her integrity, credentials and true knowledge of domestic violence. My expert was not only the victim of domestic violence herself, she had started an outreach program and women's shelter for other victims of DV.

The board next called my husband to testify against me. He answered their questions honestly, but you could tell by the manner in which the IA advocate was asking them that they were designed to "trip him up" or cause him to inflict the most damage the department could glean from him on me. Who does this? Pits a husband and wife against each other? We had children. Clearly, the LAPD didn't give a damn about the state that this situation was creating for our children. Mom hurting dad; dad hurting mom. And the current chief of police says that "there are no inherent problems" with the LAPD administrative system. Give me a break. Get real.

Once they were done filleting my husband, it was time to gut me. The chairman wasted no time. He asked me about the incidents that caused the response of the "outside agency" and concluded that I had "unnecessarily" caused the response of an outside police agency. The chairman, told me, "You gave as good as you got." Somehow, he knew that I was involved in bodybuilding and had competed in the Police Olympics representing LAPD. He wanted to know how much I could "bench." Understand I had sacrificed my time and put in a lot of hard work in an effort to get my body in the best shape that

I could, as a forty-year-old mother of four, competing for LAPD against other working law enforcement female officers, and this was how the LAPD treated me? The deputy chief knew how I represented the department, and yet he was unrelenting in his attacks against me. Thinking I heard his punk ass wrong, I asked him to repeat the question. He stated, "How much do you bench press?" I told him a whopping eighty pounds. I knew that I was not allowed to ask any questions but one begged to be asked, so I did. I wanted to know what this little factoid had to do with anything. I was really angry. Before he could answer, I reminded him that I was "a female—my husband is a male. No matter how much weight I could bench, I was not strong enough to kick his ass." I told the chairman that my husband could bench over 315 pounds—so now what? Of course, the chairman and thus the LAPD were well aware of my husband's personnel record and his propensity to get into trouble on the job. This was covered ad nauseam at his BOR the month prior, and all of my husband's previous sustained acts of misconduct had been delineated during his board. So for the deputy chief to now act like my husband was some choir boy and that I had made up the domestic discourse was disgusting.

The deputy chief reminded me that I was, at the time, a sergeant-II and that my husband was a police officer, and he opined that my rank on the department should have had some bearing when I was at home in my role as a wife, that somehow I should have been able to compel my husband to do as I ordered—really? I again interjected, against the kicks under the table coming from my defense rep, that "when I am at home, be clear—my husband is not impressed with this rocker on my sleeve. I don't get to order him around because he has only attained the rank of police officer on the department, and I am a sergeant." Are you kidding me? I wanted him to know that when I went home or end of watch (EOW), I was no different than any other woman—rank be damned.

I wondered how the deputy chief presiding over my BOR would have expected his daughter, if he had one, to respond in a similar situation. I wondered how the department thought I should have behaved when I felt threatened. I wondered what I should have done to be a better "victim" in the eyes of the LAPD. Did the department even consider that we both had guns? Did the BOR panel opine what my husband's response would have been if provoked? Didn't they hear me when I said I couldn't leave—he wouldn't let me? Did the BOR consider the fact that the "outside agency" had responded not to a "shots fired" call but to a "keep the peace" request from me? It didn't matter to this all-male BOR panel.

I guess the department had also forgotten that the month prior to my BOR, I had been "compelled" to testify at my husband's BOR where he was found guilty. Now my BOR Chairman is telling me that I am a liar and I "gave as good as I got." You can't you have it both ways, LAPD. Or, can you?

The LAPD was trying to fire me for doing what every other citizen, man or woman, had a right to do when they needed help—call the police. Where was it written that when a police officer asked for help, it was deemed "unnecessary"? If my house was burglarized, could I ask for help then? How about if my car was stolen? Was it okay to call the police then, or was that unnecessary too?

Had the BOR panel considered what effect this whole BOR process was having on my small children at home? Did the department stop for even a minute to contemplate that maybe I asked for "outside assistance from another police agency" because I was concerned for my children's safety as well as my own? The LAPD, in its arrogance, talked to me, during my BOR, in a way that would not be tolerated if I as an officer treated a citizen that way. The board made assumptions based on nothing and then arbitrarily decided to what extent they will allow an officer to mount a defense or explanation of fact.

The chairman had heard enough. My BOR was over. A decision was about to be made, and I was ordered to return the following day.

# FORTY-THREE: FORGET YOU KNOW ME, SALLY

I neared the point where, if found guilty, I would need to have character witnesses come in and speak about what type of officer/supervisor I needed to mitigate the possible penalty. I felt I needed some high-ranking and highly respected LAPD command staff to speak on my behalf.

First, I contacted the black lieutenant I had worked for in OSB–CRASH. Oh, I meant the house Negro.

I had received glowing commendations and ratings under his command. I kind of knew him personally, or so I thought. I had seen him over and over during my career, out at Lil J's, and at department functions. We had many conversations over the years about goings-on within the department. I thought of him as a friend, a mentor and someone I could count on, an older black officer with "time on the job." He was, after all, my former lieutenant and someone who could truthfully speak to my performance in the field and my contributions to the department at this critical juncture in my administrative hearing.

When I contacted my former lieutenant, who was now a commander, he sounded as if he would be willing to speak on my behalf. Before he would commit, however, he wanted to know what the charges against me were. I gave him the Reader's Digest version of the DV stuff. I could almost hear a "yes" in his tone, but as I continued with the list of charges, I added, "False and misleading statements to IA investigator."

Crickets. You could've heard a mouse pissing on cotton. He waited a few more seconds and then said, "Sally, forget you know me." (He used to call all the black female officers "Sally" when he spoke to us.)

I was stunned beyond belief. Had he just refused to help me? What was he scared of? He was, after all, a commander. What— did he have dreams of being a deputy chief when he grew up? His country ass had always told me how happy he was to have had the life he enjoyed on the LAPD plantation—I should have known. He had talked about the great assignments he had worked and how difficult it had been for him to get assigned to some of those specialized units like Metropolitan Division as a black during his era. He didn't mention that he had to bend over to get those coveted assignments. He had, "yes-sir, boss" all of his career. Loser

He never gave me the why - He just gave me the "no." I didn't need him to explain any further. I already knew why he said no – he was a house Negro.

# FORTY-FOUR: YOU'VE REACHED TOO FAR INTO THE DORSEY BEDROOM

I felt as though I had just been hit in the stomach with a medicine ball. There were precious few command staff officers whom I could ask to come to my board and speak on my behalf. I didn't think for a moment that the country-bumpkin house Negro would turn me down. Now, there were a few other house Negroes around—but I had no interest in going back down that road. I had seen what kind of impact a high-ranking LAPD officer's testimony could have at an officer's BOR when our Newton patrol captain testified against my vice officer during his BOR. I was certain that the captain's simple statement of "he can't work for me" was the nail in the young officer's coffin, so to speak. I did not want to suffer a similar fate.

By this time, I was hyperventilating. My head hurt. I was about to lose everything. I had, for the last three or four days, been the subject of a different sort of jury nullification. Each and every day as I rode in the elevator to the top floor of the Bradbury Building and walked to my hearing room, I would glance over the wrought iron railing down to the marble floor below. Most might find this venue beautiful and architectural. I found it hellish and dismal. The thoughts that took up the most space inside my head during that ride and walk were bad. They were painful. They made me want to cry. I found that as I walked along the railing, I had to physically will myself away from that railing. I had to force myself to walk the aisle standing so near the walls that I could literally feel the coolness of the tile or marble or whatever it was against my harm. I didn't trust myself standing close to that railing for very long.

I had been thinking about the what-ifs. What if I lost my job? How would I take care of my children? Where would I go to look for employment? Who would hire me with the label of "fired LAPD sergeant"? How much money could I realistically earn in this hypothetical new job? What about my house—the five-bedroom, three-bath, three-thousand-square foot dream house with the two big back yards, pool, and good area schools? We had moved in only a few short years earlier. Who would help me pull myself out of this financial struggle that was sure to come? My parents were both deceased; I was an only child. I didn't know of anyone who was willing or able to take on the burden of helping me out financially—period.

If they find me guilty, I will just jump, I thought. At least my children would be taken care of financially. I was insured up the wazoo. I knew that I had maintained my life insurance long enough for them to be unable to use the "suicide clause" as a reason not to pay my children. But who would administer my estate? Who would make sure that my young children didn't go crazy with their newfound fortune? I didn't want what had happened to another female police officer who died suddenly to happen to my children. This female had died suddenly of an aneurism, and a black female attorney had befriended her sons in an attempt to get her hands on their money. When the young men, now in their early twenties, didn't do what she wanted, she hired some thugs to break into their home and kill them. Is this how my children would end up? This was awful.

Maybe I needed a manifesto. I'm not the violent type. I don't condone the violence. I never thought for a minute about striking out at the board members, the IA advocate, or the IA investigator who brought these trumped-up charges against me. I was not going to blow my head off with a shotgun either. I surely understood how an officer could be pushed to create a manifesto. I understood how an officer could become irrational in thought when faced with the real prospect of losing everything that he or she had worked so hard for. I was certainly being wronged. It was being done in a vacuum, and there seemed to be no way to overcome the odds that were against me now.

I decided to call on that one person who had always been there for me: James (Jim) Tatreau, my former OSB–CRASH lieutenant and Newton captain. He was the same person who had told me years earlier that the LAPD machine would "eat you up and spit you out." Well this heffa was about to spit me out and I wasn't having it. Commander Tatreau was very respected on the department and he was high profile.

I met with him and explained that I needed him to be a character witness at my BOR. He didn't even ask me what the charges were. All he needed to know was "when" and "what time." I cannot say enough about this man. Over the years he had been my mentor, an ardent supporter, and a dear and cherished friend. He was willing to do what no black on the department would. He did it because it was the right thing to do. An injustice was being done to me, and he was not afraid to tell the department.

When the IA advocate called him to give his testimony about Sergeant Cheryl Dorsey, he spoke in a soft tone with that half smile and an occasional wink and nod my way in the manner that I had grown to love about him. He looked directly at the deputy chief and stated in the way he liked to start off a sentence when he was about to say something others would never have the balls to say to someone they feared on the department, "With all due respect, Chief, I think the department has reached too far into the Dorsey bedroom." Commander Tatreau told that deputy chief that he knew both me and my husband, that he liked us both, and that we were good officers. He added that specifically I had been an outstanding sergeant when I worked for him at Newton and an exemplary gang suppression officer when I worked for him in CRASH. I thought I saw him give the chairman a "what are you doing?" kind of look when he urged him and the entire board to rethink their involvement in this situation. When he finished speaking, he stood, faced me, and gave me one last wink and a smile. He left the room. I was appreciative.

There was a bit of a delay in the board rendering their "recommendation" to the chief of police. What a joke. Every officer on the LAPD understood that the chief would do exactly what the board recommended. There were instances when the chief might lessen a penalty recommended by the board—but that was rare.

The deputy chief called me back into the room. I stayed away from the railing as I entered. I don't remember all of what he was saying. It was mostly white noise. What I do remember as vividly today as I heard thirteen years ago now were these words uttered by the deputy chief: "In the first time in my thirty-five years on the department, on this one day, on this one occasion—I see a need for mercy. So I am going to grant you mercy, Sergeant. I am going to recommend to the chief of police a penalty of a five-day suspension rather than termination." I looked in the direction of the spineless department advocate for his reaction to my penalty. He showed none. I sensed that he hoped for a recommendation of my termination by the board. After my 1998 BOR, the department rewarded the house Negro and department advocate with promotions from sergeant to lieutenant in 1999 and then captain-I in 2005 and captain-III in 2006, for being a good and loyal ass licker.

My defense rep stood up and whispered in my ear to go and shake the board members' hands and thank them. My stomach was in knots. I was relieved, for sure, but disgusted. How dare that deputy chief talk to me that way? How dare he act as though he's God sitting at the throne? How dare he say that he was going to give me mercy? All I had was sheer contempt for him, the LAPD, and everything that it stood for. But I was a good soldier, and not knowing if this "recommendation" was set in cement, I figured I'd better go along to get along. I shook their funky-ass hands. I returned to my division and was told to pick which time period I wanted to be suspended. I served my five-day suspension and went on about my business. Two more years—I just needed to hold on for two more years.

This was my first-hand experience on how the Los Angeles Police Department will grind an officer down. This is what the general public doesn't understand. The department has the resources to mount an aggressive offensive against you in trying to "prove" allegations of misconduct. Since we all live pay check to paycheck, most police officers don't have the financial means to fight the department/city. The department will just wear you down.

By the time an officer is ordered to an administrative BOR hearing, he or she has already been "relieved of duty without pay." Thankfully, I was not.

Then there's the administrative and disciplinary process for command staff. You see, if you are a high-ranking LAPD official, captain and above, and get caught "dirty"—I mean, really "dirty"—then you get to "retire in lieu of termination" That means hurry up and sign that letter of retirement before a BOR convenes. That also means you get to leave with a service pension, in most cases. It can take up to a year before an officer is set to appear before a BOR. So hurry up, Captain, Commander, Deputy Chief—the clock's ticking.

*According to a Los Angeles Times article dated March 31, 2002, "Maurice Moore, a 40-year veteran of the Los Angeles Police Department who until recently was one of its highest-ranking officials is under investigation for real estate transactions that authorities believe may have laundered money from a multimillion-dollar cocaine ring headed by his son.... Deputy Chief Moore, a longtime friend and special assistant to Police Chief Bernard C. Parks, was allowed to continue in his job while the investigation was underway. Under Parks, LAPD officers accused of crimes or serious misconduct often have been ordered to remain at home during working hours until the cases against them have been resolved.*

*Parks declined to discuss specifics of the Moore case on Friday, but said the LAPD was continuing to probe the allegations against him. "At the conclusion," Parks said, "we will determine if there's anything he is culpable of."*

*In the meantime, Moore, long regarded as a friendly, approachable LAPD supervisor, has retired from the LAPD, officially winding up his service on Jan. 26. A message in Parks' monthly newsletter said Moore's long career was "distinguished by his remarkable commitment to continuous public service," adding that the deputy chief had gone for more than 30 years without taking a single day off due to illness.*

According to that article, Parks knew about Moore's activities as early as December 1999, based on a FBI letter sent to him detailing their suspicions. The was also an interim police chief, Martin Pomeroy, during that the time, who "wanted to do an analysis" of the charges before taking administrative action.

A former LAPD commander reported that the department should have immediately relieved Deputy Chief Moore of duty based on the FBI information and that if Moore had been a rank-and-file officer, the outcome would have been different. A LA city police commissioner said that he was disturbed by the handling of the Moore allegation.

You're following the story, right? That means in 1999, Chief Parks knew, based on a letter sent to him by the FBI, that his good buddy Deputy Chief Maurice Moore was implicated in serious misconduct. Parks did absolutely nothing. The department analyzed the allegations for years and ultimately allowed Moore to stay put and eventually retire as if these charges were non-existent. Give me a break. Don't tell me that there aren't inherent problems in the LAPD's internal discipline system. This is not new, and it certainly is not old. This double standard in discipline goes on today. It's the LAPD culture. It's the LAPD way. It's the LAPD: passed down from generation to generation, chief to chief. Please.

*Another Los Angeles Times article dated, September 13, 2002, stated in part, "Deputy Chief Maurice Moore from the Los Angeles Police Department was, for at least seven years, an active player in his son's cross-country cocaine ring, helping to launder hundreds of thousands of dollars in illicit profits, a confidential LAPD report alleges.*

*Deputy Chief Moore, who retired earlier this year as one of the LAPD's highest-ranking officials, allegedly retrieved, delivered, stored and then laundered drug money through real estate transactions for his son, who orchestrated the operation from federal prison, according to the LAPD's internal investigation, a copy of which was obtained by The Times."*

*I saw on a recent nightly television broadcast for a local news station that the Oscar Joel Bryant Association, known as OJB, held an "emergency" meeting to discuss the LAPD's race relations.*

*According to an LA Weekly News article written by Erin Aubry Kaplan, dated September 4, 2002, "The OJB emerged in 1968... the foundation, named for the first black LAPD officer believed to have died in the line of duty that same year, was conceived as a countervailing force to the highly unequal treatment that had too long defined L.A.'s finest and given the force much of its historical racist taint. Modeled on the many black activist and advocacy groups that cropped up in the late '60s, OJB made the working conditions of members its own cause; it was not a union, but something quite opposite—an antidote to the LAPD's Police Protective League, a union that for years was dominated by the very good old boys who were the core of the race problem that gave rise to the foundation, and who assiduously kept blacks off its board. Even in the best of times the league could hardly be trusted to represent the interests of all."*

*I found it laughable that OJB waited until 2013, to hold an "emergency" meeting. The 2002 article also reported in part, that "LAPD Sergeant Ronnie Cato, OJB President at the time, 'criticized past OJB leadership as being too conciliatory and soft on race issues'...he says he understands it perfectly. 'Look, the fear of discovery if you complain, the fear for job security on the force, is great,' he says. 'Everybody agrees with my positions privately, but they don't want to make it public. They won't say anything, but they'll call me on the phone to congratulate me... A lot of black officers didn't support him [Police Chief Bernard Parks] ,' Cato says bluntly. 'Black officers were already getting unfairly disciplined, and actually Parks made it worse. He signed off on increased disciplinary measures. He allowed officers to be fired, and let go. Members were very upset.' But, Cato adds by way of explanation, 'There were more minorities promoted under Parks than had ever been promoted in the history of the LAPD. It all depended on where you were, whether you were rank and file, or whether you were on the verge of being promoted higher.'*

*"The percentage of black officers on the force—about 13 percent—accurately reflects the number of black people in the city that it serves. The last two L.A. police chiefs have been its first black ones, and the second was championed by a white Republican mayor. But many argue that progress at the top, however impressive, is too often symbolic, and that it hasn't trickled down to the roughly 1,200 black rank and file who still observe—and often absorb—institutional racism on a daily basis."*

# FORTY-FIVE: TWO VS. ONE

Captain Jim Tatreau, who had been so supportive for many years, transferred out of Newton to assume command of the elite Robbery-Homicide Division. Our black captain-I promoted to captain-II and transferred to South Traffic. He later returned to Newton as the captain-III. What a mess.

Once the black captain returned as the officer in charge of the entire police division, the work environment for me at Newton became contentious. Whenever I saw him around the station, he would try to "shuck 'n' jive" with me because that's what house Negroes did. I remained cordial but curt. Shortly after the black captain returned as the captain-III, the speckled-back white female lieutenant also returned to Newton, as a newly promoted captain-I. Oh boy. This tag team was going to be the end of me.

Vice was a limited assignment, only eighteen months. As my vice tour neared its end, I began looking for other sergeant-II positions within the department that I could apply for. If I was unsuccessful in finding a sergeant-II job, I would revert back down to the rank of sergeant-I and return to patrol. I was fresh off my five-day suspension and not really caring about the LAPD. I had approximately two more years to go before my twentieth anniversary on the plantation. I just wanted an assignment where I did not have to work too hard, something Monday through Friday with weekends off.

Before Captain Tatreau left, I asked him about participating in the department's "cross-training program." This program was created to provide officers who held the rank of sergeant and detective to switch assignments. As a sergeant, I would work as a case-carrying detective, and the detective would supervise patrol officers. This benefited both of us because I had the opportunity to conduct follow-up investigations and the case carrying detective-I and detective-II classifications was given line-supervision responsibilities over patrol officers; something not available as a detective. Supervisory experience was a resume necessity when promoting to lieutenant. Of course, my captain granted my request.

I was assigned to the burglary table. My immediate supervisor was a black detective-III (D-III). I didn't know him personally, but like most of the blacks on the department, I had seen him around. I was happy to work for him. I had my nine to five, so to speak, with weekends off.

Shortly after I started working detectives, I decided to use public transportation to ease my commute time. I approached my D-III and asked for and received permission to use my plain detective vehicle at the end of my shift to drive between the Metrolink train station and Newton Division. Many other detectives were already doing this, or had done this in the past.

After a few weeks of me taking the train to and from work, I was approached by a lieutenant who was working on "loan" at Newton; he was normally assigned to Central Division. This lieutenant asked me about the detective vehicle I had been driving to and from work each day. I explained to the lieutenant, who happened to be a male, white officer, that I had been using the detective car and that my D-III approved its use. What I didn't know was the department had a policy that prohibited this type of use and it even had a name; satellite parking. This was news to me because I knew that satellite parking had been done by many others before me.

So the lieutenant was talking to me casually about this car situation, and when I admitted the use, he kind of let out an audible sigh and stated, "I am so glad that you didn't lie about that." I looked at him, somewhat confused, because I thought, first of all, why would I lie about something so innocuous, and second, what's the big deal? Then he told me that my captain-III, the black guy/house Negro, had sent him to "investigate" me. The lieutenant said that this black captain had another patrol sergeant follow me for a couple of days to document my activity. The black captain wanted the lieutenant to ask me about using the detective vehicle and had instructed the lieutenant to initiate a personnel complaint against me if I denied using the car. The lieutenant specifically told me that the black captain told him to charge me with "giving false and misleading statements" if I denied using the car.

Are you kidding me?! Not this again. Well, I didn't lie, because I am not a liar. I was using the vehicle with permission. Now what?

The lieutenant evidently went back to the captain-III and reported his findings after our conversation. So now, the black Captain-III sicced the female captain on my D-III. I know this because my D-III approached and asked, "Did you piss somebody off?" My D-III told me that he had been getting a lot of grief from the female captain all of a sudden. The D-III was a long-time Newton detective with almost thirty years on the department. He was a good supervisor and well thought of in the division. No one "messed" with a D-III; it was unheard of.

After several more weeks of increased scrutiny my D-III decided he had had enough. He told me that he was about ready to retire anyway—he could stay or go. But what he knew for sure was that he had no plans to stick around and let the captains make him their project. He said, "They are not going to give me a heart attack. I am going to look at my numbers and talk to my wife. If it makes sense, I will pull the plug [retire]." He did just that.

It was obvious to me that the black captain had sent the female captain and ultimately that lieutenant to do his dirty work. The lieutenant was obligated, because he didn't want to make any waves and as he was directed, but the female captain—well, that was a different story. She and I had history. I had seen her go out of her way to harass the female officers over non-important, made up issues when she was at Newton assigned to patrol. She had power and was vindictive, in my opinion. I knew I had a real situation with these two. I needed a new church home.

I discontinued the use of my detective vehicle. However, I still wanted to take advantage of the whole Metrolink ride, so I asked the PM assistant watch commander (AWC), my former OSB–CRASH sergeant and now peer, if I could have someone drive me the two or three miles down the street to the Alameda train station. I told him what had happened and how the two captains were messing with me. He said, "Sure, get a sergeant" in his ruff-gruff way. Everyone knew that right out of roll call, most of the officers spent the first twenty minutes or so goofing off, at Winchell's or someplace else. That's what the patrol officers did; the sergeants the same and for a lot longer. Rank had its privileges. So I grabbed a PM watch sergeant who drove me down the road.

Guess the female captain found out about that too. Those two asses made me a full time project.

I got summoned into Her Highness's office. She asked me about the ride I had been getting and told me to stop it. I said, "Okay." I left without much dialogue; the sight of her gave me IBS (irritable bowel syndrome).

I was not going to sit around and let these two ne'er-do-wells mess with me for much longer. In addition to the female captain and her antics, the black male captain began to sexually harass me. One thing the Los Angeles Police Department had taught me was if an officer waited for the department to decide that it was time to stop messing you over, you would be waiting a long time. I was getting off this merry-go-round. I contacted the office of the ombudsman and reported that I was being harassed.

What I didn't mention before, but I will now, is that there had been a series of encounters in the police station and at other LA city facilities with my black captain. He had begun not only to harass me at Newton, but he was sexually harassing me whenever our paths crossed. Evidently I was a good actress, and he had no idea how much aversion I held toward him.

I contacted the office of the ombudsman within the LAPD, a resource where officers can seek confidential assistance or redress. Yeah, right. "Confidential" and "LAPD" are an oxymoron. I knew better, but I had to act. I explained how tenuous and hostile the working conditions were at Newton and requested an immediate transfer out of Newton area.

I made the short drive, on duty, from Parker Center back to Newton, and I was immediately called into the office of the speckled-back hyena. I imagined she would need to be notified of my contact and request—but she knew in less than half an hour. She tried to assure me that she could "handle" the black captain, and she "really wanted me to stay." She said she had no idea and that she was understandably empathetic as a female on the department. Heffa, I was born at night, but not last night; miss me with that.

I'm out. I did a one-two punch: I filed a sexual harassment complaint against the black captain and requested an immediate administrative transfer.

# FORTY-SIX: TWENTY YEARS AND ONE DAY

I made it known to the department that I was not going to accept any freeway therapy—I wanted to remain in Central Bureau because it was geographically desirable. I transferred to Central detectives. I was not going to be placed on some god-awful shift working some crappy detail. I had too much seniority for that.

On my first day assigned to Central detectives, the captain in charge of the detective unit called me into his office. He wanted to talk to me. Once I was seated in his office, he advised me that he was going to ask another female detective to "sit in with us." Are you kidding me? What—oh, I get it, you heard about the sexual harassment suit I had filed against my former Captain, the one that was supposed to be kept confidential by the department's ombudsman. Are you concerned I may file a "false" claim against you, Captain? Get real.

He gave me his little spiel and then sent me on my merry way. I worked alone. Cool. Been there, done that. Many of the detectives didn't really have much to say to me. I had been down this road too. It was January 2000. Eight more months, and then the LAPD could kiss my black ass—but not before they "paid the lady."

A short time later, I became aware of a class-action lawsuit being contemplated against the LAPD, by nearly one hundred police officers for discrimination, harassment, unfair labor practices, and the like. I was a party to that action. The LAPD, in its arrogance, then and now, only understands one thing—drastic action.

One day, I was driving down the street, and all of a sudden, while I was stopped at a red light, a citizen slammed into the back of my plain detective vehicle. I looked in the rearview mirror of my vehicle and saw this older gentleman rocking back and forth and holding his head and neck. I got out of my car, and he exited his. No damage to my car, but his front end was all smashed up. I advised him that I was on duty LAPD and this was a city vehicle.

I requested an RA for the citizen and a supervisor for myself. The fire department eventually responded. The paramedics tended to the citizen while I spoke with one of the firefighters. He asked me if I had sustained any injury in the collision. I informed him that the rear-end impact had been fairly severe and direct. I told him that my back and neck were hurting. I noticed he was kind of nice-looking. I liked him. I just didn't know how much.

He looked at me and stated, "Don't move. I am going to give you the same treatment that we give every citizen of Los Angeles." I didn't know exactly what he meant at first. He stepped away and returned with that long wooden board the paramedics use. He placed the board/gurney gently before me and told me to lie down. He immediately wrapped my neck in a soft brace and promptly trussed my ass up like a Christmas turkey. I could not move. Next thing I knew, I was looking up at the ceiling of a paramedic unit, en route to a local hospital.

Unfortunately, I had suffered a lot of soft-tissue damage in the traffic collision. I had to be placed on "injury-on-duty" (IOD). Wow, that saddened me.

I was told to follow up with my own medical professional upon my release. I did. Turns out my injuries were significant enough to require physical therapy. It was worse than I thought, according to my medical professional. I remained on IOD status for the next several months. Physical therapy was needed, and I stayed on a strict and continuous routine.

During my time off, as I recuperated from my injuries, I began to plan my exit strategy. I had been suspended five days without pay and would therefore need to make this time up if I were to retire later in the summer as planned. I contacted the department of pensions and learned that I could "buy back" my bad days. Thank goodness. This meant that I could reimburse the city for those days when I was not officially on the payroll due to my suspension. I was given a dollar amount for the five days and agreed to cut the city a check. I wanted off the LAPD in a bad way. I did not want to stick around this hellhole for an extra code-7 (forty-five minutes). All I could think of was how bad I felt for officers who had suffered several suspensions during their careers. On August 24, 2000, Goldberg & Gage filed that civil suit against the LAPD.

My back finally was feeling better. I was ready to return to "full duty" status. My doctor obliged. He cleared me to return to the LAPD on August 26, 2000. This was one day after my twentieth anniversary and my last day on the plantation. I retired. Honorably.

Understand - the LAPD always has and always will continue to be very adept at hiding its dirty laundry from the public and minimizing the maltreatment of its officers. Transparency is in the eye of the beholder. Most citizens are ill-informed when it comes to the goings-on of the LAPD. Many of the department's reprisals are covert but lethal nonetheless. It takes an "insider" to know the appropriate follow-up question to pose when a high-ranking command staff officer or department spokesperson gives the "company line" at a press conference staged for the sole purpose of diverting the public's attention. The LAPD shelters and misrepresents wrongdoing by some command staff by ducking behind confidentiality rules relating to personnel investigations or, in my case, barring me from speaking as a stipulation to accepting a settlement. For example, I am barred from discussing the details of the sexual harassment settlement my attorney reached with the City of Los Angeles.

However, suffice it to say that the law offices of Goldberg & Gage hooked me up. My children loved our lush and tropically landscaped backyard and new swimming pool - thanks, Captain.

•••

I was headed for a simpler, well-deserved, life of leisure. I had made a clean break from the LAPD. 20 yrs.-check. Service pension- check. Sanity – check. Then circumstances and events, for which I could not have predicted and most definitely could not watch silently, began to occur. Black and Blue, The Creation of a Social Advocate happened.

I had no idea after I had written the story of my life as a young black woman on the LAPD what was to come. I expected this autobiography to be "one and done". Once I began to share the story of my professional experiences, I quickly realized that all the trials and tribulations on the LAPD had been purposed. What I had learned and become during my tenure on the LAPD was about to play a critical, vital and necessary role in discussions regarding events that were increasing tensions between police and black, brown and poor white communities. I became a much sought-after police expert, making the rounds on national and international news, which included local and cable networks regarding racial profiling, abuse under the color of authority and an unnecessary escalation in uses of force which oftentimes resulted in fatal shootings. A spate of deadly encounters and increased community - police tensions was the genesis for the next volume of my book, "Black and Blue. The Creation of a Social Advocate" is a guide to understanding police culture, deciphering police code talk and recognizing warning signs when a police detention is about to go bad; a phrase I have coined- Contempt of Cop™. This volume is singularly focused to help the reader "survive police encounters." For more visit www.sgtcheryldorsey.com and follow me on twitter @sgtcheryldorsey

# ADVOCACY

# FORTY-SEVEN: THE CREATION OF A SOCIAL ADVOCATE

*"Be ashamed to die until you have won some victory for humanity"*
   - Horace Mann

Having been put through the paces at the LAPD, I had no idea that I had been learning tough lessons that I would need to r-visit in the future.

I am a believer that God does not qualify the called - He calls the qualified.

So to that extent, I am speaking out and advocating for police reform and accountability; standing in the gap and speaking correctly, concisely and credibly for families who have suffered violence and abuse at the hands of errant police officers; corroborating complaints of mistreatment and retaliation by women in a male-dominated workplace.

My voice for those adversely effected by an abusive and powerful institution like a police department is an important one. I was not expecting the fork in the road that was ahead. The detour that would ultimately point me in the direction of a new movement; #MeToo. More on that later.

I now understood that my LAPD experiences had uniquely prepared and positioned me to speak in a way that was credible, undeniable and timely regarding the need for police reform, policy changes and a cessation in deadly police encounters. Martin Luther King wrote, "Nothing in all the world is more dangerous than sincere ignorance and conscientious stupidity." As a woman, as a mother and as a police professional I intend to share what I have seen and learned for the betterment of humanity.

So, to that end, I felt compelled to address what I knew to be institutionalized racism that permeated the LAPD and many other police departments around the nation. Minority communities have known for years that there were racist cops on their police departments; racist cops who responded to their calls for service and ultimately dealt with them in ways that were inappropriate and disrespectful. You know like when a parent is having an issue with an incorrigible teen or maybe a mentally ill relative whom they cannot control. And because the belief had been that when you had a problem you called the police for help in restoring order. Only now, the police arrive on scene and rather than bring peace and calm; some perceived threat on the part of the officer ends up in a deadly use of force. Now families are left with the dilemma of what to do next time. Many have adopted the position that when there is an issue or problem in the home – the police will be the last ones to be called. These communities have been keenly away that racism and biased officers existed within the ranks of the police departments that served them. It was after all, their lived experience.

To illustrate my point, here are a few examples. On February 14, 2014, Nair Rodriguez and her daughter became involved in a domestic dispute outside a movie theatre in an Oklahoma, city mall. Moore Police officers presumably responded to the scene to do what officers do, keep the peace. In this case, not so much. What ultimately happened was that her husband, Luis Rodriguez was confronted by several officers and mall security all of whom allegedly beat Luis Rodriguez to death. According to Nair Rodriguez, in a Daily Mail article, she had recorded the incident on her cell phone which was confiscated by police. The City of Moore, Oklahoma Police Department remains in litigation with the Rodriguez family at the time of this writing. So, the question that begs to be answered is, "If this Latino family required police assistance in the future to resolve a familial dispute and keep the peace do you think the police will be their first call?" Would these white officers have conducted themselves similarly if the disputants had been white? You decide. Calling the police for assistance and drawing their ire is not an infrequent occurrence.

On August 7, 2010, a black woman, Tamela Eaton called the Cleveland police department to report a car that had been blocking her driveway. Officer Frank Garmback ( former partner of Timothy Loehmann who shot and killed Tamir Rice) and his then partner responded. What happened next was unclear as stated in reports. However, according to those same reports and a civil suit that was filed by Eaton, she cited "such reckless, wanton and willful excessive use of force proximately caused bodily injury to (Eaton)." Eaton had been arrested and charged with a crime as a result of the incident. She was later acquitted in November 2010. It was reported in December 2014 that a U.S. District Court in Cleveland paid out a $100,000 settlement to Eaton as a result of her call for police service. Now, who do you think Tamela Eaton will call the next time a car has blocked her driveway? Why did those white officers escalate a call for service from a black community member into a chargeable offense? I'll let you be the judge.

So, on October 17, 2006, when the Federal Bureau of Investigation (FBI) released a redacted version of their report on *White Supremacist Infiltration of Law Enforcement* few were surprised by the reported findings.

According to the report, in part, there was an acknowledgment that "ghost skins" a term used by white supremacist to define those who covertly display their beliefs to blend into society, existed. The inference and admission being that "ghost skins" existed on police departments across the nation. This fact was evidenced in the memo which further reported that in Los Angeles, California, a U.S. District Judge found that in 1991, members of a local sheriff's department had formed a neo-Nazis group which routinely harassed black and Hispanic communities. It is understandable how then interactions and encounters between police and community quickly escalate to abuses under the color of authority.

In a 2015 speech, then FBI Director, James Comey admitted, *"All of us in law enforcement must be honest enough to acknowledge that much of our history is not pretty.... At many points in American history, law enforcement enforced the status quo, a status quo that was often brutally unfair to disfavored groups."*

The following year, in October 2016, during a speech, Terrence Cunningham, president of one of the largest police organizations in the United States, the International Association of Police Chiefs (IACP) said this, *"...There have been times when law enforcement officers, because of the laws enacted by federal, state, and local governments, have been the face of oppression for far too many of our fellow citizens. In the past, the laws adopted by our society have required police officers to perform many unpalatable tasks, such as ensuring legalized discrimination or even denying the basic rights of citizenship to many of our fellow Americans."* Cunningham admitted that, *"...this dark side of our shared history has created a multigenerational—almost inherited—mistrust between many communities of color and their law enforcement agencies...*

Cunningham then apologized this way, *"...For our part, the first step in this process is for law enforcement and the IACP to acknowledge and apologize for the actions of the past and the role that our profession has played in society's historical mistreatment of communities of color.*

While I appreciated the IACP president's apology on the one hand, I thought it to be disingenuous on the other. Cunningham acknowledged historical mistreatment of communities of color as though he had been referencing abusive police tactics that occurred back in the early 1900s. Factually, this mistreatment is going on right now- real time. I would have appreciated hearing from Cunningham what steps the IACP would take regarding policy reform and accountability. From what had been released, substantive change was never addressed during Cunningham's speech. So, for me, the mere admission of problem without a resolution or solution rang hollow. Disenfranchised and adversely affected communities know this – what are you and your organization going to do sir?

So, let me speak truthfully regarding the issues and the actuals behind these reported facts. Let's not just address the circumstances and the stats. Let's address and acknowledge the real people who have lost lives. Let's say their names. Oscar Grant. Ezell Ford. John Crawford. Sam DuBose. Sandra Bland. Eric Harris. Freddy Gray. Jordan Edwards. Stephon Clark. Zachary Hammond. Philando Castile. Samantha Ramsey. Kelly Thomas.

Police abuse and excessive, unnecessary force, deadly force is not an aberration. Police abuse is a too frequent occurrence in communities of color and where poor whites reside. Be clear, everyone is in danger. So, remember, this may not be you now, but you might be next.

On April 26, 2014, 19-year-old Samantha Ramsey was leaving a large outdoor party, in Boone County, Ohio. Sheriff's Deputy Tyler Brockman fired a round at her car as she drove past the deputy when she failed to comply with his demands to "stop". She later died. The sheriff's office later agreed to pay the family $3.5 million in a settlement. Will this police department be your first choice the next time a group of unruly, underaged teens gather to drink and party?

In the summer of 2014, on the heels of an NYPD officer choking and killing Eric Garner and Ferguson, Missouri officer fatally shooting Mike Brown - Ezell Ford had been shot and killed in city of Los Angeles by two LAPD gang officers. Enough is enough. A social justice advocate had been created.

I decided to attend a community meeting which was being held at the Paradise Baptist Church in Los Angeles, California.

It had been reported LAPD police chief Charlie Beck would be attending. This would be my first opportunity to advocate for a family who had lost a loved one at the hands of police. These kinds of occurrences had not been happening or at least not widely reported and certainly not with this frequency since the time that I had retired; but being retired afforded me the ability to speak in a way that active duty police officers could not and most retired officers would not. So, I geared up to confront the police chief of the LAPD; my former department.

The local area news had reported the circumstances of the Ezell Ford police shooting. Based on my knowledge of LAPD policy and procedures as well as my LAPD training, I was prepared. I expected Chief Beck to speak as most chiefs had during police involved shootings. I was ready for what I like to refer to as "code-talk." I recognized and understood police double speak. But I had questions.Questions that I intended to pose in front of the Ford family that would require the responses that I felt the family deserved.The answer to the why? And, what will be done by the department? As a mother, I wanted to be at that community meeting. As an LAPD sergeant, I needed to be at that meeting.

I was reminded of the words of Horace Mann, *"Be ashamed to die until you have won some victory for humanity."* Ezell Ford did not deserve to die. There had been no articulated rationale for his detention by those LAPD gang officers. To that point, it was, in my mind, inhumane to think that a young black man, hanging out with friends, minding his own business would be shot and killed for refusing to respond when beckoned by cop.

Chief Beck spoke briefly as did the president of the Police Commission; LAPD's civilian review board and others. All of them pretty much towing the company line. Transparency. Full and thorough investigation blah, blah, blah.

Eventually, the floor was opened to community members in attendance. Folks seated all around the church sanctuary jumped from the seats and formed a line. By the time I could do the same there were already twenty or so people ahead of me in that line. As the first few community members began to question and lambaste the officials in attendance, I politely began to work my way to the front of the line as I explained to each person in front of me who I was and why I needed to jump the line. Each obliged one by one. Eventually, I made it to the front.

I stood before the family members who had attended and the community, my community and identified myself as retired LAPD sergeant Cheryl Dorsey. Of course, chief Beck knew exactly who I was. In the presence of the LA City Inspector General, the president of the Los Angeles Police Commission, Steve Soboroff and others, I queried the chief as to the probable cause those LAPD officers had when they detained Ezell Ford. Chief Beck provided the expected non-answer in front of the Ford family; but I had accomplished my goal. I wanted to make the chief uncomfortable. I did not want to allow him to simply brush the family off with the usually police department jargon. I wanted to, if only in that moment, hold the LAPD accountable to the Ford family. It was the least I could do – as a woman, as a mother, and as a LAPD supervisor who knew better. A social advocate had been created.

Ezell Ford's story did not initially reach the same level of national news coverage as other fatal police encounters that had occurred a few weeks prior. So, to that end, using this platform, my platform and because I feel a kindred spirit relationship with his mother Tritobia Ford, whom I have come to know, I want to share with the reader what happened in the aftermath the fatal police shooting of Ezell Ford.

On June 9, 2015, the *Los Angeles Times*, reported that *"the Los Angeles Police Commission issued a mixed ruling Tuesday in last year's killing of a mentally ill black man, finding that one officer was wrong to use deadly force but clearing another in the fatal shooting.*

The Commission also opined in their findings and *"faulted both officers for their decisions to draw their weapons at different points during the confrontation with Ezell Ford and disapproved of the tactics used by one of the officers."*

Although the police commission disapproved, LAPD police chief Beck sided with his officers. Having a civilian review board, like the LAPD has without teeth behind their "recommendations" seemed pointless. Police chiefs have tremendous power and autonomy over their departments. What they say goes. This was true in the fatal shooting of Ezell Ford. And this has also been true in the fatal police shootings that have followed.

Police chiefs, sheriffs and commissioners have refused to find fault with their officers' actions. They continue to give some officers the "gift of resignation" and while rarely terminating others. But I'll tell you what always happens, without fail after a fatal-police shooting or use of force - buckets of money is thrown at the families at the expense of tax payers. The involved officers are not held financially responsible. The officers live to offend again. Some of these officers have been allowed to simply move on to another police department after resignation or termination; a la Betty Shelby; a la Timothy Loehmann, a la Darren Wilson and so many others; whose personnel records the public can not follow due to confidentiality and the cover of the Police Officers Bill of Rights.\*\*\*

As I continue to speak out about these atrocities and the others, criticisms directed towards me from those who are purported to be cops (mostly white based on social media avatars) is often swift, unrelenting, profane and downright ugly. My credentials routinely come into question- this continues today.

So, let me set the record straight, there is not another female, black or white on the Los Angeles Police Department with twenty, solid years of patrol experience- then or now. Those twenty years I spent in patrol were under the command of Police Chiefs Daryl Gates, Willie Williams and Bernard Parks;

and my experiences will never to be duplicated.

Here is my curriculum vitae. I patrolled the streets of Los Angeles during a time when PCP drug activity was a mainstay in "sherm alley" and cocaine use was on the rise; the LAPD battering ram was used to plow into the homes of suspected criminals; drive-by shootings between warring gang factions were a constant; Hammer Task Force operations which were launched from the Los Angeles Coliseum and OSBC CRASH (the gang unit I worked at the time) played a vital role in those gang sweeps; the OJ Simpson murders happened, the Olympics, Northridge earth quake, Rodney King beating and subsequent LA Riots. Those times have come and gone. It is because of these lived experiences that I know firing a gun or choking someone to death could have, in some instances, been avoided.

# FORTY-EIGHT: TAKE A KNEE. NO ONE'S IMMUNE

What is the point of having a platform if you are not willing to use it? In his February 2015 speech, former FBI Director James Comey said this, *"...Every American should feel free to express an informed opinion—to protest peacefully, to convey frustration and even anger in a constructive way. That's what makes our democracy great."*

To that end, music moguls, actors and athletes from the NFL and NBA have used their platforms; some to speak out and to protest silently. They understood that they were not immune. Or maybe they were fed up. Because just "being a black" means you are not immune.

On the heels of the murders of Eric Garner, Mike Brown, Ezell Ford, Tamir Rice, John Crawford, Sam DuBose, Terence Crutcher, Sandra Bland and the police assault of Floyd Dent, and police shooting of Charles Kinsey, Levar Jones and others; San Francisco 49rs quarterback Colin Kaepernick refused to stand for the playing of the national anthem in silent protest against police abuse in minority communities.

On August 26, 2016, Kaepernick initiated a silent protest because he believed abusive police tactics were being unnecessarily used on blacks and minorities in the United States. That was his stated reason when he first refused to stand during the playing of the national anthem and that continued to be his stated reason; even though some had tried to re-direct the conversation and make his protest about something else. Kaepernick paid a hefty price for exercising his 1st amendment right; freedom of speech. Kaepernick was not alone. He had been eventually joined by other notable athletes like Dwayne Wade, LeBron James, Chris Paul and Carmelo Anthony have also used their platforms to shine a light on issues affecting minority communities in the United States.

Here's why we take a knee. On August 26, 2017 a year after Kaepernick began his silent protest, according to published reports, Seattle Seahawks defensive end Michael Bennett had been unnecessarily detained, physically assaulted by police officers, handcuffed and thrown in the back of a police car. Bennett's crime; being a black man out on the streets in Las Vegas Nevada. Apparently, Michael Bennett was not immune.

Bennett had been returning to his hotel room in Las Vegas, Nevada after the Mayweather vs McGregor fight when shots fired were heard. According to Bennett, in a written letter, several hundred people were also in the area at the time the shots were fired, and everyone started running; including Bennett. Bennett described what happened next, in part, this way:

*"Las Vegas police officers singled me out and pointed their guns at me for doing nothing more than simply being a black man in the wrong place at the wrong time.*

*A police officer ordered me to get on the ground. As I laid on the ground, complying with his commands to not move, he placed his gun near my head and warned me that if I moved he would "blow my fucking head off." Terrified and confused by what was taking place, a second officer came over and forcefully jammed his knee into my back making it difficult for me to breathe. They then cinched the handcuffs on my wrists so tight that my fingers went numb."*

Bennett continued, *"The Officers' excessive use of force was unbearable. I felt helpless as I lay there on the ground handcuffed facing the real-life threat of being killed. All I could think of is I am going to die for no other reason than I am black, and my skin color is a threat… I kept asking the officers, What did I do? and reminding them I had rights they were duty bound to respect.*

*The Officers ignored my pleas and instead told me to shut up... After confirming my identify I was ultimately released without any legitimate justification for the Officer's abusive contact..."*

Bennett survived the police encounter. This is why we take a knee.

Michael Bennett perhaps had the good fortune, if you want to call it that of having the title "NFL player" after his name. What about the many other black men who don't have the benefit of celebrity or fame attached to their names.

In July 2014, sixty-nine-year old William Wingate; a black man was falsely arrested and charged by former Seattle police officer Cynthia Whitlatch. Whitlatch accused the elder black, man of swinging a golf club, that he used while walking, at her. Wingate was subsequently jailed for thirty-hours and charged with a misdemeanor. A later review of Whitlatch's police car dash-cam revealed that the officer had lied and falsely charged Wingate. The charges were eventually dismissed. If you are a senior citizen and black, you are not immune This, is why we take a knee.

On September 4, 2014, Levar Jones was shot by former South Carolina State Trooper Sean Groubert. Jones exited his car during a traffic stop and when the former trooper directed him to present his driver's license, Jones turned away, reached inside his car and was shot by Groubert. Jones survived the incident. If you are a young, black male motorist, complying with an officer's order, you are not immune. This, is why we take a knee.

Then there is the case of Floyd Dent, who in January 2015, had been stopped, handcuffed and beaten by former Inskter, Michigan police officer William Melendez. As a result, the very violent police assault, which had been recorded by the officer's in-car dash cam, Floyd Dent had been hit sixteen times and choked so hard - he passed out. Dent was arrested and charged with possession of cocaine which was later thrown out of court by a judged. If you are an unarmed, black man, not resisting nor interfering with an officer's orders – you are not immune. This, is why we take a knee.

# FORTY-NINE: SURVIVING POLICE ENCOUNTERS

What should you do when stopped by the police? Be careful. Your next move could be life altering. We have already learned that there are linguistic disparities when some officers interact with minority community members. So, it is imperative that you conduct yourself accordingly.

I am advocating for your survival. Be clear, there is no guarantee that having read this chapter will ensure that you survive a police encounter. I'm just offering additional tools for you to add to your tool chest. Because if all you have is a hammer - than everything you see is a nail.

More examples of what has happened when police contacts have gone awry. Speak the way I do not because any of this is a newsflash; but to corroborate what minority communities have complained about and dealt prior to the advent of cell phone recordings, YouTube and other social media platforms. So, I acknowledge that some cops have initiated a stop for the sole purpose of creating an opportunity. By creating an opportunity, I mean a "fishing expedition". I know that this occurs, and the reader knows that this occurs. If only police administrators could be so honest.

On August 10, 2016, the U.S. Department of Justice, Civil Rights Division reported in part, that the Baltimore Police Department (BPD) engaged *"in a pattern or practice of making stops, searches, and arrests in violation of the Fourth and Fourteenth Amendments and Section 14141. BPD frequently makes investigative stops without reasonable suspicion of people who are lawfully present on Baltimore streets. During stops, officers commonly conduct weapons frisks—or more invasive searches— despite lacking reasonable suspicion that the subject of the* search is armed. These practices escalate street encounters and contribute to officers making arrests without probable cause,36 often for discretionary misdemeanor offenses like disorderly conduct, resisting arrest, loitering, trespassing, and failure to obey. Indeed, BPD's own supervisors at Central Booking and prosecutors in the State's Attorney's Office declined to charge more than 11,000 arrests made by BPD officers since 2010."

On November 13, 2017, CBS Chicago reported that, in Evergreen Park, a suburb in Cook County, *police stopped just under 94,000 motorists from 2012 to 2016, records show. It's a staggering number compared with nearby towns, such as Oak Lawn (48,995 stops); Alsip (16,618); and Hometown (4,746).*

*Police officers in Illinois must record the ethnicity of every driver they stop, thanks to legislation co-sponsored by former President Barack Obama, back in 2003 when he was an Illinois state senator.*

*That data, submitted each year to the Illinois Department of Transportation, shows a startling divide in who gets pulled over in Evergreen Park.*

*About 74 percent of Evergreen Park's 20,000 residents are white. Yet, 67 percent of stops last year involved minority drivers.*

*Similar disparities existed in 2015 (66% minority vs. 34% white), 2014 (66% minority vs. 34% white), 2013 (69% minority vs 31% white), and 2012 (69% minority vs. 31% white)."*

 So, when I share with you, what I have known to exist and to be true, based my lived professional police officer experiences, that some police officers look for an in some cases create opportunities to engage minorities one must agree that it is imperative to understand how best to conduct yourself to survive that police encounter.

Earlier, in June 2017, Stanford University Professor Jennifer Eberhardt co-authored a systematic analysis of police body camera footage in collaboration with the Oakland, California Police Department. The study found that "officers consistently used less respectful language with black community members than with white community members, according to the Stanford research."

According to Professor Eberhardt, "Our findings highlight that on the whole police interactions with black community members are more fraught than their interactions with white community members".

Our community did not need a university study to tell us what we have seen as it played out on national news as in the case of Sandra Bland. Police chiefs can no longer, credibly pretend as if the black community did not get it right. So, while they continue to lie and mitigate disrespectful language, unnecessary escalation in uses of force and deadly force we as a community must act wisely.

We have seen the disparities in treatment between the ways in which officers pursue blacks versus the way police pursue white suspects. The outcomes usually very different – even when the root cause of the pursuit was similar.

Reprint from Huffington Post – written by Cheryl Dorsey

*"After a massive 48-day manhunt, three deputy U. S. Marshals saw accused cop killer Eric Frein "moving through tall grass..." and they "could see his hands... he had no weapon." Frein was taken into custody near an abandoned airport hangar without incident. This was very different from the Christopher Dorner manhunt which ended in a shootout and Dorner's death. Very different from the confrontation and detention of accused jaywalker Mike Brown in Ferguson Mo. This was not at all like the detention and capture of "reasonably suspicious" Ezell Ford in Los Angeles.*

*As a retired LAPD sergeant, I know that officers are taught "time* is on our side"; there's no need to 'rush in'; we can wait the suspect out." Why didn't the LAPD and San Bernardino Sheriff's, after surrounding the cabin where Christopher Dorner had been hiding just wait for a while. What was their urgency? It had been reported that, Dorner had been spotted several times during the 9-day manhunt as he eluded authorities; much like Eric Frein. Why did Darren Wilson apparently need to confront Mike Brown for refusing to get out of the middle of the streets?. Why not just wait a while let him continue to walk to the sidewalk? What did the LAPD gang officers need to "talk" to Ezell Ford about that was so urgent that the officers grabbed him precipitating a confrontation which ended in his death. Why not just wait a while - "talk" to him on another day.

Eric Frein was described as a survivalist with an extensive shooting background; someone with a grudge against law enforcement and someone who had prepared for months if not years to ambush a police officer. Eric Frein had been named as one of the FBI's 10 Most Wanted. Am I to assume that Eric Frein was "less frightening" to law enforcement than Dorner, Brown or Ford.

It was reported that Eric Frein had either left or abandoned an AK-47, ammunition and two pipe bombs as though they were bread crumbs for the pursuing officers to discover.

Yet, in the matter of Eric Frein there were no accusations of "scaring the police"', no "hand-hiding" and no "reaching for his waistband". There were no flash bangs thrown. There were no structures burned to the ground once Frein had been spotted. Nope, , Eric Frein had been allegedly caught with his guard down. Eric Frein was simply "ordered to lie face down" and handcuffed.

There seems to be striking similarities between the Christopher Dorner manhunt and the Eric Frein Manhunt; well except Eric Frein is white and Christopher Dorner was black. Eric Frein and Christopher Dorner both appeared to have pre-planned their attacks. Both were considered armed and dangerous. Both were reported to be expert shooters. Both killed law enforcement officers in a cold-blooded and calculated manner. But only one was "ordered to lie face down and was handcuffed."

I do not condone the actions of either Eric Frein or Christopher Dorner.

I am, however, bothered by the apparent disparity in the way police officers "handle" black and brown people. We are not the "boogie man". What was the urgency in taking down Christopher Dorner? What was the exigent circumstance that precipitated the Mike Brown Shooting? What was so "scary" about Ezell Ford's actions? When you have a real bad actor as in cop-killing, white, Eric Frein and a multi-agency strike force can bring about a non-lethal conclusion to his capture - shouldn't that be the norm? I'm just asking.

I admit there is a lot that I don't know about the capture of Frein, however, what I do know is that a young black man, in South Carolina, was asked to show his driver's license to an officer and was shot several times. I know that a passenger, in a car, in Hammond, Indiana was ordered to show his identification and was tasered and arrested when he failed to comply. I know that the coroner, in Oklahoma, ruled the death of Luis Rodriguez a homicide after officers struggled with him in a movie theatre. If Dorner, Brown, Ford or Rodriguez had been white would they still be alive? I'm just asking."

# FIFTY: WHAT'S CHANGED

On the 25th Anniversary of the LA Riots and during an appearance on CNN International with anchor Isha Sesay we discussed what's changed since the LA Riots. There was civil unrest in south central Los Angeles in April 1992 after four LAPD officers were acquitted in the video-taped arrest and beating of a black man, Rodney King. Sadly, not much has changed. I would argue, matters are worse. It seems as if all trust had been eroded – on both sides. And the situation has been exacerbated by unapologetic police department administrators whom, in most instances, haven't seen a use of force they can't support.

A look back in time.

In November 1991, the Los Angeles Times reported on a major "position paper" which had been presented to the Los Angeles Police Commission, This came after the beating of Rodney King by those four white LAPD officers. The concerns being expressed, in part, at that time by the president of the Oscar Joel Bryant Association, a black police officers group stated the following:

"As products of this community, African-American officers are deeply concerned that the safety, quality of life and level of police service be equally provided to all citizens of Los Angeles."

Further, the paper contends that "in the areas of discipline, coveted assignments and recruitment, there is strong evidence to suggest that discriminatory practices have had a high level of tolerance within the department."

"These practices," the paper says, "have had a detrimental effect on African-American officers."

"Cmdr. Robert Gil said Gates has sent a letter to the association president, Sgt. James Craig, in which he noted that the Christopher Commission, formed after the King beating, recently raised some of the same issues in its review this summer of the LAPD. Gil also said that Gates has asked an internal LAPD executive committee to "review and analyze" the association's concerns.

The group maintained that the LAPD has an "unfair disciplinary system" that lowers morale and creates a stressful work environment. "Some African-American officers have lost confidence in the fairness of the entire disciplinary process," the paper said.

"The myth is projected that people residing in this area are criminals and a constant threat to officers," the paper said."

" . . . This lack of training and stereotyping is also the primary cause for many African-Americans being stopped and proned out for allegedly matching a commonly used description for a robbery suspect."

So, what's changed? Not much. In 2013 things appeared to be much the same as in 1991. We can assume this to be true based on the actions and grievances of fired LAPD officer Christopher Dorner and others who widely complained in local news reports.

Here's just a sampling of police deadly encounters which played a part the break down and distrust that currently exists.

On July 14, 2014 an unarmed black man (Eric Garner) was choked to death by New York Police Department (NYPD) officers for his alleged failure to comply with officers' orders during an investigation into the selling of single cigarettes on the street. One of the NYPD officers on scene used what has been referred to by some as a prohibited choke hold as Mr. Garner repeatedly screamed, "I can't breathe, I can't breathe". Several other NYPD officers, including a female sergeant stood and watched the life being choked out of Mr. Garner as they collectively ignored his plea.

A few short weeks later, on August 5, 2014, a twenty-two-year-old black man (John Crawford) was murdered as he casually shopped in a retail store. Mr. Crawford's sin, if you will, was that he had retrieved a BB gun from the retail store's shelf and been seen carrying the BB gun inside the store as he continued to shop. On duty police officers responded to a radio call of a "man with a gun" inside the store and shot and killed Mr. Crawford. Four days after that, on August 9, 2014, an unarmed, black teenager (Mike Brown), in Ferguson, Missouri was shot and killed for allegedly jay walking. I watched in horror, thinking that each nationally televised fatal police incident that followed was the worst thing to have ever happened – until something worse than that happened.

On November 24, 2014, a twelve-year old, black child (Tamir Rice) was murdered while playing with a pellet gun in the park. Well, surely it can't get any worse than that right? Wait, wait a minute, there's more.

On April 2, 2015, 73-year old, pay-for-play (former) volunteer reserve deputy Robert Bates shot and killed an unarmed black man (Eric Harris) who ran from police during an undercover sting operation for alleged illegal gun sales. According to news reports, "Bates said he was merely trying to tase Harris, who was already underneath a pile of deputies attempting to handcuff him." No sir, you wanted to punish Mr., Harris. You wanted to hurt Mr. Harris because he ran. There were already several deputies restraining Mr. Harris; this was another case of "Contempt of Cop ™" plain and simple Bates was eventually arrested and convicted of 2nd degree manslaughter. He received a four-year prison sentence.

What I found most bothersome about this police encounter was that a poorly trained, unqualified, friend to the Sheriff (Stanley Glanz) could "play cop" during a high stake, undercover sting operation. This fact was exacerbated by a report in the Tulsa

World that former sheriff Glanz falsified Bates training record. A clear demonstration of what I have said for years, that the systemic and cultural problems on some police agencies truly start at the very head of that agency and then works its way down to the officers.

So, we cannot act surprised to learn that Glanz' deputies who were on scene during that incident, after Mr. Harris had been mistakenly shot, were recorded making very disturbing comments to Mr. Harris as he took his last breaths.

Mr. Harris could be heard as he cried out, "He shot me! He shot me, man. Oh, my god. I'm losing my breath," to which former deputy Mike Hukeby, replied, according to news reports as he sat straddled on Mr. Harris' chest, "you shouldn't have ran ... shut the fuck up." While another deputy, identified in news reports as Joseph Byars told Mr. Harris, "fuck your breath".

Imagine if you will, the last thing your loved one heard was a police official whose job it is to protect and serve saying, "fuck your breath."

Put yourself in the place of Eric Harris' mother who now knows and must live with the fact that the last image her dying son had was that of a law enforcement officer who looked him in his eye and without one shred of decency nor compassion told him to "shut the fuck up." It was unconscionable. It was heartless. It was despicable.

The FBI later cleared the former Oklahoma sheriff's deputy of violating Eric Harris' civil rights. So, what's changed? Not much.

According to the NY Daily News, both Hukeby and Byars were reassigned after they received death threats. Some the question that I have is how many other Eric Harris' were out there. Clearly this was not the first time that these two deputies treated a person of color with so little regard. And what about the other deputies who stood around and watched – not once trying to intervene. I get that Eric Harris was a suspected illegal gun dealer. He may very well have been a "bad dude." But we have a judicial system; a jury of our peers who determine guilt and punishment. That is not the job of a police officer or in this case a deputy sheriff. As a mother, my heart is broken.

On April 4, 2015, former officer Michael Slager pumped eight rounds into the back of an unarmed black man who had been stopped for a traffic infraction; an inoperable third tail light. The fact that disgraced former officer Slager unnecessarily ended Scott's life was exacerbated by the lie he initially told when Slager alleged that Walter Scott had taken his taser.

Then, on July 10, 2015, an unarmed black woman (Sandra Bland) was wrongfully dragged from of her car, as the in-car police dash camera recorded the entire incident. After being prompted by former officer Brian Encina, Ms. Bland expressed dissatisfaction over the issuance of a traffic citation. She was subsequently arrested and three days later found dead in a jail cell; purportedly from a suicide.

Wait, I'm not done. On July 19, 2015, former University of Cincinnati police officer Ray Tensing lied when he said that he was being "dragged" by a motorist (Sam DuBose) to justify shooting into the car of Mr. DuBose' - killing him. There were other officers on scene who also reported falsely that Tensing had been drug by the driver of the car. Tensing was charged with murder and after two deadlocked juries, according to the Washington Post, prosecutors decided against a third trial. The prosecutors in the case polled several jury members, black and white and were told that they "would never convict a police officer".

I have often said that great deference is given to a police officer. Most want to believe that if we say something – it's the truth. I am here to tell you that some police officers will lie. Some police officers have been proven to be liars. Truth is Spoken Here.

The senseless police shootings and murders of unarmed black men and women continued.

Remember that July 18, 2016, shooting of unarmed Charles Kinsey; the behavorial therapist assisting his severely autistic patient? North Miami police chief Gary Eugene was fired in part for his mishandling of that shooting investigation. North Miami Police Cmdr. Emile Hollant, who was in charge and on scene at the time of the incident, was also fired after an internal affairs investigation by North Miami police determined that Hollant hindered the investigation into the shooting and misled the police chief. In other words, according to CBS 4 Miami, Hollant was "...fired for allegedly lying about his part in the shooting.."

On September 16, 2016, unarmed black man (Terence Crutcher) was murdered as he walked with his hands raised above his head. Former officer Betty Shelby was charged with his murder and acquitted by a jury. Less than two months following her acquittal, Shelby resigned. "Sitting behind a desk, isolated from other officers and Tulsans, isn't for her" according to news reports. In other news, "Her attorney told News On 6 she sat in a tiny cubicle with no windows, doing nothing but pushing paper, adding that Shelby was made to be a beat cop."

On August 10, 2017, Betty Shelby was sworn in during a televised ceremony of one as a reserve deputy sheriff in the Rogers County Sheriff's Office; an unpaid position with the possibility of a full paid assignment later down the road. Okay, so let me get this straight, this heffa is so set on killing another unarmed black man that she will work for free? Who does this? I am going to be ill. So, what has changed? Nothing. Not one damn thing.

According to the Tulsa World, Shelby said this after being sworn in, "As a reserve deputy for the Rogers County Sheriff's Office, I will continue to serve the great state of Oklahoma and strive to improve the relationships between law enforcement agencies, organizations and our community through education and community involvement," she said. "I will work and contribute to the sheriff's department's mission of providing the highest quality of law enforcement services."

I could go on and on, but I must stop. This must stop.

Every police encounter described above could have been and should have been handled differently. Poor tactics, coupled with a rationale to escalate each individual situation to a use of force resulting in an in-custody death was unconscionable. Moreover, in each case described buckets of monies have been thrown at the families without any evidence of a substantive consequence in the case of the officers involved. As we have learned in the case of Betty Shelby she was given the gift of resignation as most officers are and then promptly hired by a neighboring police agency in Tulsa.

Twenty-five years after Rodney King was beaten senseless by four LAPD officers at the end of a car chase- not much has changed.

# FIFTY-ONE: DEADLY FORCE HAS UNINTENDED CONSEQUENCES
### REPRINT LA PROGRESSIVE BY SGT CHERYL DORSEY

27-year-old is Erica Garner, social justice activist and daughter of slain New Yorker Eric Garner died an untimely physical death during the recent holidays; however, I believe she metaphorically died in July 2014 when NYPD officer choked her father Eric Garner to death.

After three long years filled with police department denials and justifications regarding the use of that prohibited chokehold that caused her father to utter those haunting words, "I can't breathe, I can't breathe!"

A chokehold, according to NYPD policy, is only to be used "when an officer's life is in danger." While allegedly selling illicit cigarettes – "loosies" – on the sidewalk hardly seems "life threatening", a grand jury declined to prosecute Pantaleo in Garner's death.

The rationale often given by law enforcement personnel of "failure to comply with an officer's orders" was insufficient and conscionable. In other words, non-compliance – even if true – based on my 20 years of LAPD training and experience does not justify the use of deadly police force.

In September 2017, an NYPD Civilian Complaint Review Board (CCRB) recommended disciplinary action against Pantaleo in Garner's death. Be clear, this finding means very little. While an independent civilian review board is desirable and necessary, their recommendation has no teeth. So, while the CCRB "recommended" discipline, the NYPD's Commissioner has complete autonomy and is the final adjudicator what discipline, if any is given.

Not that prior disciplinary action always deters bad behavior. This was true in the 2012 fatal police shooting of Ramarley Graham, an unarmed black teenager from Brooklyn. Much like Pantaleo, former NYPD officer Richard Haste's conduct had been problematic and well documented.

According to CCRB reports, Pantaleo had been disciplined for police misconduct in the past and had been sued three times prior to the Garner incident. In each case, charges were dismissed, and in one case a settlement was reached.

The progressive news website Think Progress also released leaked documents showing that Pantaleo had 14 individual allegations filed against him and seven disciplinary complaint, four of which had been sustained by investigators.

Disciplinary actions that allow officers to continue in their misconduct – or providing others with the gift of resignation only to be rehired by another police department or worse still to remain on the job as in the case of Pantaleo – is insulting to the families. Discipline can include a penalty of additional training, a written reprimand, reassignment, suspension or termination. So much for deterrence, right?

In most cases, however, officers who commit abuse under the color of authority get little more than a slap on the wrist and the opportunity to move on to another police department and continue with their lives like Pantaleo who married last year.

So, while Pantaleo may at some point be disciplined (yet again), he continues to enjoy all the benefits associated with employment: good pay, a good pension and an ability to breathe – something he clearly denied Eric Garner.

One can only assume this weighed heavy on the heart of Erica. While I make no medical claim as to what caused her death, I'm sure repeated national broadcasts of her father, at the age of 43, being choked to death by a NYPD officer – and her subsequent fight for justice, accountability and reform – may have caused undue stress.

At the end of the day, such stress – coupled with grief, anxiety and probable financial hardships – are unintended consequences of police abuse and far exceed the boundaries of police procedure and protocol.

So, we must pick up the mantle. We must demand officer accountability and substantive administrative action when police misconduct occurs.

Erica Garner probably understood that intuitively. She embraced the cause, fought the good fight and honored her father's memory by courageously trying to fuel a movement that would end the cycle of police abuse, racial injustice – and, in the process, stem the tide of pain and suffering that families like hers have come to know.

In Erica's absence and memory, myself and others are deeply committed to that fight – and equally pledged to advocate for justice, reform and accountability.

# FIFTY-TWO: CONTEMPT OF COP™

Contempt of Cop™ is a real thing. I watched incident after incident as each made headline news around the nation where police officers, in most case, escalated an encounter to a use of excessive force and in some cases deadly force. These officers would later falsely report a failure to comply on the part of the citizen; an attempt to disarm the officer of his taser or weapon; or some other perceived threat. Based on my training and experience as a patrol officer and patrol supervisor I opined that these officers had made a conscious decision to punish the alleged violator; Contempt of Cop™.

Police officers are trained to use deadly force as a last resort. Deadly force is that thing that we do when we, as police officers, have exhausted every other tactical tool available. Officers are trained to use only that force necessary to overcome the resistance of a suspect to effect and arrest and then de-escalate the situation once the suspect is in control/custody.

Officers are not trained to shoot an alleged perpetrator because that person is failing to comply with orders or won't shut their mouth. Folks being unhappy about being cited for a traffic violation is to be expected. And now because of the onslaught of aggressive and seemingly unnecessary detentions citizens are filming police interactions in minority and poor white communities.

Reprint from Huffington Post – written by Cheryl Dorsey

*"Beatriz Paez is just one of the many recent victims of what I like to call "Contempt of Cop"; fortunately, Paez lived to talk about her encounter.*

*Ms. Paez witnessed plain clothes officers detaining several individuals at gunpoint and decided to record the incident on* her cell phone. One of the officers, a U.S. Marshal, told Paez to stop recording and when she failed to obey his order the unidentified marshal charged towards her; snatched her phone out of her hand and hurled it to the ground. But he wasn't done - the marshal then stomped on the phone and punted it down the sidewalk. Luckily, Paez had someone else recording her as she recorded the officers.

As a retired twenty year veteran sergeant of the Los Angeles Police Department (LAPD), I understand that some police officers have an absolute expectation that if they tell you to do something, you better. When you don't, sometimes, there is a price to pay.

Police Officers have tremendous power. That small group of officers who have garnered so much of the public's attention lately have the ability to take hours out of your life as in an unlawful detention on a Friday followed by a weekend in jail if the individual does not have the financial wherewithal to make bail. An errant officer could cost someone hundreds or maybe thousands of dollars by issuing a traffic citation and towing your vehicle. An over zealous officer can stop you, drag you out of your car, beat you up, requiring expensive follow-up medical treatment once released from jail on that bogus "resisting" arrest and battery on a police officer charge or you just may end up losing your life.

Contempt of Cop is not real you say? Ask Floyd Dent of Inkster, Michigan, who was recently exonerated of all charges after he had been brutally beaten by [fired] Inkster Police Officer William Melendez aka RoboCop after Dent allegedly committed a traffic infraction. Melendez has been charged with two felony counts. Ask Mario Givens who was yanked from his residence by fired SC Officer Michael Slager; investigating a burglary at Givens' home. (The same Slager who killed Walter Scott during a traffic stop.) Givens was tasered and booked for "resisting" arrest when Slager decided Givens did not really live there. The charge was later dismissed.

These incidents are sadly commonplace. Police initiate a traffic stop or their other favorite — an investigative stop; escalate a seemingly benign encounter to a use of force incident and then arrest the citizen for either resisting or battery on a police officer. Both of these charges are difficult to refute without the benefit of a video recording.

Here are just a few more examples of contempt of cop. Remember Marlene Pinnock, the homeless grandmother walking along the Santa Monica freeway in Los Angeles and former CHP officer Daniel Andrew who straddled Pinnock MMA-style and punched her repeatedly in the face and head when she failed to obey his order. CHP paid Pinnock $1.5 million. San Bernardino County Sheriff's recently paid Francis Pusok $650,000 after Pusok attempted to evade officers on horseback. They were the lucky ones.

Tragically, 52-year-old Walter Scott, during a traffic stop for a broken third tail light, exited his car and ran on foot eluding 32-yr old [fired] officer Michael Slager and paid with his life. Apparently, when you run from a police officer and as in this case and the officer lacks the physical stamina to catch you - five shots to the back is the penalty.

Need More proof? Eric Harris ran from Tulsa City Deputy sheriff's during an undercover sting operation and was told as he [Harris] took what were probably his last breaths by one of the deputies, "you f*cking ran". So, let's be clear — if you run from the police there is a price to pay. Gun dealer or not — when did police become judge, jury and executioner?

I could go on and on. Contempt of Cop is real. There does not appear to be any other explanation for the loss of life in these next incidents. Ezell Ford, a mentally ill man in Los Angeles who did not want to "talk" with LAPD gang officers during an "investigative stop"; Kelly Thomas, another mentally man who was beaten by a [former] Fullerton Police Officer who was reportedly overheard saying, "I'm gonna f*ck you up" as he placed black leather gloves on his hands and Freddie Gray in Baltimore, an alleged "career criminal" made eye contact with an officer and then ran; Gray died from a partially severed spine and broken vertebrae. Career criminal or not — you don't get to kill him officer.

My thoughts: Bad police tactics can lead to bad shootings. Poor planing and a lack of communication between partner officers can lead to excessive force or even deadly force. An inability to empathize and relate to the community served can also lead to devaluation of a human life.

During my twenty year career, while working south central Los Angeles, I had my fair share of alleged criminals run from my partner and I. That's what criminals do; most don't want to go back to prison. So if an officer understands that fleeing suspects are inherent to police work; officer, get ready to exercise officer.

Why would an officer feel justified in shooting someone simply because they ran? I'll tell you why - because these officers have been able to get away with murder; literally. Police Chiefs circle the wagons, the department begins to craft a[fish] tale and then the victim/suspect is vilified.

Bad guys do bad thing; I get that. Whether a suspect is a so-called "thug", a drug user, a gun seller or just dumb in public [for running] - police officers should not be allowed to shoot and maim or kill them on the spot for a perceived slight.

When police officers become personally involved; when police officers believe the failure to obey an order is a direct affront to them - excessive force and sometimes deadly force follows.

I understand that if sense was common everybody would have it. I understand that common sense is not something that can be taught. I understand that compassion and empathy is not a learned behavior. That's who you are at your core. Police officers found wanting in this regard should be plucked from the rank *and file and banned from serving on another police department. Recurring and intermittent psychological evaluations might help identify those troubled officers. Let's start there."*

So understand, suspects running from an officer is inherent to police work. If a suspect takes off running, as a police officer you now have two choices; 1) get ready to get some exercise or 2) let the suspect go. It is when officers take noncompliance or attempts to evade arrest personal that Contempt of Cop becomes an issue.

As a frequent guest commentator on CNN, Inside Edition, Fox News and HLN TV as well as various radio networks, I have regularly spoken on the Contempt of Cop™ phenomenon. While I am certainly not a psychologist, there appeared to be many more instances of Contempt of Cop™ which involved male officer vs male citizen than female officer vs citizen; although there are no official statistics on this that I am aware of. As a woman, I/we are just wired differently and charging a suspected criminal like two rams on a steep cliff is not what first comes to mind. If you understand and accept that becoming a victim of Contempt of Cop™, then let's have a real discussion about how avoid it.

In addition to me pointing out what I think should be the obvious given what has been played out in front of us on the national news I want to also share ways in which "Surviving Police Encounters" can also be a real thing. I have created a series of lectures, forums and workshops wherein situation simulations will be presented, discussed and solutions will be offered to help you survive that police encounter. Now, there are no guarantees. Be clear. But if you recognize the red flags that some officers raise just before they are about to "put hands" on you this may give you reason to conduct yourself in a way you are more likely to survive that police encounter.

Here are, in my opinion, a couple of quick examples of Contempt of Cop ™. In the instance of Sandra Bland and former officer

Brian Encina. When Encina returned to Ms. Bland's car with the completed traffic citation and asked her why she seemed "upset" about the ticket; she responded in a way any reasonable person might at the thought of paying hundreds of dollars for something that was bogus to begin with. Encina, in my opinion, then escalated what was a done deal; the ticket had been written and the encounter was technically over but for Ms. Bland's signature on the citation. Encina appeared to become upset himself and ordered Ms. Bland to "put the cigarette out". What then pursued was a contempt of cop situation with threats being made by Encina to "light you up" with his taser for his perceived non-compliance. Encina escalated the situation which resulted in a use of force incident. Ms. Bland was later arrested for that thing that all police officers will arrest someone for – resisting, interfering; when they have nothing else, but they have put hands on you and now they must take you to jail for something. They can't just let you go.

In many instances when an unnecessary use of force has occurred, followed by an arrest by the offending police officer based on manufactured probable cause for interfering or resisting arrest; charges are later dropped if you had been fortunate enough to survive the police encounter. But what about the inconvenience of having been arrested in the first place. What about the financial hardships that follow an individual who was held on bail, potential loss of employment and attorney's fees. This not only adversely effects the person arrested; but also, their family.

In the police detention of Eric Garner, who was accused of selling single cigarettes on a sidewalk in the city of New York, he had been confronted by several police officers and ordered to "turn around". According to the officers' version, Mr. Garner failed to "comply" with their orders and was subsequently choked to death; Contempt of Cop™.

Police officers are not trained to choke someone who refused to turn around. Police officers are not trained to shoot someone in the back when they run away. If sense were common everyone would have it. You can't teach an officer common sense. An officer can't open a police manual and read about. Police officers are taught however, to escalate and de-escalate a use of force during an encounter. Officers are not trained to punish people who are uncooperative, mouthy and attempt to evade arrest. An uncooperative arrestee s inherent to police work. If a suspect has decided to run the officer has two choices; get ready to get some exercise or let the suspect, go. After all, that suspect probably lives in the area and the officer works in the area; get 'em another time.

An example of an egregious failure to de-escalate a police encounter involved former McKinney, Texas officer Eric Casebolt.

On June 5, 2015, officers responded to a call which involved a group of black teenagers who were attending a pool party in a community where many of the teens allegedly did not live. Video recording of the incident showed Casebolt as he chased various teenagers, on foot, in different directions as he barked orders. As the teens attempted to scatter, Casebolt directed his attention toward a young, black, bikini-clad teenager, grabbed the young girl, hurled her to the ground and then straddled her. When the teenager protested the officer's abuse Casebolt became more physically aggressive with the teen. Police officers are not taught to straddle bikini clad teenager; if sense were common, everyone would have it. The teenager was later arrested and charged. Contempt of Cop™. The officer failed to de-escalate the situation. The use of force was unnecessary. Casebolt later resigned from the department

There were signs and red flags. When a police officer moves around from police department to police department like an athlete changes teams; there's a problem. Many times, there is a history of bad behavior, poor performance standards or misconduct in the officer's personnel file; as in the case of Timothy Loehmann who shot and killed twelve-year old Tamir Rice.

Casebolt had worked for two other police agencies before he had been hired by McKinney PD. He had previously worked as a trooper for the Texas Department of Public Safety and in Oklahoma as a city police officer, according to reports. His reason for leaving those agencies was unknown.

In July 2015, Seneca police lieutenant Mark Tiller shot and killed nineteen-year old Zachary Hammond as he drove his car away from an alleged "drug sting operation." Tiller escalated a police encounter to a deadly force incident rather than de-escalating the situation. Contempt of Cop™. Tiller had not been convicted in the matter because he said he "believed he was going to be run over" by Hammond. The judge in this case however, described a video recording that captured the incident as "troublesome" and said it "raised questions." Tiller was later fired.

An Associated Press article, in Balch Spring, Texas, reported that in April 2016, fifteen-year old Jordan Edwards was murdered by former police officer Roy Oliver. Oliver and his partner had responded to a radio call of "drunken teens at a party." Edwards had been riding in a car with friends and the driver ignored Oliver's order to "stop" as they were leaving the party. Edwards was shot in the back. Contempt of Cop™. Oliver was arrested and indicted for Edwards' murder and four counts of aggravated assault. That case was pending.

What parent would expect that having allowed a child to attend a party would result in a phone call advising that the police had just shot your child as he was leaving the party. So, as a mother myself, I am concerned that it in my community, it is no longer a matter of "if "a loved one may fall victim to Contempt of Cop™ any more but more like – when. We need an intervention. We need resolutions and solutions.

Roy Oliver, he had a long history of hostile and aggressive behavior according to court records filed. There had been documented evidence that he was perhaps psychological unfit to be a police officer. It was reported in a news story that "as far back as the eighth grade, Oliver carried a knife and a stun gun, wore paramilitary clothing and was a member of a group called 'Caucasians in Effect' in which he posted swastikas in public places..." In a 2011 pre-employment psychological examination it was reported that "Oliver may feel so insensitive to threat that his judgment may be impaired in evaluating the risk of danger" and "his sense of entitlement may be so strong that the possibility of his behaving in an antisocial manner must be considered."

In 2013 Oliver was reportedly, "uncooperative and used profanity in his responses to an attorney" during a jury trial. Two weeks before Jordan Edwards' death, Oliver was "accused of committing aggravated assault on two women during which he displayed a firearm." Perhaps, a psychological re-evaluation was warranted in the Oliver case.

If police departments fail to provide adequate and regular psychological re-evaluations of its rank and file beyond first hire; unnecessary fatal police encounters because of Contempt of Cop™ will continue. If police officers are not held personally accountable for violating police policy and/or law this will continue. Errant officers are given the "gift of resignation" and, in some cases, move on to another police department.

The same may have been true of fired police officer Michael Slager. After being stopped for a traffic violation, Slager attempted to use a taser on Walter Scott. Scott ran and then Slager pumped eight rounds into his back as he ran way, killing him. According to The Post and Courier, Slager, had previously tasered two other men; Mario Givens and Jerome Stanley. Slager had not been held accountable for those actions.

Mario Givens attempted to file a personnel complaint against Slager; it was dismissed. Both men later filed a civil suit against the department and dropped their charges against Slager after a financial settlement was reached. Would a psychological re-evaluation of Slager after the Givens and Stanley incidents have prevented the murder of Mr. Scott? We will never know.

Young people, old people, men and yes women need to educate themselves on what is required to stand a chance of surviving police encounters. It is important to know your rights; but it is imperative to "know that officer" who just pulled you over. It is a matter of life and death to recognize the red flags and warning signs. You may have just been pulled over by a "Michael Slager" or a "Ray Tensing" or a "Betty Shelby".

You had better comply with whatever that officer has just told you to do. "Holding court curbside" with certain officers will get you tasered, choked or murdered.

Become educated on how to best deal with an over-zealous, drunk with power cop. Avoid making your family the next newly made millionaire in your town because, "you know your rights!" Survive the police encounter.

Be clear, even if you live through the police encounter and subsequent detention, this does not necessarily mean that you are out of the woods-so to speak.

As in the case of Roswell GA police officers Courtney Brown & Kristee Wilson who were relieved of duty after their in-car police bodycam showed the officers laughed and concocted an arrest of a female motorist based on the flip of a coin after allegedly stopping her for speeding. The actual arrest of Sarah Webb which occurred in April 2018, had not been made public until the police video was leaked to a local news station in July 2018.

The released police video resulted in reckless driving charges being dropped by the prosecutor and the officers relieved from duty pending an internal investigation.

Now let me ask, do you think this was the first time these two officers used the flip of a coin to decide someone's fate? How many other victims of Contempt of Cop™ currently exist in the city of Roswell, Georgia? How many others have lost their freedom and gained a police record because of the flip of a coin? And, why did it take Police Chief Grant so long to take administrative action?

Being a victim of Contempt of Cop™ can cost your freedom, your dignity, time, money and sometimes your life. You've been warned!

# FIFTY-THREE: COMPLY AND COMPLAIN

During a symposium on the campus of Prairie View A&M University; the 2018 Royce West Forum and Lecture Series on Race, Trust and Police Legitimacy at the Texas Juvenile Crime Prevention Center, College of Juvenile Justice and Psychology, my message to the students regarding surviving police encounters was simple– "make it home".

It was exciting to engage and converse with so many young people who were really interested in making a difference in their community. Young people, many of whom want to do more than just complain about mistreatment and perceived ills. They want to actively engage and get involved in the process of resolving this crisis.

We have seen what happens when someone is stopped by a police officer and initial compliance is an issue- bad things happen. Sometimes compliance is insufficient in ensuring we will live through the encounter. So, we do the best we can to reduce the possibility of being harmed or killed because our mere black existence frightens some police officers.

Add to this, citizen complaints to police dispatchers about black folks doing the things we have always done – things they do. Suddenly, these activities in which black people are engaged in, in public spaces like parks and coffee shops are seemingly also cause for concern and police intervention. Therefore, it is important to comply regarding the mistreatment and complain later. Complain to mayors, police chiefs and any independent review board as well as going public using social media platforms will hopefully help to bring about reform.

Reprint LA Wave Newspaper – written by Cheryl Dorsey

*"Starbucks CEO Kevin Johnson plans to close more than 8,000*

U.S. locations on May 29, 2018, to conduct racial-bias training to prevent discrimination in his stores.

After initially defending his officers' actions, Philadelphia Police Commissioner Richard Ross has apologized to Rashon Nelson and Donte Robinson, the two black men who were arrested while waiting for a business meeting at a Philadelphia Starbucks.

I am not comforted by Ross' apology. The commissioner admittedly stated he made the situation worse when he initially defended his officers' actions, yet Ross still contends that "race did not play a role in the officers' actions."

Ross, who is black, did what we have seen other police administrators do when one of their own acts out of order; circle the wagons, try to explain the inexplicable and attempt to protect his department.

While Ross has promised to enact policy change for his officers going forward when dealing with "defiant trespass," the question that begs to be answered is, "Will this change include sensitivity training and a common-sense approach to dealing with the minority community?"

Commissioner Ross, you do understand that there is a distinct difference between enforcing the "letter of the law" versus the "spirit of the law?"

Apparently, Commissioner Ross serves at the pleasure of the Mayor Jim Kenney, whom undoubtedly had a little something to do with Ross finding the need to "articulate his changed perspective."

Naturally, "no charges were filed" against the men. That is often the case when police officers abuse their authority and act with impunity. Police officers have tremendous autonomy in the discharge of their duties.

In an instance like the one involving Nelson and Robinson, the officers certainly had options. Unfortunately, common sense did not prevail. I always say if sense was common, everybody would have it.

Thankfully, the young men in this situation did not lose their lives. But an apology is insufficient.

Officers don't start off by being over-zealous. Perhaps the Philadelphia Commission on Human Relations should conduct a personnel review of the two involved officers' history in dealing with the minority community. It is important to ensure that there aren't more problems. Is there a pattern of this type of behavior?

As a retired 20-year veteran police officer/supervisor (sergeant), a black woman and mother of sons, it is my hope that whatever Starbucks employee training, police policy changes by Commissioner Ross and review by the Philadelphia Commission on Human Relations come from this unfortunate incident, that corporations and police departments will use this teachable moment to ensure a respectful, dignified response to and a better cultural understanding of the communities in which they find themselves situated."

Police officers have a myriad of reasons as to why they might initiate an encounter. It is important to understand that there are circumstances, which may seem unreasonable at first glance, that are unknown to the detainee when stopped by the police that are in fact justified.

In many cases, when officers are responding to a call for service they are relying on and reacting to information given to them by a 9-1-1 operator; this information, which sometimes includes a suspect description, may be incorrect either accidentally or on purpose.

So, as a citizen there is some responsibility to adhere to an offers orders as well as some culpability if you don't and situations escalate to a use of force incident. That means, running from the police, failing to turn around and submit to being searched and/or handcuffed or just refusing to present your identification can escalate a situation and, in some instances, has ended in a deadly encounter.

And then there are those times when some police officers are just looking for a fight – so to speak.

On January 26, 2018, what should have been a 10-minute officer-initiated Q&A ending with a parking ticket being issued or stern warning quickly escalated to a violent assault and arrest.

Given the circumstances in totality and the early morning hours-spirit of the law vs letter of the law was on display. Common sense should have been the order of the day - instead what Sterling Brown, guard on the Milwaukee Bucks received was-Contempt of Cop©.

Approximately five months following Brown's detention and arrest, the Milwaukee police department released body cam footage of the violent encounter between several of its officers and Sterling Brown earlier that year.

The lone patrol officer had been waiting for Brown to return to his car which appeared to have been parked across several marked parking spaces in what appeared to be a mostly vacant, desolate Walgreens parking lot at 2 a.m. on a still dark and rainy early morning.

As Brown neared his car, the officer could be heard as he confronted Brown using an unnecessarily harsh, aggressive and disrespectful tone.

Research has shown that police often speak very differently to black motorists than they do to white motorists upon contact. That morning was no different.

The officer's tone and the way he questioned Brown was

snarky, aggressive and seemed to beg for a similar response from Brown. The officer could be heard asking Brown questions that in my police supervisor mind were intended to escalate the situation; first verbally and ultimately physically.

As a twenty-year veteran sergeant of the Los Angeles Police Department, I have often managed and resolved similar conflicts during an officer-initiated traffic stop. As the professional on scene, the officer's job was to advise Brown of the reason for the encounter, issue Brown a traffic ticket (at his discretion) and let Brown go on about his business.

So, for Milwaukee Mayor Tom Barrett to infer otherwise is insulting and disingenuous. Sterling Brown nor any other citizen has the responsibility to diffuse and de-escalate a police encounter situation. The officers on scene that morning were purportedly trained professionals and an unruly, uncooperative detainee (Not that Sterling brown was either) is inherent to police work and does not give any police officer license to assault under the color of authority.

But the isolation, location and early morning hours seemed almost too irresistible for this officer.

So instead, this first officer requested additional units and continued to badger Brown as he awaited his back-up. At one point the officer can be heard when asked by Brown, "what are we doing? The officer's response was, "we are waiting."

This first officer initiating the confrontation requested additional units- not because Brown presented a threat; Not because Brown was being uncooperative; but because once the cavalry arrived they were going to "put in work." Police talk for "Brown was about to get his ass handed to him."

The body cam showed Brown was compliant as the officer stalled and awaited the arrival of back-up units. The officer asked Brown for his identification and Brown complied.

But the back-up unites hadn't arrived yet, so the officer needed to stall. And to fill the time the officer continued to berate Brown.

As more and more responding units arrived adrenaline and excitement no doubt began to rise. Most of the officers exited their patrol cars and took a position of advantage - circling Brown as they awaited the signal.

Brown now surrounded and alone in this desolate, dark, wet, parking lot. Must have surely believed that he was about to be the next Eric Garner, Sandra Bland or Michael Brown.

These officers were not there to protect- but they were about to serve.

This positioning and re-positioning of the officers continued for several more minutes, as more black and white calls hastily pulled up to the scene, slamming their police cars abruptly into the park position with the menacing red and blue lights illuminating the once semi lit parking lot.

The responding officers, all male and seemingly white, each appeared to take turns peppering Brown with questions- no doubt designed to be upsetting and off-putting. Yet Brown remained composed and compliant.

The officer who first started this mess was seen talking and visiting with other units as they arrived and now mostly filled the parking lot with their presence. A few of them remained seated in their patrol cars as the first officer intermittently conversed with them; leaving the newly on scene officers to be "tagged into the fray".

Let's face it, who wants to stand in a parking lot on a dark and wet night while six or ten cops ask you the same questions over and over? No one.

Brown continued to comply. He dares not complain. Sterling

needed to make it home.

This was no doubt about to get ugly. Sterling Brown was alone and a black male, in an isolated convenience store parking lot at 2 a.m. in the morning, surrounded by a squadron of police cars with flashing red and blue lights.

Suddenly, one of the responding officers could be heard yelling, "take your hands out of your pocket."

Based on my years of experience on the LAPD, when an officer yells out some command like "stop kicking me, don't move, or take your hands out of your pocket"; this is akin to the starting gun being sounded at a track meet.

Like a pack feral dogs, several off the officers, without provocation by Sterling Brown, swarmed him and began barking commands from every direction. Then, Taser! Taser! Taser!

Of course, Brown was subsequently arrested for that thing that cops love to arrest a detainee for when they have nothing else; resisting, interfering. These are the "go-to" charges when officers put hands on someone and now they cannot just let that person go. That person must go to jail for something. Never mind, that it will be a district attorney reject days later.

These officers on that night understood the process. It's the culture. It's condoned. It's the blue wall.

Research indicates racial bias exists. Why? Because it is acquiesced, condoned and then minimized and mitigated at every level within some police departments and then further justified by some Mayors who exacerbate the situation with their tacit approval.

I know firsthand that some white officers yearn to work in those neighborhoods where black and brown folks are plentiful. On the LAPD, the code word for those neighborhoods were "busy divisions".

I've heard many white officers gushing at the possibility of being assigned to a "busy division" in south-central Los Angeles. I also know firsthand that some white officers enjoy working "morning watch"- that is generally after 10 p.m. Why? Because under the cover of darkness, these errant, over-zealous officers can conduct themselves in a manner much like they did on January 26, 2018.

It wasn't a coincidence that so many officers showed up for a mere alleged parking violator. My guess is that those officers on scene at 2:00 a.m. were like-minded. We can surmise this to be true because not one of them stepped in and said, "that's enough".

Yeah, it's been reported, in what I term police code talk by Milwaukee Police Chief Alfonso Morales that the involved officers were "disciplined"; whatever that means.

Understand, Chief Morales decides what "discipline" looks like and the fact that he refused to answer any questions during his press conference spoke volumes. But what Chief Morales was reported to have done on the day the body cam footage was released was to assure the community that the involved officers as well as any bystander officers would absolutely retain their jobs.

In other words, they will live to offend again. Or in the case of Sterling Brown; bully, berate and beat up another lone, black male citizen if he is unlucky enough to be observed by one of Milwaukee's finest, exiting a convenience store at 2 a. m.

Discipline can be as simple as a paper penalty or reprimand. Since this incident has been under the radar all these months, my guess is the discipline was minimal at best. What we know is that all the officers involved STILL HAVE THEIR JOBS.

Now that Chief Alfonso Morales has let the public in on his little secret, no more circling the wagons. Time for substantive accountability and consequences for the officers involved.

So, Mayor Barrett and Chief Morales, Sterling Brown and the community which you proclaim to protect and serve are going to need more than just an apology on this one.

And as we patiently wait for police chiefs and ultimately their officers to "do the right thing" recognize that as law abiding citizens there is a very important role that you must abide. Comply. There is nothing disrespectful about going home- intact, after a police encounter. Everyone approaches these encounters with a little trepidation. You want to go home – the police want to go home. So, when Harith Augustus was stopped by Chicago police for allegedly carrying a concealed weapon neither knew anything about the other.

Rather than comply with the officers' orders and desires to search him, Augustus chose to spin away to avoid the grasp of one of the officers on scene. It did not end well.

Harith Augustus was shot and killed. Harith Augustus was in deed carrying a weapon concealed underneath his shirt. Whether or not he was licensed to carry is of little consequence to his family. He's dead. It would have been so much smarter if Augustus had just complied with the officers and allowed them to investigate the circumstances of his gun possession and if in fact the possession had been legal, perhaps he might still be alive.

Police officers are sometimes given information from the police dispatch operator, prior to arrival on scene, that forms the basis by which we act when confronting an individual. We want to go home too. Making demands and trying to hold court curbside will end badly. Police officers are trained to gain control of a situation and thus citizen compliance during a detention is a mandate. It is the affirmative responsibility of every citizen to allow an officer to do their job. Comply. And. Complain.

There is certainly a myriad of reasons why an officer may engage a citizen and currently there is a new phenomenon that black folks must navigate through. You've heard of bar-b-que Betty, Permit Patty and Coupon Carl; those white folks that suddenly have been reporting black folks to the police for doing the things that we have been involved in, unmolested forever.

Until police departments can come up with a remedy to curtail the Bettys and Carls  black people need to comply and complain not if- but when it happens to you.

And here's what the complaint should look like. Create a paper trail of your complaint, contact police chiefs, mayors, city leaders like council persons, independent police review boards, inspectors general who may have police oversight and demand a financial penalty be assessed to any 9-1-1 abuser who diverts emergency services as in the cases of Betty, Patty and Carl.

It is an easy fix and this foolishness would stop yesterday if the abuser was charged for emergency services required to respond to a family bar-b-queuing in the park. A quick tally of the hourly wages for six officers and one sergeant billed to the offender will deter that behavior. I suggest further that the offender be flagged in the police data base and a second offense should result in a misdemeanor arrest.

So as cute as those memes are – let's put some teeth behind our disdain. Get involved, engaged and demand justice from your local police/legislators.

Comply. And. Complain

# FIFTY-FOUR: SOLUTIONS, RESOLUTIONS & SOCIAL ADVOCACY

You have been warned. Manufactured probably cause and reasonable suspicion (activity) are being used by some officers to engage minority and poor white communities. These encounters often end in unnecessary uses of force, fatal police shootings and continue to on happen a regular basis in communities of color. Expect nothing to change unless and until community members get involved, engaged and educated. Change and police reform will come from within police departments, so to that end I say – join! Changes in the ways in which police officers can engage communities will necessarily involve legislation, to that end I say – focus!

"The Racially Targeted Tobacco Crackdown Coming To A City Near You"

Reprint from OZY – written by Cheryl Dorsey

Imagine a police officer snatching a "suspicious" Black man off the street to spend the weekend in jail. The probable cause? Dealing Newport cigarettes.

A growing under-the-radar movement to criminalize menthol cigarettes is starting us on a slippery slope toward just such a scenario on a street corner near you. San Francisco was the first city to ban the sale of flavored tobacco products, including menthol cigarettes, followed by Contra Costa County, California, and the city of Oakland.

In Minnesota, St. Louis Park banned the sale of flavored tobacco, while Minneapolis, St. Paul and Shoreview passed new limits on its sale. Both chambers of the New Jersey legislature now are considering prohibition against the sale and distribution of menthol and clove cigarettes, which would be the nation's first statewide ban.

Why is this so important? The World Health Organization points out that menthol is used more frequently by younger smokers, women and minorities, and it is more enticing for people both to start and continue smoking. While fighting tobacco addiction is a worthy public health goal — and menthol products can be especially dangerous — criminalization is an imperfect solution.

At this point, a business in these areas would face only a fine or the loss of a license for selling the banned items — and it's no offense for someone to possess menthols. But these policies set minority communities on a dangerous path. As a retired veteran sergeant in the Los Angeles Police Department, I am most concerned about the unintended consequences of targeting menthol. Why not ban all tobacco products?

You have to start with the legacy of the War on Drugs in the 1970s and the War on Crime in the 1990s, both of which caused soaring incarceration rates of Black men and women. Considering that more than 80 percent of Blacks who smoke prefer menthol tobacco, I see an additional pathway to the penal system.

Let's not pretend that some police officers don't already have a plethora of ways at their disposal to engage members of minority communities under the guise of probable cause, reasonable suspicion and investigative stops. There are plenty of examples of how these "investigative stops" can quickly escalate into lethal uses of force.

An unsuspecting Black male no longer needs to just "fit the description" as a reason for detention. Officers in places where menthol tobacco is banned could begin to stop and question someone who may smell suspicious. As a patrol officer and patrol supervisor for over two decades, I know first-hand how creatively an officer can articulate probable cause. So much for enforcing rules based on the spirit of the law — the letter of the law rules the day. Errant, drunk with power officers have a new tool in their petty probable-cause arsenal. And since great deference is given to an officer's version of events, I see potential for wide-ranging abuses.

This kind of heavy-handed authority allows for an arrest on a Friday evening with a court date on Monday, followed by a district attorney rejecting the case for prosecution due to insufficient evidence. In such a case, the low probable-cause threshold had been met and the arrestee was ultimately released. The system considers it no harm, no foul. But the officers just took 72 hours from someone's life, knowing there was insufficient cause to prosecute. Police officers have a symbiotic relationship with prosecutors and understand which arrests are deemed viable by the district attorney before a jury. And there is never a consequence for officers who abuse the system in this manner.

These confrontations easily could turn ugly. One can almost see the confusion, disbelief and resistance in a suspect, leading to an alleged "failure to comply" that will surely follow the initial contact. Next comes a resisting arrest charge, or worse — death.

We've seen this before. Eric Garner, Sandra Bland, Ezell Ford — all were victims of what's known in law-enforcement circles as "contempt of cop," when they allegedly failed to comply with an officer's order. Remember, it was tobacco that caused Garner's fateful police encounter: He was illegally selling individual cigarettes. So, rather than criminalize those who smoke and create unnecessary police interaction with selectively enforced tobacco laws, why not educate people better on tobacco's dangers?

To start, let's educate people on the perils of a menthol ban. There's still time left to stop this discriminatory movement in its tracks before the smoke spreads any further.

*The author is a retired sergeant in the Los Angeles Police*

Department."

Legislation that allows errant police officers to hide under the shelter of the Police Officer's Bill of rights must be passed. Most police chiefs serve at the pleasure of a mayor – voice your resolve at the ballot box to effect substantive policy change and police reform that will better quality of life concerns in your community. Since Law enforcement organizations have staunchly opposed previous legislative attempts to strengthen the use of force standard it is imperative that the community get engaged.

I have long supported officers who have been found guilty of malice and violating shooting policy should be held personally responsible for any financial civil judgement.

*To that end, the Baltimore Sun reported in part," As many as nine Baltimore police officers could have to pay tens of thousands of dollars in damages after juries found they acted with "actual malice" in the course of making arrests ... Lt. Gene Ryan, the police union's president, told his members that the city had "generally supported" officers in the past by paying punitive damages as well as compensatory damages awarded in civil jury trials." Ryan informed his members that "...Davis, a former federal judge who joined the city last year, has changed that policy.*

*What this means is that police officers are now required to pay these punitive damage awards, which can amount to thousands of dollars, out of their own pockets."*

*But the former Baltimore City Solicitor confirmed that this has long been the city's policy. He said the Baltimore law department has held for years that taxpayers are not responsible for paying punitive damages when a jury finds the officers acted with malice. He said such cases arise rarely because the city often settles cases before trial.*

*The article went on to report, that "...two men, Leo Joseph Green and James Green, won a jury verdict against Officers Nicholas Chapman, Daraine Harris, Brian Loiero, Marcus Smothers and Nathan Ulmer. The suit alleged battery, false arrest and violations of constitutional rights stemming from an incident that occurred June 13, 2013, in the 6000 block of Moravia Road in Northeast Baltimore.*

*The jury called for $147,100 in compensatory damages, as well as $40,000 in punitive damages. One of the officers faces paying $15,000, with the others responsible for smaller amounts."*

If officers are held personally responsible, this foolishness will stop – yesterday.

In California lawmakers have proposed a dramatic change in the standard under which police officers can use deadly force, following the deadly police shooting of Stephon Clark. According to reports the legislation would authorize officers to use deadly force "only when it is necessary to prevent imminent and serious bodily injury or death -- that is, if, given the totality of the circumstances, there was no reasonable alternative to using deadly force, including warnings, verbal persuasion, or other nonlethal methods of resolution or de-escalation," according to Democratic Assemblywoman Shirley Weber of San Diego, a co-author of the measure. The proposal would also establish that a homicide by an officer is 'not justified if the officer's gross negligence contributed to making the force 'necessary,' according to the proposal." The bill is known as the Police Accountability and Community Protection Act.

Recognize red flags and warning signals when detained by police and comply with officers' orders to make sure you stand a chance of surviving that police encounter. Then create a paper trail to memorialize the incident and send the written complaint to everyone in that officer's chain of command. A 2017 research study has validated and demonstrated the manner in which some officers run roughshod in minority communities. I have said many times that there are two departments within the LAPD; one south of the Santa Monica freeway (south central Los Angeles) which is comprised of mostly black and Hispanic residents and the LAPD north of the Santa Monica freeway which encompasses some of the more affluent areas of Los Angeles. I know that officers will not treat residents in West LA Division or North Hollywood Division the same way they do in 77th Division (south central Los Angeles) or South East Division. Now there is a study that speaks to my truths.

In June 2017, the results of a study which was co-authored by Jennifer Eberhardt, a professor of psychology at Stanford University was made available. The study included a *"systematic analysis of police body camera footage which showed that police officers tended to speak less respectful to black residents than to white residents."* According to the reported study, *"the racial disparities in respectful speech remained even after the researchers controlled for the race of the officer, the severity of the infraction, and the location and outcome of the stop."*

The researchers had demonstrated in part that, *"white residents were 57 percent more likely than black residents to hear a police officer say the most respectful utterances, such as apologies and expressions of gratitude like 'thank you'. Meanwhile, black community members were 61 percent more likely than white residents to hear an officer say the least respectful utterances, such as informal titles like "dude" and "bro" and commands like 'hands on the wheel"*

So, with that in mind, I want the reader to return home safely after a police encounter. It is my hope that the reader will also share this information with loved ones to make sure that they too survive the police encounter.

Having survived the police encounter, from the stand point of being able to walk away from a detention uninjured is the first part; the second is not going to jail unnecessarily.

In that February 2016 speech FBI Director James Comey, also stated, that *"...Serious debates are taking place about how law enforcement personnel relate to the communities they serve, about the appropriate use of force, and about real and perceived biases, both within and outside of law enforcement. These are important debates."* I agree. Won't you join me?

Police officers cannot serve a community that does not trust them. A community cannot trust a police department that does not serve them. Let's all survive the police encounter and effect real change. Let's create an environment wherein both community and police co-exist and celebrate their shared humanity.

Join the movement - visit www.sgtcheryldorsey.com and follow me on twitter @sgtcheryldorsey

**COMING SOON!**
**Black and Blue – The Creation of a Whistle Blower**

As we work together to chop down into bite size pieces the bureaucracy that exists in some police departments, I recognize that bureaucracy and abuses of power exists in many large institutions across America. The internal problems I encountered while an LAPD officer were not unique to law enforcement. My goal has always been to help others, who find themselves similarly situated to, better understand the system; speak your truth; and commit to the fight. These were valuable life lessons which I would again find myself needing to deploy during my time as a senior investigator for the Los Angeles Unified School District, Office of the Inspector General.

As I reach another crossroad on this journey called life, I am compelled to speak out against workplace discrimination, [sexual] harassment and retaliation.

I have written extensively about my circumstances while employed by the Los Angeles Unified School District (LAUSD)

for several print and digital media. I will share those stories and eventually in "The Creation of A Whistle Blower" provide a comprehensive step-by-step guide to dealing with, navigating, and managing this process.

#MeToo. I was first harassed and then retaliated against by my supervisors for complaining about disparate treatment and reporting malfeasance which I believed to be occurring in the office where I worked; Office of the Inspector General.

There has been much reported in national news regarding sexual harassment being committed by powerful men in the workplace. To that I say harassment most often occurs at the hands of powerful men – but it is not always sexual in nature. These abuses are being reported in the movie industry, on police departments and, this time- in a school district.

Here is how this David vs Goliath story goes...

In 2015, while employed as a senior investigator assigned to the OIG Investigations unit, I filed a complaint of discrimination and harassment.

My complaint had been ignored by everyone I contacted within the LAUSD; [then] superintendent Ramon Cortines, Deputy Superintendent Michelle King, General Counsel David Holmquist and the Board of Education: Steven Zimmer, Monica Garcia, Dr. George McKenna III, Dr. Ref Rodriguez, Scott Schmerelson, Dr. Richard Vladovic a violation of the District's whistle blower policy.

After filing the March 2015 discrimination/harassment complaint; an unrelenting retaliation campaign followed. The three very powerful men in charge at the OIG, Investigations Unit whom I affectionately refer to as "the unholy trinity": Inspector General (IG) Kenneth (Ken) Bramlett, Deputy Inspector General Frank Cabibi and Supervisory Investigator Jorge Urquijo led the way.

In October 2015, I sought refuge from the retaliation and met with Cortines and Michelle King; requesting whistle blower protection and an immediate investigation.

In January 2016, I was subjected to the combined weight and might of the OIG & LAUSD.

Since the District's powerful administrators could not quiet me I was sent home and an LAPD-style task force was convened.

The "Dorsey Task Force" members consisted of approximately thirty (30) employees from the OIG, OGC, Student Safety Investigation Team (SSIT) and Staff Relations under the command of the first black woman to lead the Los Angeles Unified School District, Superintendent Michelle King.

LAUSD General Counsel David Holmquist, dispatched a battery of attorneys; Lynn Ibarra, Lorri Gosset and Kathleen Collins. Apparently, Superintendent Michelle King thought it more important to investigate me, for previously undocumented district policy violations, rather than relegate one staffer to investigate my complaint of retaliation and malfeasance.

Be clear; complaining comes with consequences. This is not an anomaly nor unique to me.

- In December 2014, LAUSD awarded Archie Roundtree $3.3 million dollars in a whistle blower law suit which involved retaliation.

- In October 2015, the LAUSD was slapped with a $1 billion-dollar lawsuit to end "teacher jail".

- In July 2017, Saif Hussain filed a lawsuit against the LAUSD claiming he had been fired for reporting harassment.

In February 2016, I again contacted [then] superintendent Michelle King requesting her assistance by way of an investigation. The very next day, OGC attorney Lynn Ibarra emailed me directing me, 'not to contact Michelle King, she is aware of your concerns and the District is working toward a resolution."

Let's walk through the resolution, shall we?

- March 1, 2016, LAUSD served a sustained Notice of Unsatisfactory Service (NOUS); I was not interviewed; denied due process.

- April 2016, Melinda LeDuff Menefee, Staff Relations Manager, sent a veiled threat by way of a settlement offer demanding that I resign and stop blogging about the District; with a promise that declining the offer would result in more discipline. I declined.

- On April 8, 2016, OGC Atty Lynn Ibarra notified IG Ken Bramlett & Deputy IG Frank Cabibi that more discipline was coming; "time is of the essence."

- May 9, 2016, the promise was kept; I was served a second NOUS and directed to a hearing to be chaired by Vivian Ekchian, who was a deputy superintendent.

- On June 9, 2016, Ekchian, during my hearing told my attorney to hurry up, she "had a graduation to attend." A communication, given to me during discovery, from OGC Attorney Kathleen Collins to IG Kenneth Bramlett stated, "skelly provides opportunity to be heard". (So, you're not even gonna pretend to be fair?).

- On June 10, 2016, IG Ken Bramlett sent Ekchian a copy of my "Whistle Blower" blog(s) in which I complained about LAUSD retaliation with the caption, "for your reading pleasure". Was Bramlett trying to sway Ekchian's decision?

- June 13, 2016, Vivian Ekchian issued a letter of agreement with OIG, OGC, Staff Relations recommending my termination.

- June 14, 2016 the Board of Education along with [then] Superintendent Michelle King adopted Ekchian's recommendation.

- June 15, 2016 I was fired.

- Power – absolute power is not gender specific. I believe the path to 333 S. Beaudry is littered with the bodies of mistreated LAUSD employees. Evidence of road kill. The remains of those who had the temerity to complain. A warning sign to others who might.

- If you believe you have been the victim of racial discrimination by former Deputy Inspector General Frank Cabibi during his previous employment at LAUSD; US Dept of Justice (DOJ), Glendale, CA; US Dept of Agriculture; Immigration & Naturalization Service, or DOJ OIG– email lausdroadkill@gmail.com

- If you have reported misconduct and believe you have been denied due process, marginalized and retaliated against by the LAUSD; this is a call to action – email lausdroadkill@gmail.com

Find the strength to come forward and speak truth to power. #MeToo #TimesUp

Reprint EURWeb – written by Cheryl Dorsey

*In March 2015, after I filed a race and gender discrimination complaint against my supervisor, Frank Cabibi, [former] Deputy Inspector General, Office of Inspector General (OIG) at the Los Angeles Unified School District (LAUSD), I was targeted.*

*After complaining, I was subjected to collusion, collaboration and conspiracy. A hostile, toxic work environment came first. I was set-up to fail; sabotaged, and singled-out. The retaliation campaign was facilitated by LAUSD administrators who violated their own policies and protocol. All the while, impugning my professional reputation, character and work ethic.*

Then superintendent Michelle King ignored my whistle-blower complaint, a violation of the LAUSD policy. Frank Cabibi lived to offend again. On March 9, 2018, Cabibi was forced to resign in lieu of termination; a closely guarded LAUSD secret.

Michelle King allowed the allocation of thirty plus District staffers including in part, OIG Inspector General (IG) Kenneth (Ken) Bramlett, Frank Cabibi and Supervisory Investigator Jorge Urquijo whom I refer to affectionately as the "unholy trinity"; OGC General Counsel David Holmquist, attorneys Lynn Ibarra, Kathleen "Kate" Collins and Lorri Gossett; current interim Superintendent Vivian Ekchian; OIG staffers Kent Kuniyoshi, Cira Zamora, Melinda LeDuff Menefee -all apparently purposed to malign my reputation.

I was sent home and ordered to have no contact with OIG staff. In a certified letter, IG Ken Bramlett, promised that I'd be "contacted when the investigation was complete." Well, I was never "contacted".

In March 2016, a Notice of Unsatisfactory Service (NOUS) was issued sustaining the charges; with a "no discipline" recommendation. This is important because "no discipline" means the employee can't grieve the discipline. Sneaky, right? That March NOUS stood as is and became foundation for the next NOUS I was served.

In May 2016, I was served a second Notice of Unsatisfactory Service (NOUS); recommending termination.

On June 10, 2016 while Vivian Ekchian, considered my employment status Bramlett sent her an email with links to articles I had written complaining about the retaliation, "for her reading pleasure".

So, then it should come as no surprise that Ekchian recommended my termination and the Board of Education adopted the recommendation on June 14, 2016.

Well, Melinda LeDuff Menefee you were right about two things; "she won't be getting her job back" and "we haven't heard the last of her."

THE DEPOSITIONS.

I had an opportunity to sit across a conference table from Melinda LeDuff-Menifee and the rest during their depositions, in conjunction with my civil suit. I felt it important that I be present. From the emails communications I read through discovery; it appeared that many of them were having a grand ole' time at my expense as they celebrated and did virtual victory laps around the Beaudry administration building at pivotal stages in my termination process. So, I watched and listened intently knowing full well that I would eventually do that "thing" that the LAUSD most despises; write about it. I was singularly focused on providing a lil' disinfectant to the Los Angeles Unified District's dirty little secret.

It was entertaining to witness LeDuff-Menefee and various others involved in my termination proceeding, at various times, shove every member of the unholy trinity under the school bus. Now that Deputy Inspector General Frank Cabibi had been forced to resign, speaking truthfully seemed to be somewhat easier.

An admission under oath by LeDuff-Menifee that Frank Cabibi was "highly resistant" to following LAUSD policy in pursuit of my termination was helpful and appreciated. But I do just have one question sis; Why would you put your name on a document that, by your own sworn admission, had been crafted while violating LAUSD protocols as well as the CSEA Bargaining Agreement?

Deputy Inspector General Frank Cabibi affirmed during his recorded deposition that "as a matter of fundamental fairness the subject of the investigation should have an opportunity to present their side of whatever the alleged misconduct is..."

Specifically, Cabibi under oath acknowledged that, "it is essential" to interview the subject of the investigation, "Because that's the person that has information that they may share with you that you might not have." However, according to Cabibi, OGC attorney Lynn Ibarra conducted the investigation and, "I'm not gonna be able to say that for some other investigative entity. They have their protocols and they do whatever they do. In my investigations that I've conducted, in a majority of them I've interviewed subjects." Well okay Frank, but you, sir, signed off on the NOUS in March 2016 and May 2016; attorney Lynn Ibarra did not.

During Urquijo's sworn testimony he said (in part) an investigation required the "target's responses... They may have mitigating circumstances that may provide you information that would dispel any of the witnesses. I've seen cases where there's vendettas ... there are situations where employees who don't have full knowledge of what's going on ... They don't like the person and here you go ... That and also incomplete information that on the surface it looks that way, but once you dig deeper you'll find different." Um, Jorge, did you just describe a vendetta against me?

Jorge Urquijo and Frank Cabibi both admitted during their depositions that neither had interviewed me on the charges for which I had been terminated; yet both signed off.

Any conspiracy questions I may have had were certainly put to rest thanks to the sworn deposition of LAUSD Human Resource Manager, Melinda LeDuff-Menefee. LeDuff-Menefee stated that Ekchian had called her [Le-Duff-Menefee] as Ekchian was scurrying out of my administrative hearing on June 9, 2016- on her way to a graduation. I had been previously told that Ekchian had an "appointment" and would need to end my hearing, which began at noon, promptly at 2 O'clock pm. Melinda LeDuff-Menefee, admitted that Ekchian had halted my hearing, as promised, and advised LeDuff-Menefee to draft the paperwork as she [Ekchian] was sustaining my termination.

Now understand, my administrative hearing regarding my termination had barely ended. And as Ekchian, left the Beaudry building my fate had apparently already been decided. Let that sink in for a moment. My existence had been decided in the turn of a door-knob, the flick of a car ignition switch. My ability to maintain a roof over my head, feed myself; provide for myself and my children had been solidified as this hearing officer hurried off to a graduation. And to add insult to injury- when asked during her sworn deposition, Ekchian could remember few details about my termination hearing.

Seemingly, Ekchian was not interested in reviewing the voluminous folder presented by my attorney with rebuttals to the charges during my hearing. Apparently, Ekchian had paid little attention to the oral presentations made by both myself and my attorney as to how Ken Bramlett, Frank Cabibi and Jorge Urquijo violated LAUSD policy and the contract bargaining agreement. And apparently Ekchian did not have an appetite to review our prepared written declarations which were read aloud and given to her for consideration.

Nope. Ekchian had made up her mind on the way to a graduation. It is important to note that in 2018 Ekchian, while acting interim superintendent for the LAUSD, was skipped over for promotion to superintendent; the job was given to District outsider Austin Beutner. Currently Ekchian is second in command at the LAUSD.

Cabibi further admitted under oath regarding my retaliation complaint that I "also had the right to expect that the district would take that complaint seriously... that the district would vigorously investigate that complaint".

Bramlett acknowledged under oath that he ignored my pleas to stop the retaliation testifying that "there had been no retaliation against her nor would there be... I believed Mr. Cabibi."

During Bramlett's sworn deposition, he conceded, that my not being interviewed was a "serious violation of due process".

Did they unholy trinity just confirm they violated my due process rights?

To the extent that the unholy trinity have nearly 90 years of professed investigative, supervisory and management experience between them, I find it disturbing that they would support a disciplinary process that denies due process.

I'm certain I'm not alone. And neither are you."

For all the celebrations that occurred within the LAUSD administration building on Beaudry Avenue in 2016 amongst those assembled to manufacture reasons to fire me – it was a very different by the time June 2018 had rolled around.

The Unholy Trinity no longer existed. Frank Cabibi was unceremoniously shown the door in March 2018 amid allegations of making "racial and sexually tinged remarks" and in June 2018 the Board of Education declined to renew Inspector General Kenneth Bramlett's contract which was due to expire at the end of the fiscal year; June 2018.

According to a published report by SCPR, which read in part that, "...Two sources who requested anonymity to discuss a personnel matter confirmed board members will allow Bramlett's contract to expire as scheduled at the end of June... The sources said some board members were concerned Bramlett was overseeing a "hostile work environment" in L.A. Unified's Office of the Inspector General, citing around a dozen complaints filed by employees in that office alleging harassment and discrimination.

While Bramlett himself was not the target of most of these complaints, the sources told KPCC Bramlett appeared not to take the allegations seriously, contributing to the hostile climate."

To that, Bramlett reportedly disputed the assertions of the

sources; "I take all complaints very seriously and have actively looked into every single one," Bramlett's statement said. "Our audits and reports are carefully planned, reviewed and executed. I am very appreciative of the thorough and laser-focused work of the entire Office of Inspector General team."

Well sir, I know of at least one complaint that you apparently did not take seriously – mine. By your own admission during your sworn deposition. Rather, you stated that you failed to investigate my complaint because Frank Cabibi told you that I had not been retaliated against nor discriminated against.

The SCPR article went on to report that, "...One source said L.A. Unified board members Mónica García, Kelly Gonez and Nick Melvoin voted against renewing Bramlett's contract in closed session on Tuesday."

This is important because LAUSD Board member, Dr. George McKenna was also deposed in June 2018 prior to the Board of Education's decision being made public, stated under oath that while he was aware of my discrimination and retaliation complaint after having met with me in person in his office; as just one of several Board Members it was not his role to "get involved in staff issues". Clearly the Inspector General Ken Bramlett continues to enjoy the full support of Dr. George McKenna; a black man.

According to the LA Times, the Board of Education explained their decision not to renew Inspector General Ken Bramlett's contract in part, "...Complicating the decision were complaints that the inspector general had failed to act quickly when his top deputy, Frank Cabibi — who recently resigned — was accused of making racially and sexually tinged remarks.

Black and Blue, The Creation of a Whistleblower – coming soon!

# ABOUT THE AUTHOR

An acclaimed author, retired Los Angeles Police Department Sgt. Cheryl Dorsey has written an autobiography, Black and Blue, The Creation of A Social Advocate Vol II, which provides an unfiltered look into police culture, LAPD's internal disciplinary processes, and techniques to de-escalate and diffuse tensions during police encounters as well as best practices to report police misconduct with a level of credibility that is effective, relevant and irrefutable. Sgt. Dorsey is a highly sought police expert on significant criminal justice issues making national headlines. She has been a frequent commentator on CNN, Fox News, OWN, CNN International, HLNTV, Inside Edition, MSNBC as well as KPCC and KABC Talk Radio.  Sgt. Dorsey has also appeared as a guest police expert on Brazilian TVGlobo, Tavis Smiley, Dr. Drew, Dr. Phil and TD Jakes Shows. She has also been featured on several TV Crime Series such as "It Takes A Killer", "Corrupt Crimes" and "Dead Files".

Cheryl Dorsey is a Los Angeles native. In 1978, she began a career in law enforcement where she worked for the State of California, Department of Justice. In 1980, Cheryl joined the Los Angeles Police Department. During her career, she worked exclusively in patrol and specialized units in all four geographic Bureaus within the City of Los Angeles; South, Central, West and Valley. In addition to various patrol division assignments, Sgt. Dorsey was assigned to traffic division, Newton Area vice and the infamous gang unit in Operations South Bureau; known as Community Resources Against Street Hoodlums (C.R.A.S.H.)

Sgt. Dorsey's lived and professional experiences as an African-American woman, mother of four sons and law enforcement supervisor form the basis for her honest and unique view from behind the blue wall.

As an LAPD insider, Sgt. Dorsey highlights criminal, social or public policy injustices affecting disenfranchised communities throughout the nation. As a mother and police professional, Sgt. Dorsey exposes institutional social and police abuses, as well as social justice disparities, while introducing strategies and commentary on how to systematically attack those injustices and empower audiences on how to navigate within that system, when necessary, and help change that system, when possible.

Printed in Great Britain
by Amazon